MORAL POWERS: NORMATIVE NECESSITY
IN LANGUAGE AND HISTORY

MORAL POWERS:
Normative Necessity in Language and History

Anthony Holiday

ROUTLEDGE
London and New York

First published in 1988 by
Routledge
11 New Fetter Lane, London EC4P 4EE

Published in the USA by
Routledge
in association with Routledge, Chapman & Hall, Inc.
29 West 35th Street, New York, NY 10001

Printed in Great Britain

British Library Cataloguing in PublicationData

Holiday, Anthony
    Moral powers: normative necessity in
    language and history.
    1. Ethics 2. Cynicism
    I. Title
    171'.7   BJ1535.C9
    ISBN 0-415-00304-0

Library of Congress Cataloging-in-Publication Data

ISBN 0-415-00304-0

Contents

Abbreviations

NB   *Notebooks 1914–1916*, G.H. von Wright and G.E.M. Anscombe (eds), G.E.M. Anscombe (trans.), Basil Blackwell, Oxford, 1961

TLP   *Tractatus Logico-Philosophicus*, D.F. Pears and B.F. McGuinness (trans.), Routledge and Kegan Paul, London, 1961

LLW   *Letters from Ludwig Wittgenstein with a memoir*, B.F. McGuinness (ed.), L. Furtmuller (trans.), Basil Blackwell, Oxford, 1967

RLF   'Some remarks on logical form', *Proceedings of the Aristotelian Society*, supp. vol. ix, 1929

BB   *The Blue and Brown Books*, Basil Blackwell, Oxford, 1958

RFM   *Remarks on the foundations of mathematics*, G.H. von Wright, R. Rhees and G.E.M. Anscombe (eds), G.E.M. Anscombe (trans.), Basil Blackwell, Oxford, 1978

PI   *Philosophical investigations*, 2nd edn, G.E.M. Anscombe and R. Rhees (eds), G.E.M. Anscombe (trans.), Basil Blackwell, Oxford, 1958

Z   *Zettel*, G.E.M. Anscombe and G.H. von Wright (eds), G.E.M. Anscombe (trans.), Basil Blackwell, Oxford, 1967

OC   *On certainty*, G.E.M. Anscombe and G.H. von Wright (eds), D. Paul and G.E.M. Anscombe (trans.), Basil Blackwell, Oxford, 1969

ROC   *Remarks on colour*, G.E.M. Anscombe (ed.), L.L. McAlister and M. Schättle (trans.), Basil Blackwell, Oxford, 1977

LC   *Lectures and conversations on aesthetics, psychology and religious belief*, C. Barrett (ed.), Basil Blackwell, Oxford, 1966

CV   *Culture and value*, G.H. von Wright and H. Nyman (eds), P. Winch (trans.), Basil Blackwell, Oxford, 1980

RFGB   'Remarks on Frazer's Golden Bough', J. Beversluis (trans.) in C.G. Luckhardt (ed.), *Wittgenstein sources and perspectives*, Harvester Press, Hassocks, 1979

For my Mother and in memory of my Father

Preface

This book is the product of research for a doctoral thesis, undertaken at Linacre College, Oxford, between 1983 and 1987.

My thanks are therefore due, in the first instance, to the Trustees, Director and staff of the Africa Educational Trust for the financial and moral support afforded me during this period, and to the Principal and Fellows of my college for their friendship, advice and encouragement. I owe a deep debt of gratitude to my supervisors, Rom Harré, Jerry Cohen, John McDowell and Steven Lukes. I have special reasons for my feelings of gratitude to Rom Harré, who not only saw my research through all its stages from the project's inception, but, long before I came up to Oxford, provided an invaluable stimulus to my thinking during a difficult period when I was a political prisoner in Pretoria.

Other persons, too numerous to mention individually, have assisted me, sometimes by commenting on various drafts of my manuscript; or through discussion of the notions contained in them; or, very often, by lightening the weight of my ignorance through their teaching. In this last regard, I cannot omit to acknowledge all I have learned about Wittgenstein from Peter Hacker and Gordon Baker of St John's College, Oxford, whose careful and rigorous scholarship taught me something of the difference between a clear exposition and an interpretation. I must also thank my friend, Adrian Moore, for the generosity with which he placed his sympathetic and acute intelligence at my disposal. I should like to thank Rainer and Ilse Born for their unstinting hospitality during my visits to Vienna and Linz. I derived much benefit and encouragement from Rainer's thoughtful comments on drafts of my chapters on Wittgenstein and the theory of core-language-games. I have also benefited from conversations with Stuart Shanker, John Roach and Katherine Morris.

Introduction

The chief aim of this essay is to subvert an attitude towards the moral dimension in our lives which I have chosen to call ethical cynicism. This term has been selected in an effort to pick out features of the attitude in question which differentiate it in subtle but important ways from, and render it somewhat more virulent than, its gentler and more detached cousin, moral scepticism. For, although cynicism, in my sense, is certainly connected with notions included in the philosopher's use of the term 'moral scepticism', there are components in the cynic's world view which need not be available to the sceptic. While cynicism is certainly indebted to the Humean dichotomy between 'ought' and 'is' and to a denial of the very possibility of moral knowledge that flows from it, hostility to moral realism does not do enough to explain the pervasiveness of cynicism in our present-day dealings with one another, especially as regards our political dealings. Cynicism, in my usage, is indeed the offspring of Humean scepticism, non-cognitivism and relativism in ethics. However, these are only the negative branches in its ancestry, and it has had more assertive forebears, including not only positivism, scientism and emotivism, but also genuine traditions of discovery, particularly in the human sciences.

The modern moral cynic, as I recognise him, is equipped with a good deal more than the stock of arguments with which the traditional non-cognitivist confronts the moral realist. He is, in a special sense, worldly wise; he is master of a set of manipulative techniques, made possible by advances in the study of politics, psychology and the social sciences, and has a grasp of the theories which underpin his technology. He is, in the true meaning of the word, a *professional*, at home in the managerial world, in the intelligence gathering 'community', in journalism and, above all, in politics, because his true calling is the attainment and exercise of *power*.

My cynic is a latter-day Thrasymachus or a Callicles. In much the same way as possession of rhetorical skill and worldly ambition obscured the point of Socratic talk about justice for those Athenian men-of-affairs, so the power which mastery of our contemporary manipulative techniques confers, coupled with the fascination concerning that power's worldly applications which it engenders, bolsters the cynic's moral scepticism and makes the moral realist's perspective especially opaque to him. In short, it is the modern cynic's possession and understanding of power and its mechanisms which does most to render him impervious to realist arguments. With the best will in the world, he cannot see the point of discourses which are not about, or are uninformed by, some theory of power. It is not that he is merely unintelligent, obstinate or intellectually dishonest; he really cannot get inside realist perspectives for the very understandable reason that they do not seem to him to touch his life and the way the world compels him to live it. Even the term 'moral realism' may seem to him to be something of a misnomer, since he considers himself to be a realist, not just in some superficial or vulgarly pragmatist sense, but inasmuch as he genuinely knows a great deal about the functioning of the human world and can give his knowledge a reasonable theoretical gloss.

Once these facets of the cynic's condition are taken seriously, it becomes evident that a different argumentative strategy is required to meet his case. Such a strategy would have to address the central place which notions of, and theories about, power occupy in his world view. On the assumption, then, that the cynic will be responsive only to counter-arguments which incorporate a theory concerned with power, I propose to offer him a theory of moral powers — a theory which will show that moral values are immensely potent sources of power, lying at the very heart of our life together as social beings. A consequence of this theory is that the preservation of these values is a precondition for the exercise of other power-begetting techniques which preoccupy the cynic.

This theory employs a form of transcendental argument in order to demonstrate that the preservation of certain moral norms is a necessary, although not a sufficient, condition for the very possibility of language, as the later Wittgenstein conceived of it, and for the rise and fall of historical epochs, as that process was conceived of by the mature Marx. In order to establish this claim, I argue for the following positions:

(1) That just as the existence of certain minimal natural regularities is an external prerequisite for the possibility of human language, so the existence of certain moral regularities is an internal precondition for the realisation of that possibility. (2) That there is a conceptual affinity between the Wittgensteinian account of language and the Marxist theory of history,

such that the two complement and even require one another in various respects.

(3) That language should be counted among the productive forces which are the primary determinants of historical change according to Marx's theory, so that

(4) The correctness of (1) generates a presumption in favour of there being a significant degree of overlap between moral, semantic and historical necessity, enabling us to identify the 'ought' of morality with the 'is' of the publicly accessible realms of linguistic coherence and historical change.

Because arguments favouring theses (1), (3) and (4) require a preparation in the form of explication and interpretation of Wittgensteinian philosophy and Marxist theory, the ensuing sequence of chapters does not conform to the above outline. Considerations designed to establish thesis (1) are presented in Chapter 2. Thesis (2) is established by interpretations offered, partly in Chapter 1 and mainly in Chapter 3. Theses (3) and (4) are defended in Chapter 4.

As far as the interpretative chapters are concerned, while they pretend to be neither definitive nor complete descriptions of either Marx or Wittgenstein's thought, they are as uncontroversial as I can make them. They may, however, appear contentious in three respects. Firstly, I have given more weight to Wittgenstein's moral and religious preoccupations than would be accorded to them by such scholars as Baker and Hacker, and I have treated Marx's system in the same way, despite the interpretations of such experts as Cohen and Althusser. I have learned much from these authors, and believe that their approaches yield valuable insights. At the same time, I believe that my way with Marx and Wittgenstein's texts is at least as fruitful and accords more thoroughly with their own view of their respective projects than the usual opinion.

Secondly, I have refused to treat either Marx or Wittgenstein as if their earlier views could be radically segregated from their later ones. Althusser's treatment, although it must be regarded as a seminal one, makes far more of the division between the earlier Fuerbachian and Hegelianised writings and Marx's mature doctrine than I have thought appropriate. As far as Wittgenstein is concerned, I expect that my general search for continuities would be approved by most scholars writing today. It is possible, however, that some will find debatable the dialectic of irony which seems to me to bring the *Tractatus Logico-Philosophicus* and the *Philosophical investigations* together.

Finally, there is the connection I try to draw between Wittgensteinian philosophical semantics and the Marxist theory of history. As far as I can establish, there is no concrete historical evidence that Wittgenstein had so much as read Marx, despite his having visited the Soviet Union and his association with Sraffa, whose connections with Italian communism and with Gramsci are well known. I have therefore relied almost entirely upon conceptual evidence, internal to the texts, arguing chiefly that Wittgenstein's progress away from logicist essentialism with respect to language is prefigured by Marx's movement away from an Hegelian version of the same dogma with respect to history. Because, as far as I am aware, writers on this topic have not so far tried to forge the link in this way, any attempt to do so must, in the nature of the case, be the object of critical scrutiny and debate.

These three features of my exegesis — emphasis on the ethical preoccupations of the authors with whom I am concerned, insistence on the continuities in the thought of both, and arguments favouring affinities between them — hang together and relate to my own most central claim about the importance of value-preservation. For purposes of establishing that claim, however, the third of these features is probably of most importance, because it is essential to the project of defending an historicised portrayal of language — that is, a conception of language as inseparable from everything we are as historical creatures, and of our own historicity as being bound up with the fact that we are language-users. Once this view of these matters is adopted, and logicist essentialism as an account of the necessity which governs language and history is rejected, questions as to what kind of internal necessity is genuinely at work here must be revisited: for although later Wittgensteinian and mature Marxist doctrines allow us to say that language and history respectively depend for their existence on the existence of certain material regularities *external* to their being *qua* human artifact, the question which logicism had originally seemed to answer concerning the *internal* necessity at work here confronts us once more. The very intimacy we associate with the way in which the historico-linguistic side of ourselves is combined with what we take to be our own nature, coupled with the connotations attached to the word 'internal', tempted us to think of 'internal connections' in the logician's sense of the term when wonderment at the coherence of language and history took hold of us. However, the enigma did not evaporate once the image of a human world determined by a logical essence no longer captivated us, for these realms of our social selves still seem relatively autonomous from brute nature and, thus, still seem to exhibit a unity which cries out to be dealt with on its own terms.

My response to this question is to sketch an account which does double duty as a realist theory of ethics and a realist approach to the philosophy of language. I shall argue that the function of certain religio-ethical codes and practices is to preserve the integrity of the languages we all speak, understand and are liable to misunderstand; and that such codes and practices are themselves part of language, existing, so to speak, at its very core, from which centre they exert a cohesive influence, somewhat akin to the power of a gravitational force. If this enterprise succeeds at the semantic level, it succeeds also at the level of moral philosophy, for it bridges the fact/value divide by identifying moral and semantic reality. The advantage of this from the ethicist's point of view is the restoration of ethical life and action to the realm of the rational by showing its indispensability to speech and, hence, of the construction of the patterns of rational discourse that we in fact construct. Moral philosophy is hereby liberated from the deadening engagement with all the varieties of Humean sceptical epistemology and from the tedious debates concerning prescriptivism, emotivism, relativism and varieties of hedonism, all of which are to some extent the result of our failure to give realist positions in ethics the foundation they require.

It must be said, however, that whatever advantages accrue to the realist cause from the adoption of my theory, the theory itself, although relying on the soundness of much in Marx and Wittgenstein's thought, deviates from what the latter held to be legitimate philosophical activity. The deviation consists in my attempt to provide a *theoretical* explanation of the relation of morals to language. In so doing it exemplifies what is, by Wittgensteinian lights, a dangerous tendency to be metaphysical. While Wittgenstein might have approved the impulse which thrusts in that direction, he would have mistrusted the result.

To mistrust, however, is not to dismiss, nor is it to detect an error. It is rather the preliminary to critical explorations which may result in such detection. To theorise is not to be in error, but only to run the unavoidable risk of error. Great philosophy is as full of theories as it is full of errors, and the former are often sources of the latter. However, it is not a philosopher's mistakes which ought to interest us so much as the route which led him to make them. All the same, a philosopher who tries, as I have done, to use Wittgensteinian concepts in the elaboration of a theory of his own, has a special duty to remain as faithful to the main lines of his creditor's thoughts as can be managed. To this end, I have tried to cast my account of the transition from the philosophy of the *Tractatus* to that of the *Investigations* in an expository mould. This account, given in my opening chapter, remains, however, not an exposition, but an interpretation. In so far as this interpretation bears on my semantico-ethical theory (as distinct from its bearing on my claim that there is an affinity between Wittgenstein and Marx), it is designed chiefly to establish the point that the moral dimension of the *Tractatus* is of paramount importance, not only for a right understanding of that work, but for a proper appreciation of Wittgenstein's attitude to his calling as a philosopher. Once this point is taken seriously and set beside the other continuities linking the Tractarian to the post-Tractarian corpus, the absence of any real attempt to deal with the problem of ethics in the *Investigations* — in which there is only a single laconic reference to the ways in which we might learn the meaning of the word 'good' (PI, i, para. 77) — emerges as a striking lacuna. My theory may be seen as an attempt to fill this void by making creative use of precisely those notions which were most crucial to Wittgenstein's critique of the logical essentialism of the *Tractatus* — the language-game trope and the concept of a form of life.

1

Necessity in
Wittgensteinian Semantics

1.0 Introduction

What are the necessary conditions for the possibility of language?
If this very Kantian question makes sense, then who ever does
make sense of it will see some hope of making sense of the term
'semantic necessity', apart from the trivial sense it makes to say
that semantic necessity is the necessity governing the possibility
of meaning or meaningful language. We shall get no further with
the question until we know what conception of language in
general is before us; for the notion of 'semantic necessity' must
evidently be tied to some or other philosophical, scientific or
pseudo-scientific picture of what language is, and will alter as and
if the picture changes. The present chapter is an account of the
changing picture of language, entertained by Ludwig Wittgenstein, and of the metamorphosis his concept of semantic necessity
underwent as his perspective shifted. Beginning with some
remarks on the nature of, and relations between, the Wittgensteinian texts, the chapter goes on to describe the intellectual
context in which they were produced and critically explore both
the Tractarian and post-Tractarian accounts of language. It
concludes with a discussion of the vexed topic of depth grammar.

In conducting this survey, I have accentuated (although, I
hope, not exaggerated) the role which Wittgenstein's ethical and
religious concerns played, from the very first, in shaping his
images of language and the world. I have also tried to bring out
the ironic dimension of his writing, which is a key not only to his
own method of doing philosophy, but to the way it connects with
a dialectical tradition which culminates in Marx's theory of
history. All this is designed to introduce the thesis that the
necessity which governs language is of a moral, not of a logical,
kind. It will be the task of the succeeding chapter to elaborate a

theory which supports this claim. My immediate aim, however, is to indicate that the thesis is consonant with the spirit of Wittgenstein's philosophy, and that the germs of the theory are, despite his own stringent efforts to guard against theorising, present in at least some of the things he wrote. In the Preface to the *Philosophical investigations*, Wittgenstein expressed a hope that his writing might 'stimulate someone to thoughts of his own' (PI, p. viii).[1] The ensuing account of his doctrine is intended to show that thoughts expressed in subsequent chapters have indeed been stimulated by Wittgenstein's writings and not by some fanciful misreading of them.

1.1 Wittgenstein's texts

Excepting the *Blue and Brown Books*, which are duplicated notes, dictated to students, Wittgenstein saw the publication in his lifetime of only one book, the *Tractatus Logico-Philosophicus*, which appeared in 1921, and fully intended (as far as we know) the publication of only one other. This was the *Philosophical investigations*, which appeared in 1953, two years after his death. Notwithstanding the undoubted importance of much of the material subsequently released by his executors, these two great works must be regarded as the main keys to his philosophy of language, and a proper appreciation of the relation in which they stand to one another is a prerequisite for a correct approach to the thoughts they express. However, because the later work explicitly repudiates doctrines set forth in the first, it is tempting to think of Wittgenstein's philosophy as an essentially fissured product, the halves of which bear only the relation of contrast to each other. This impression is sustained by the striking differences in style and structure which distinguish the two texts. It is lent further credibility by the fact that the *Investigations* ranges over a broader subject area than does the *Tractatus*, being far more concerned with what is now called the philosophy of mind than was the first book. Indeed, as we shall see, Wittgenstein's own convictions concerning the mistakes of his Tractarian period prompted him to favour broader surveys, as against in-depth excavations, in the later period of his life.

Like most half-truths, however, this tale of the 'two Wittgensteins' obscures more than it explains. It fails, notably, to explain why he should have wished to publish both texts between the covers of a single volume in the belief that his new thoughts 'could be seen in the right light only by contrast with and against the background of my old way of thinking' (PI, p. x).[2] Two modes of thought which are different *toto mundi* are not set in the right light by being placed in the closest possible spatial proximity to one another. To think that they are is like supposing that works by, say, Constable and Van Gogh are best understood by being seen together in the same room. We know, moreover, that the Tractarian and post-Tractarian doctrines are not irreconcilably at odds on every point, and that Wittgenstein did not think them to be so. 'Wittgenstein', Anscombe recalls, 'used to say that the *Tractatus* was not *all* wrong: it was not like a bag of junk professing to be a clock, but like a clock that did not tell you the right time.'[3] The project of presenting his old and new perspectives as Wittgenstein once wished to do must, therefore, have been inspired by some motive more subtle than the crude impulse to rebuke and expose past mistakes. When the later author speaks of the interest of comparing the multiplicity of our linguistic tools with what logicians have said about the structure of language, and adds elliptically, 'including the author of the *Tractatus Logico-Philosophicus*' (PI, i, para. 23), we are being invited to remember, among other things, that the author is the same man in both cases.

These comments on his own work suggest what a closer examination will confirm. They insinuate that, in the last decade of his life, Wittgenstein hoped that the *Tractatus* and the *Investigations* would be read as ironic commentaries upon one another, such that new thoughts often mock old ones, although old thoughts, too, are capable of echoing derisively amidst the new — which, in any case, require them in order to be understood. In the end the single-volume plan was never realised: instead, the dialectical character of the *Investigations* was produced very largely by the introduction of an interlocutor, who presents Wittgenstein's earlier positions, thus creating a somewhat Hegelian impression of an old 'Self' striving to rediscover itself in a 'Self' that is new. It may well be that these efforts to recreate his own self-criticisms sometimes have the effect that Kenny[4] discerns of masking the considerable continuity between Wittgenstein's earlier and later views. What is certain is that continuities are present, often where we least expect to find them.

Conjunctures and disjunctures coexist within the body of these texts and only attention to both will reveal the character of the whole.

1.11 Conjunctures

Three connecting strands tend to unify Wittgenstein's ideas about language and the philosophy of language, namely:

(1) his conviction that meaning is tied to use;
(2) his sense of language as a relatively autonomous ongoing concern which requires to be investigated in its own right; and
(3) his anti-theoreticism.

These are only the main bonds of continuity, but they are the ones least shrouded in ambiguity.

(1) It is usual and correct to contrast the Russellian and Tractarian tendency to identify the meaning of a name with its bearer with the post-Tractarian slogan that: 'The meaning of a word is its use in the language.' (PI, i, para. 43) Yet already in the *Tractatus*, Wittgenstein is committed to the notion that the meaning of a name cannot be determined apart from its use. He says there, for instance, that a sign does not determine logical form unless it is taken together with its logico-syntactical employment and that 'if a sign is *useless*, it is meaningless' (TLP, 3.327–3.328, original emphasis). An elliptical remark in his discussion of the pseudo-propositional status of mathematical equations is even more explicit: 'In philosophy the question, "What do we actually use this word or this proposition for?" repeatedly leads to valuable insights.' (TLP, 6.211) These dicta, of course, derive from the Fregean stipulation that a word has meaning only in the context of a sentence. In the *Investigations*, the doctrine is much more pervasive, and is connected with the focus on practice which is a central feature of that work. It is worth noticing, however, that the so-called 'use-theory' is Fregean and Tractarian in origin, and coexists with a denotational theory which features in the *Tractatus* and with the criticisms of Frege which occur in both books.

(2) Throughout his work, Wittgenstein attempts to remain

faithful to the notion that language is a medium in which human creatures inescapably dwell, so that philosophical perplexity about language is really only a special form of a general sense of wonder at the human condition. Language and world are seen as part of a single, inseparable reality, not as two distinct realms which must somehow be held together by a conceptual glue. This realist intuition is easier to descry in the post-Tractarian writings than in the *Tractatus*, because the metaphysical atomism we find there is liable to obscure it. The Tractarian atoms must indeed be thought of as extra-linguistic *things*. For the early Wittgenstein, however, the form of any one of these simple objects is the bare possibility of its occurrence in some state of affairs (TLP, 2.0141), and the totality, not of things, but of facts, is what the world is (TLP, 1.1). A fact, for Wittgenstein, is a statement in language that something is or is not the case. He is saying that our factual talk — such talk as is genuinely propositional — is certainly talk about an objective world, although our meta-linguistic talk about facts is, nonetheless, talk about talk. The same brand of realism is on offer in the *Investigations*: 'When we say, and *mean*, that such-and-such is the case, we — and our meaning does not stop anywhere short of the fact; but we mean; *this — is — so*.' (PI, i, para. 95, author's emphasis)

(3) Finally, and far less controversially, Wittgenstein is consistent throughout his writings in presenting philosophy as being a non-theoretical — in the sense of being a non-scientific (although by no means anti-scientific) — practice. He was emphatic on the point from the very first: 'Philosophy is not one of the natural sciences.' It was not 'a body of doctrine' but an 'activity', consisting essentially of 'elucidations' (TLP, 4.11–4.112). In the *Blue Book*, he warned his students that the tendency among philosophers to ask and answer questions as science does leads 'into complete darkness' (BB, p. 18). The same methodological precepts are operative in the *Investigations*: 'And we may not advance any kind of a theory. There must be nothing hypothetical in our considerations. We must do away with all *explanation*, and description alone must take its place.' (PI, i, para. 109, original emphasis) By these lights the philosopher's researches are of an entirely logico-conceptual sort. He makes no discoveries about what occurs in the world in the sense that a scientist or even an explorer does. Nor is he a reformer of any aspect of the world. Philosophy may not 'interfere with the actual use of

5

language', not try to give it a foundation. 'It leaves everything as it is.' (PI, i, para. 124) As we shall see, Wittgenstein himself failed to conform to these anti-theoretic provisos, and it is debatable whether he truly believed any philosopher could conform to them. What is not debatable is that they represented for him an ideal of the kind of philosophy he wanted to do and see done, and that they are the source of his claim to be doing philosophy in a new key, using these strictures as criteria for the assessment of philosophical artistry or skill.

1.12 Disjunctures

To emphasise these constant features is not at all to deny the very real and radical departures and innovations which segregate the post-Tractarian from the Tractarian texts. Indeed, one such difference concerns just this last-mentioned matter of philosophical method, and is illustrative of how closely unity may approximate to diversity within the totality of the Wittgensteinian fabric. For while both the earlier and the later writings stress the non-explanatory character of philosophical work, the *Tractatus* sees that work's goal as a clarificatory one in the sense that the activity is supposed to give 'sharp boundaries' to our thoughts (TLP, 4.112). The *Investigations*, in contrast, deals in concepts with blurred edges, draws fuzzy boundaries or refuses to draw them at all. (PI, i, paras. 71, 76 and 77) The style and texture of the later writings reflect this change in Wittgenstein's appreciation of what is appropriate to his new aim of providing an overview of the surface-scape of language, rather than an analytical account of its logical depths. The later writings have a sketch-book-like appearance which contrasts sharply with the rigidly programmatic character of the first great book. They give a sometimes misleading impression of being highly diffused pieces of conceptual cartography, the intersecting nodes of which are not readily perceptible. These features are connected with crucial doctrinal changes. The early calculus model of semantic necessity has been replaced, firstly by the notion of a system of sentences, and then by the image of a network of language-games. Metaphysical and logical atomism have been abandoned, and logicist essentialism — the theory that language is determined by an inner logical essence — has given way before Wittgenstein's determination to restrict himself to a fine-grained description of what lies open to view.

1.13 Frayed strands

The sheer range and complexity of the matters covered in the Wittgensteinian corpus — especially if account is taken of the mass of material that has appeared since the publication of the *Investigations* — makes a neat division into conjunctive and disjunctive themes both undesirable and probably impossible. Some tendrils of the earlier thought seem to reach tantalisingly close to threads in the later texts, although it is impossible to say with any certainty whether contact has been made. A trilogy of related matters deserves mention in this regard. They are: the picture theory of the proposition, the saying/showing distinction, and the status of logic.

The picture theory. In his first book, Wittgenstein held that the *Tatsachen* of which the world consisted were pictured by us to ourselves (TLP, 2.1), that the elements of such pictures represented objects (TLP, 2.131), and that a proposition was a picture of reality (TLP, 4.01). It has been a matter of some controversy whether this theory, or any form of it, survived the demolition of so many other Tractarian doctrines. Kenny held that the theory was later thought by Wittgenstein to need supplementing rather than as being straightforwardly false, and that 'the theory of meaning as use is a complement rather than a rival to the picture theory.'[5] A similar view, together with an attempted refurbishment of the theory, designed to disambiguate Wittgenstein's use of the term 'representation' and related concepts, has been defended by Stenius.[6] Indeed, if we focus attention on certain remarks in the *Investigations*, such as the observation that comparisons between a proposition and a portrait or a genre-picture 'have point' (PI, i, para. 522), it is very tempting to think that some or other version of the original picture theory must be salvageable. On the other hand, if we are attending to the exceptionally powerful cohesion that exists between the various elements of the Tractarian philosophy, we shall find ourselves in sympathy with Hacker's[7] staunch refusal to countenance the idea that it is possible to isolate a core of the theory which could have survived once logical atomism had been abandoned. Shifts of attention tend to produce different views of the matter. To say this, however, is not at all to say that there is no correct position in this important scholarly dispute: rather, it is to suggest that the dispute itself is partly the product of the character of the texts that concern us.

Saying and showing. Genuine propositions, for the early Wittgenstein, always picture no more nor less than two possibilities: these are the possibilities that something is or is not the case; that some or other fact of the matter is or is not thus and so. Moreover, he held that any such genuine proposition *showed* its sense. 'A proposition', he said, '*shows* how things stand *if* it is true. And it *says that* they do so stand.' (TLP, 4.022, original emphases) What propositions thus mysteriously show is not the worldly reality they are able fully to represent, but the logical form they must have in common with reality in order to represent it (TLP, 4.12–4.121). Thus it is that 'What *can* be shown, *cannot* be said.' (TLP, 4.1212, original emphases) This realm of the unsayable is coextensive with what lies outside the world — namely, its sense, and this realm will include religio-ethical values: 'the sense of the world must lie outside the world . . . *in* it no value exists — and if it did exist, it would have no value.' (TLP, 6.41, original emphasis)

The question which at once presents itself is this: if Hacker is right in thinking that the picture theory cannot survive the demise of logical atomism, must not the saying/showing distinction, which is so intimately connected with the Tractarian rendering of this theory, equally suffer extinction? A possible response to this argument is to point out that the saying/showing distinction predates the inception of the picture theory. The textual evidence for this is the notes Wittgenstein dictated to G.E. Moore in April of 1914, in which the propositions of logic are said to *show* the logical properties of language and the universe, but to *say* nothing (NB, p. 107). The first formulation of the picture theory in the *Notebooks* does not occur until September of that year, at which point we find the entry: 'That a sentence is a logical portrayal of its meaning is obvious to the uncaptive eye.' (NB, p. 5)

This consideration, however, is insufficient to disestablish the bond between the saying/showing distinction and the full-blown version of the picture theory as developed in the *Tractatus*. It is no licence either for reading the distinction into later texts, or for resurrecting it, as I have tried to do elsewhere,[8] by seeking cognates for the notion of 'showing' in the concepts of 'practice' and 'ritual' as these emerge in the *Investigations* and in the *Remarks on Fraser's Golden Bough*. The most that can safely be said is that 'rediscoveries' of the distinction are likely to be reconstructions of it, bearing only a distant familial likeness to the original ancestor.

Logic. The Tractarian attitude to logic is consistent with that of logical essentialism — the belief that all necessity is logical necessity and that a hidden logical essence governs language. Wittgenstein's later texts are, in large part, the tale of a titanic struggle to rid himself of this vision of logic's role and status, yet his preoccupation with logic persisted. In the last months of his life, he could still write that 'everything descriptive of a language-game is part of logic' (OC, para. 56), and he continued to insist that colour classification was a logical matter (ROC, iii, para. 12), being fascinated by the problem on that account. Here the impulse to believe that old and new conceptions must somehow belong together is very powerful. The words 'logic' and 'logical', we feel inclined to say, cannot take on an entirely different meaning in the mouth of the same philosopher, especially if we suppose him to be using them, as we all do, to refer to the rules for valid inference. However, an impulse just as strong to think that, after all, two very different uses of 'logic' are being employed arises when we examine the later work: for in the post-Tractarian philosophy, the logical seems synonymous with the grammatical, and both enjoy a kind of free-floating existence on the surface of language, such that the rules which govern them are seen to serve mutable human ends. This relative independence of logic may be expressed by saying that, say, Occidental and Oriental musical systems have different logical structures or grammars, but that, of course, no music at all would be possible were the physics of sound radically different from the way it is. It is in this matter of logic and logical necessity that we are most liable to go wrong in reading Wittgenstein's texts, and are most liable to imagine consistency and system when they are absent and to ignore them when they are genuinely present. The best prophylactic against such errors is to borrow a metaphor from the *Investigations* and treat the sum of these writings like a 'torn spider's web' (PI, i, para. 106), a maze of delicately woven strands, some of which are continuous, while others are irreparably broken, some of which are are so fine that it is impossible to tell whether or not they are whole.

1.2 The conceptual background

If the Wittgensteinian conceptual web is in a somewhat tattered condition, this must largely be due to the polarised state of the philosophical tendencies which were present in the intellectual milieu in which it was woven. These speculative currents may roughly be classified as Kantian idealism, various shadings and offshoots of empiricism, and the dialectical tradition inaugurated by Hegel and Marx. To these three sets of competing influences must be added others of an aesthetic and religio-ethical sort, which seem to have acted as a constant predispositional screen through which the thoughts of the great modern philosophers were filtered. Although Kantianism seems to have left the most vivid imprint on the early period of Wittgenstein's formation, there is little to suggest that he was ever 'converted' to any one of the specifically philosophical standpoints he encountered. If the mass of biographical material published since his death teaches us anything about Wittgenstein as a thinker, it is that unqualified commitment to any school of thought or religious persuasion was alien to his curious personality and singular mode of life. His aphorism: 'the philosopher is not a citizen of any community of ideas' (Z, para. 455) is a motto which reflects his determination to transcend influences and strive for originality. Nonetheless, he combined his extraordinary capacity for intellectual detachment with a fervent receptivity to currents of thought and speculative traditions, in an era in which the currents ran strong and the traditions often conflicted.

1.21 Kant and Kantianism

The original cast of his mind predisposed Wittgenstein to take very seriously the idea that a philosopher's *primary* task is to *think*, rather than to read or to soak himself in the ideas of others. It is difficult to ascertain to what extremes he took this notion in guiding the life of his own mind, but he certainly seems to have regarded scholarly absorption in the great books of past phil-osophers as a distinctly subordinate activity to the attempt to generate thoughts of his own. It is consequently not possible to say with any certainty that he actually made a close study of Kant's own writings. On the other hand, his friend and pupil, Drury, recalls Wittgenstein speaking to him 'of the great depth to be found in Kant's writings',[9] and Lee reports a conversation in which Wittgenstein describes Kant's method of starting with what we know and going on to examine the validity of our suppositions about our knowledge as 'the right sort of approach'.[10] However, whether Kant's ideas were transmitted directly or, as seems more probable, through the influence of powerful intermediaries, the Kantian and Tractarian doctrines are clearly comparable in two crucial respects. Firstly, as Kant sought to set limits to what can be known in experience, so the *Tractatus* traced the limits of what can be said in sensible language. The significant difference here, of course, is that the Bounds of Sense are experiential in the former case and logico-semantical in the latter. The *Tractatus* is not an epistemological treatise. Secondly, Wittgenstein shared with Kant an ambition to revolutionise philosophy by quenching the aspirations of all prior metaphysics. It cannot be fortuitous that Kant's prefatory boast in the first edition of the first *Critique* 'that there is not a single metaphysical problem that does not find its solution, or at least the key to its solution here',[11] should be echoed by Wittgenstein's claim in the preface to the *Tractatus* that he had found 'on all essential points, the final solution of the problems' (TLP, p. 5).

The first philosopher to impress Wittgenstein was Schopenhauer, easily one of Kant's greatest debtors. A youthful reading of *The world as will and idea* so enthralled Wittgenstein that, as he later told Von Wright,[12] his first philosophical beliefs consisted of a Schopenhauerian epistemological idealism. The vogue enjoyed by the writings of the neo-Kantian and fiercely anti-Hegelian Schopenhauer among the educated elite of Vienna at the turn of the century was contemporaneous with, and is partly explained by, a vociferous anti-Hegelian movement among scientists and philosophers of science.

Hegel's intervention into the preserves of natural science was itself a reaction to the atomism and mechanism of the radical Enlightenment. Hegel resisted this world view by relating the movement of human subjectivity, as it is expressed in history, art, religion and in philosophy itself, to the processes studied in biology, chemistry, physics and mechanics. The Hegelian *Geist* is imperfectly expressed in these physical processes. Its self-realisation is hampered to the degree that they are mechanical, abstract, simple and 'self-external'. Thus, subjectivity or consciousness seeks to unfold itself in ever more complex and 'concrete' material forms through a dialectical motion, the moments of which are negation, sublation and higher synthesis. Hegel had no scruples in applying his dialectical method even to the fundamentals of classical mechanils, extracting the concept of mechanical motion from a supposed interaction between time and space. He informs us that:

> This *vanishing* and *self-regeneration* of space in time and of time in space, a process in which time posits itself spatially as *place*, but in which place too, as indifferent spatiality, is immediately posited as temporal: this is *Motion*.[13]

Not only did Hegelian *Naturphilosophie* abolish the distinction between empirical science and philosophy — a distinction which, as we have noticed (1.11), Wittgenstein consistently tried to preserve — it subordinated empirical research to the mysterious, self-questing movement of speculative thought. For Hegel, while grandly conceding that philosophy must 'be in agreement with our empirical knowledge of Nature', at once adds that a science's origin in such knowledge is one thing, while the science itself is another. 'In the latter', he says, 'the former can no longer appear as the foundation of the science: here the foundation must be the necessity of the Notion.'[14] This attempt to secure suzerainty for dialectical philosophy over science provoked an understandable antipathy towards Hegelianism from experimental scientists.[15]

It is equally understandable that, in at least some of its manifestations, the anti-Hegelian revolt should have taken on a Kantian form. Kant's critical philosophy was partly inspired by a respect for Newtonian physics which approached reverence. His epistemology did not claim to supersede the pronouncements of established science, but sought rather to give them a secure foundation. There is, therefore, a certain naturalness in the circumstance that Heinrich Hertz and Ludwig Boltzman, the two Viennese philosopher-physicists who so profoundly influenced Wittgenstein, should have been neo-Kantians.

The impact of Hertz's *Principles of mechanics* on the thinking that produced the *Tractatus*, in which he is directly referred to only twice (TLP, 4.04 and 6.361), is particularly striking, and almost certainly extends into the later writings, as Barker suggests.[16] As Kant had asked how synthetic *a priori* judgements were possible, so Hertz asked how an *a priori* natural science was possible, and tried to demonstrate that possibility by a purely deductive reconstruction of Newtonian mechanics, using only the concepts of space, time and mass, which, à la Kant, he treated as arising from internal intuition.[17] The object of this exercise was to display the logical structure of mechanics without employing the concept of force, thus showing that the nature of force had been grasped by physicists. The result was an unadorned and elegantly constructed argument which stands to the complexities of Hegelian metaphysics as *Jugendstil* agricultural design stands to baroque.

As the *Tractatus* was later to teach the isomorphism between language and world in terms of a theory of propositional pictoriality, so Hertz proclaimed that there was a conformity between thought and nature which enabled the mind to form images of objects:

> We form for ourselves images or symbols of external objects; and the form which we give them is such that the necessary consequents of the images in thought are always the images of the necessary consequents in nature of the things pictured. In order that this requirement may be satisfied, there must be a certain conformity between nature and our thought.[18]

Boltzman's anti-Hegelianism is more forthright than that of Hertz. He speaks at one place of Hegel's writings as an 'unclear thoughtless flow of words'.[19] He appears, however, to have made no very systematic study of traditional philosophy and was prone to be suspicious of it,[20] so it is not at all clear that he would have thought of himself as a Kantian. What justifies his being labelled as such is the fact that, like Hertz, he employs Kant's notion of a 'representation' in an effort to delimit the scope of scientific knowledge from within. The founder of 'statistical mechanics', Boltzman modified Hertz's account of mechanics, making it the basis of a general method of analysis in physics as a whole. For Wittgenstein, the particular appeal of Boltzman's method lay partly in the use it made of the idea of a space of theoretical possibilities — predecessor to Wittgenstein's own notion of logical space — and also in its striving for ever higher standards of accuracy and simplicity. Boltzman had written: 'The final and sole decision about the usefulness of the picture lies in the condition that it represent experience as simply and accurately as possible.'[21] Wittgenstein's own devotion to these qualities doubtless explains his wish to study under Boltzman. The aspiration was frustrated by Boltzman's suicide in 1906, but it is, perhaps, a mark of how deeply Wittgenstein felt the loss that he chose to study aeronautics at Manchester, when, as Mays notes,[22] he could have studied physics under Rutherford there.

To these potent sources of Kantian influence, emanating from the philosophy of physics, we must of course add that exerted by Frege, whose innovations in logical theory so captivated Wittgenstein, and whose debt to Kant's reflections on the status of arithmetical truths and to the very Kantian notion that mathematics *qua* science stands in need of a foundation was surely considerable. Quite apart from such identifiable sources as those already discussed, however, we must remember that the Viennese culture which first nourished Wittgenstein's intellect was in many respects a post-Kantian culture,[23] a world in which the problem of the mind's propensity to overstep the limits of rationality in its efforts to discover where they lay preoccupied musicians, painters, novelists and journalists alike.

1.22 Empiricism

The term 'empiricism' denotes an extremely broad communion and one, moreover, with which Wittgenstein probably never fully identified. If we give any sort of credence to the idea that he brought a unique way of thinking to philosophy, it will be obvious that he cannot have seen himself as a champion of empiricism or of any other 'ism'. Furthermore, if we include under the heading 'empiricism' the Lockean ideational theory of meaning and the doctrine that the meaning of a name is its extra-linguistic bearer, then it would seem that the post-Tractarian, and arguably even the Tractarian, Wittgenstein was not only not an empiricist, but an active opponent of empiricism. By parity of reasoning, in so far as conventionalism is designed to be a defence of empiricism — as it was for the Vienna Circle positivists — Wittgenstein was not a conventionalist, and it is mistaken to describe his philosophy of mathematics as 'full-blooded conventionalism', as Dummett has done.[24] Indeed, early efforts by positivists like Ayer (in his *Language, truth and logic*) to portray Wittgenstein as a champion of their cause have played no small part in obscuring the genuinely Wittgensteinian notions of semantic necessity which I hope to illuminate.

This said, the fact remains that Wittgenstein did not and, in the nature of the case, could not have escaped the influence of empiricism. This is especially clear when account is taken of what has just been said about the impress of Kantian thought on his philosophy: for to be, in any sense, a Kantian is almost by definition to have empiricist or phenomenalist predispositions which one wishes to reconcile with other beliefs instead of altogether erasing them. Kant's first *Critique* is, after all, precisely an attempt to harmonise the claims of Continental rationalism with those of British empiricism and Humean phenomenalism. As he himself tells us, it was Hume's attack on the rationality of belief in the causal nexus which first interrupted his 'dogmatic slumber' and redirected his enquiries.[25] It is therefore unsurprising to find Hume's views on causality echoed in the *Tractatus*, with Wittgenstein asserting, *inter alia*, that 'what the law of causality is meant to exclude cannot even be described', that inductive procedure has no logical, only a psychological justification, and that 'the sun will rise tomorrow' is an hypothesis which we cannot *know* to be true (TLP, 6.362–6.36311). It does not much matter whether, as Anscombe asserts, Wittgenstein had never read more than a few pages of Hume.[26] It remains perfectly reasonable to suppose that the empiricist elements in Kantian discourse fertilised the soil in which more direct implantations of various species of the doctrine by Russell, Moore and members of the Vienna Circle could take root to some extent and flourish for a while.

Of these empiricist influences, that of Russell was probably the most potent. It was his reading of *The principles of mathematics* as an aeronautical research student in Manchester that weaned Wittgenstein from Schopenhaurian idealism and acquainted him with Frege's philosophy of mathematics. It is noteworthy that the *Principles*, while containing a trenchant critique of Kant's theory of space,[27] also evinces an admiration for the 'simple' and 'admirable' principles of Hertz's dynamics[28] which would certainly have appealed to Wittgenstein. The transition from neo-Kantian to more overtly empiricist approaches to the problems of language, logic and the foundations of mathematics was, perhaps, thereby made to seem a smoother and more natural development than it may now appear to us.

This early work of Russell's, moreover, included his first published attempt to resolve the problems presented by denoting expressions.[29] In it Russell gave a very flexible interpretation of the doctrine that name-meanings are to be identified with named objects. His account allowed in principle for a name to count as a genuinely referring expression even when what it named was not a genuinely existing object, as in the case of mythical beings or logically impossible entities. In his 1905 paper, 'On denoting', Russell vigorously curtailed these liberalities. He rejected Meinong's solution, which granted a kind of existence to such logically disreputable entities as round-squares. He also rejected, on grounds of its artificiality, Frege's use of the *Sinn/Bedeutung* distinction to cope with such denotationless denoting phrases as 'the King of France' by stipulating that the *Bedeutung* in such cases should be a null class. Russell saw that no theory of the sentence which failed to deal more adequately with apparently denotationless denoting expressions could escape violation of the law of excluded middle: for by that law, either 'the present King of France is bald' or 'the present King of France is not bald' must be true, yet no King of France can appear in the most exhaustive list of bald and hirsute things. In typical anti-Hegelian fashion, Russell quips: 'Hegelians, who love a synthesis will probably conclude that he wears a wig.'[30]

Russell's own solution to this and similar paradoxes presented by descriptive phrases — first expressed in the rather cumbersome notation of 'On denoting', and later simplified by the introduction of quantifiers in *Principia mathematica* — was to drop the assumption that denoting expressions like 'the present King of France' ought, from a logical point of view, to be treated as names. Instead, he treated them as incomplete symbols, to which significance could be ascribed solely on the basis of their contribution to what was to be understood by the sentences in which they occurred. Thus, even if there were (as there is not) one and only one person presently reigning as monarch of France, that person would not, on Russell's theory, be what the phrase 'the present King of France' signifies. That the appearance which such definite descriptions gave of being names was an illusion preserved only by their surface grammar could, Russell thought, be demonstrated by logical analysis. Accordingly, all phrases of the form 'the such-and-such is thus-and-so' were to be translated according to the schema 'One and only one thing ϕs and it is also ψs'. Ambiguous cases, like 'the present King of France is not bald', could be settled by determining the scope of the existential quantifier. If that sentence is taken to mean that there is one and only one present King of France and he is not bald, it can correctly be formalised:

$$(\exists x)\{\{P_{x'}(y)[Py \supset (x=y)]\}\cdot \sim B_x\}$$

If, on the other hand, what is intended is that it is not the case that there is one and only one present King of France, bald or otherwise, the formalisation will run:

$$\sim(\exists x)\{\{P_{x'}(y)[Py \supset (x=y)]\}\cdot B_x\}$$

In the first case, the descriptive phrase was said to have primary occurrence, and in the second case, secondary occurrence.

Thus, the theory of descriptions saved Russell's original dogma that the meaning of a name is its bearer, even if it did so at the cost of drastically reducing the number of expressions which could be allowed to count as logically proper names by subjecting them to the epistemological requirement that they be objects of immediate acquaintance. Although this is not an ideational theory of meaning, as Locke's theory was, it is certainly an empiricist theory inasmuch as it identifies the meaning of a name with an extra-linguistic object given in sense-experience, and the Tractarian Wittgenstein expresses a kind of allegiance to it when he says: 'A name means an object. The object is its meaning' (TLP, 3.203), although in the *Investigations* he was to criticise the error of confounding a name's meaning with its bearer (PI, i, para. 40).

The influence of Russellian empiricism was augmented to some extent by Wittgenstein's encounters with what might be termed the 'commonsensical empiricism' of G.E. Moore. To say this is not to ignore Wittgenstein's disagreements with Moore; but, in *On certainty*, the former is still wrestling with the latter's 'proofs' of the existence of externals, and, given the relatively lengthy history of their association at Cambridge, it would be wrong to assume that Moore's special brand of empiricism, itself fed by the ideas of the Austro-German philosophers, Meinong and Brentano, should have made no impression on Wittgenstein.

What, finally, of the empiricist currents carried to Wittgenstein by members of the Vienna Circle? This matter is notoriously complex and controversial. It seems certain that in 1929 Wittgenstein had temporarily embraced a version of the verification principle.[31] It also seems clear that members of the Circle, having made of the slogan, 'The meaning of a sentence is the method of its verification', a battle-cry for use in the defence of their own version of empiricism, took themselves to have derived it from

Wittgenstein. The arguments in favour of the proposition that this belief was founded on a misreading of the *Tractatus* need not detain us at this point. Wittgenstein was not a positivist. There was a period, however, intermediate between the collapse of his first system of thought and the full emergence of his new way of looking at language, when he and the positivists shared some common ground, and it would be ungenerous not to ascribe this circumstance, in some degree at least, to the influence of minds as cultivated as those of men like Schlick, Carnap and Waismann.

It is important to notice that the above-mentioned sources of empiricist influence on Wittgenstein's thought are united by a common factor which they share with the sources of Kantian influence detailed in the previous section (1.21). The thinking of Russell, Moore and the Viennese positivists was markedly anti-Hegelian. Russell's writings are peppered with jibes at Hegel. Moore's early paper, 'The refutation of idealism', signalled the beginning of the end of the Hegelian period in British philosophy. As champions of advanced discoveries in the natural sciences, members of the Circle shared Boltzman's distrust of Hegelian metaphysics, especially when it presumed to discuss physics. Kantianism and empiricism may therefore usefully be regarded as combining to form one source of the tensions in the polarised philosophical backdrop to Wittgenstein's own thought. The other polarity is a dialectical tradition, to which I now turn.

1.23 Hegel and Marx

A difficulty in linking Wittgensteinian thought with the dialectical philosophy shaped by Hegel and Marx is that, although Wittgenstein was a Viennese by origin and wrote philosophy almost exclusively in German, he is widely thought of as belonging to an Anglophone philosophical tradition. That this should be so is entirely understandable. His friends and devotees among the philosophers of his time — Russell, Moore, Malcolm, Geach and Anscombe — were mainly English, and the only university post he ever held was at Cambridge. Recognition of his stature as the first genius of twentieth-century philosophy is largely the result of the work of English commentators, while his philosophy has been, relatively speaking, neglected by Continental scholars. The task of connecting his ideas with those of the German dialecticians is further complicated by Wittgenstein's own eccentricities as a reader of the philosophical classics, and his reticence about the precise nature of what he read. The fact remains, however, that Wittgenstein was a highly educated, German-speaking Austrian, and that, as such, he had inherited the ideas of Marx and Hegel as part — and as a very central part — of his culture. They were to the nineteenth-century Germanic world of ideas a kind of zenith, just as Wittgenstein's speculations now seem to demarcate a pinnacle of sorts in our own century's life of the mind. On these grounds alone, it seems scarcely credible that he should have been unacquainted with the writings and mode of thought of the two founders of modern dialectical philosophy.

There is, in fact, some indirect evidence that Wittgenstein was acquainted with Hegel's work. Rush Rhees recalls Wittgenstein remarking two or three years after the latter's 1935 visit to the Soviet Union 'that he had talked to a woman professor there about philosophy, and that she had told him he ought to read more Hegel'.[32] This seems to imply that, at the time of his visit to the Soviet Union, Wittgenstein had read at least *some* Hegel. If this was indeed the case, it would help to explain the affinities with Hegelianism which some commentators have discovered in Wittgenstein's later writings. Taylor, for instance, has drawn attention to points of *rapprochement* between Hegel's discussion of 'sense certainty' in the opening chapters of the *Phenomenology of spirit* and Wittgenstein's famous argument against the possibility of constructing a private language in the *Investigations*,[33] while Lovibond[34] has founded her attempt to construct a realist ethic on an Hegelian reading of Wittgenstein.

Historical evidence of Wittgenstein's acquaintance with Marxism is marginally less tenuous, but still indirect. According to Drury, Wittgenstein had read Lenin's philosophical writings, but thought them 'absurd'.[35] In response to Moran's enquiries concerning Wittgenstein's knowledge of Marx's writings, Rush Rhees answered that he had evidence only that Wittgenstein had read part of the first volume of *Capital*, was familiar with the 'tenets' of dialectical materialism, and thought that the Marxist notion of a 'developing reality' could be made sense of — for instance, by reflecting on how the meaning of the expression 'what is so' develops as the methods for showing what is so develop. Rhees also gathered that Wittgenstein had Marxist ideas in mind when he used the phrase 'transition "from quantity to quality"' (PI, i, para. 284).[36] These recollections gain substance from

Moran's reconstruction of Wittgenstein's conversations with Soviet philosophers during his largely mysterious visit to their country. Moran reports Soubotine's recollection of a report by Sophia Janovskaya, late Professor of Logic at Moscow University, who had gathered from Wittgenstein's talk that he was interested in Soviet philosophy and followed its development.[37]

The prudent assumption which this paucity of direct evidence dictates would seem to be that Wittgenstein owed the larger part of such understanding of Marxism as he possessed to his colleagues and friends. In that case, the prime source of Marxist influence seems most likely to have been the economist Piero Sraffa, to the stimulus of whose criticism Wittgenstein attributed 'the most consequential ideas' of the *Investigations* (PI, p. x), and whose name appears, along with such figures as Hertz, Boltzman and Frege, in Wittgenstein's own listing in 1931 of thinkers who had influenced him (CV, p. 19). The grounds for supposing Sraffa to have been a purveyor of specifically Marxist notions are, of course, his association with the Italian communist leader and theoretician Antonio Gramsci, and the fact that Sraffa invokes Marx's name at several places in order to illustrate the connection between his (Sraffa's) critique of marginalist economic theory and the theories of the 'old classical economists'.[38] Some caution is appropriate in evaluating this data; for while it is true that Gramsci, in 1924, describes Sraffa as being 'certainly still a Marxist', who could be 'resuscitated' and made into an 'active element in our party',[39] it is also true that this hope was not realised. In the same year, Gramsci wrote that Sraffa had 'not yet succeeded in destroying in himself all the ideological traces of his democratic-liberal intellectual formation, normative and Kantian, rather than dialectical and Marxist'.[40] It should be noted, moreover, that although Sraffa's *Production of commodities by means of commodities* presents no criticisms of Marx, its anti-marginalist critique has been seen as providing a basis for attacking Marx's labour theory of value.[41]

A further difficulty is that — apart from Malcolm's[42] anecdote about the Neapolitan gesture with which Sraffa precipitated Wittgenstein's doubts about the identity of 'logical form' which the *Tractatus* had postulated as holding between a proposition and that which it describes — there is no published record of the two friends' conversations. Nonetheless, it seems unthinkable that the two should not have discussed Marxist philosophy. The fact that Sraffa was not a committed Marxist, in the party-political sense, does not gainsay the fact that Marxism and the Gramscian versions of it made a profound impact on him in the 1920s or the fact that he continued to visit Gramsci in prison and to organise international campaigns on his behalf.[43] Moreover, if account is taken of the atmosphere prevalent in Cambridge in the 1930s, when pro-communist sentiment reached a kind of zenith among Britain's educated elite, it is hard to believe that Wittgenstein could have escaped all and any forms of Marxist influence, even had he not known Sraffa and never visited the Soviet Union. Wittgenstein's friend and pupil Francis Skinner was only prevented by ill-health from joining the International Brigade during the Spanish Civil War, and other friends, like Roy Pascal, George Thomson and Nicholas Bachtin, all had Marxist sympathies. There are no better grounds for supposing that Wittgenstein was impervious to Marxist ideas, particularly in the period when the thinking which produced the *Investigations* was in its formative stages, than there are for taking him to have been incorrigibly resistant to Kantian and empiricist traditions in the gestation period which produced the *Tractatus*.

Readings of Wittgensteinian philosophy, therefore, which have sought to discover a Marxist inspiration in the treatment of semantic necessity to be found there, are unfairly treated if they are dismissed as eccentric. Indeed, once prejudices against such readings are overcome, many (perhaps too many) possible connections seem to present themselves. It seems clear, for example, that in the discussion of rules and rule-following in the *Investigations* (PI, i, paras 185–242), an internal connection is postulated between understanding a rule and acting on it and, hence, between the meaning of an expression and its use. What this connection comes down to is a thesis concerning the unmediated interaction between purposive human activity and conceptual grasp which a Marxist would describe as 'a unity of theory and practice'. It also seems evident that, because Wittgenstein's later philosophy treats all grammatical rules as essentially public standards for determining whether an expression is meaningful and what, if anything, it means, language, the bearer of ideas, is tied to historical institutions and, hence, to social processes in a way which accommodates Marxist theory. Another possibility is to speculate on whether Wittgenstein appropriated Marx's ideas about the fetishisation of commodities and applied them in a critique of previous theories of meaning. Just as for Marx the commodity form conceals its true origin and the source of its value in socialised human labour by presenting its social nature as a relationship between things, so for Wittgenstein (the speculation runs) the form of our linguistic expressions deceives us into thinking that they mean what they do independently of the uses to which we put them.

The availability, particularly of Wittgenstein's later philosophy, to speculations of these sorts has prompted the beginnings of a minor literature in which his name is linked with that of Marx. Thus, Rubenstein[44] argues, *inter alia*, that Marx and Wittgenstein concur in thinking that matters of fact, particularly matters of social fact, are internally, or conceptually, related, and that dialectical logic plays a major role in the work of both. Susan Easton believes there is a 'basic similarity between humanist Marxism and Wittgensteinian social philosophy' inasmuch as 'both are interested in systematically distorted communication and both see philosophy *qua* self-reflection as a means of freeing us from the "bewitchment of our intelligence" by language'.[45] Like Rubenstein, Easton thinks that Marx anticipates Wittgenstein's argument in favour of an internal connection between ideas and activity by his refusal to separate language as an expression of ideas from activity.[46]

The trouble with these interesting conjectures is that both Rubenstein and Easton rely on highly contentious interpretations of the strands of thought they wish to connect. Rubenstein, for example, refuses to call Marx either an idealist or a materialist because he thinks that Marx 'describes an interrelatedness between man and the world of objects that erodes distinct boundaries between the two'.[47] Easton, for her part, insists on treating Marx as a 'humanist', although conceding that 'there are certain strands which emphasise Marx's rejection of humanism'.[48] Because her treatment draws heavily on Hegelian elements in Marx's work, Easton is made anxious about possible charges that she has reduced Marxism to idealism. She is driven by this anxiety to assert not only that Marx was not an idealist, but that Hegel was not one either. Most seriously, both writers fall into the trap of focusing exclusively on the *contrasts* between the *Tractatus* and Wittgenstein's later philosophy, while ignoring the conjunctive features to which I have tried to draw attention (1.11). This is an understandable mistake, since it is in the later writings that evidence of a Marxist influence is to be found. However, it has the effect of losing sight of the character of Wittgenstein's intellectual development as a genuine *process*, containing both new and old features as real processes do. This, in turn, obscures for Easton and Rubenstein the real nature of the affinity they seek. This consists, as I shall try to show as this essay progresses, in a parallel between Wittgenstein's movement away from logicist essentialism of a neo-Kantian sort towards a materialist account of semantic necessity and Marx's journey away from logicist essentialism of an Hegelian kind towards a materialist account of historical necessity.

1.24 A moralist's concerns

As I remarked earlier (1.2), the influences acting on Wittgenstein all had to pass through the filter of his own religio-ethical and aesthetic preoccupations which — since for Wittgenstein they were all consubstantial — we may group under the rubric of his 'moralism', meaning by this his predisposition to put matters of moral evaluation at the centre of everything in his life and work. It is this predisposition which has constantly to be taken into account in trying to penetrate Wittgenstein's specifically *philosophical* purposes: for although it is entirely possible for a philosopher to be a fervent moralist without allowing his fervour entrance to his professional life, this was not Wittgenstein's case. For him, intellectual strivings were inextricably bound up with the striving after moral excellence, and the quality of a person's intellect was inseparable from the quality of his moral life. To his friend, Paul Engelmann, Wittgenstein wrote: 'I am working reasonably hard and wish I were a better man and had a better mind. These two things are really one and the same — God help me!' (LLW, p. 4). He wrote this in March 1917, while serving with the Austrian army on the eastern front and working on the notes which ultimately became the *Tractatus*.

It is characteristic that among those notes, dealing as they mostly do with the technical problems of philosophical logic, we should find an entry in January of that year dealing with the ethics of suicide (NB, p. 91). Further testimony to Wittgenstein's belief in the interweave of moral with philosophical concerns is provided in a letter to Malcolm, written in 1944:

> . . . what is the use of studying philosophy if all that it does for you is to enable you to talk with some plausibility about some abstruse questions of logic etc., and if it does not

23

improve your thinking about the important questions of everyday life . . .[49]

This sense of moral mission is intrinsic to all his major writings, and explains the powerful impression they convey that, in wrestling with the problems of logic and semantic necessity, their author is trying to implant a new ethical vision into both his and our lives.

As is very often the case, Wittgenstein's preoccupation with morality was saturated with — indeed, could not be considered separately from — his almost obsessional concern with religious matters. He was not, as he told Drury,[50] a religious man, but could not help seeing every problem from a religious point of view. If we bear in mind the fact that Wittgenstein came to think of the methods of philosophy as so many different 'therapies' (PI, i, para. 133), then we will not miss the point of his remarking that 'People are religious to the extent that they believe themselves to be not so much *imperfect as ill*' (CV, p. 45 original emphases). To the extent that he feels on his own impulses, as it were, the enigmas he confronts in his reflections, Wittgenstein's ideal philosopher is always a religious man. The ethical notion of 'trust' was tied up with his conception of religious faith, as it was with his later philosophy of language. Superstition resulted from fear and was a kind of false science, while religious faith was 'a trusting' (CV, p. 72), and a language-game is only possible if one trusts something' (OC, para. 509).

These religio-moral facets of Wittgenstein's character were doubtless fed by his reading of Augustine, Kierkegaard, Tolstoy and the Gospels. They were also sustained by his extraordinary aesthetic sensibility, his capacity to respond creatively to music, literature and the plastic arts. The fastidious purism of the *Jugendstil* movement in architecture — of which the house he designed for his sister at 19 Kundmanngasse is a perhaps eccentric example — was, it must be remembered, part of a moral and political protest movement on the part of Viennese architects and artists. That Wittgenstein felt himself part of their protest is shown not only by his friendship with the architect, Adolf Loos, but also by his 100,000-crown gift in 1914, of which the painter Kolkoschka and the poet Rilke were among the beneficiaries.[51]

The lesson of all this is that we shall miss the spirit of Wittgenstein's philosophy and, hence, of his evolving doctrine of semantic necessity, if the moralistic dimension of his make-up is lost sight of. This warning is all the more necessary inasmuch as the great bulk of Wittgensteinian philosophy is not about morality, and is not in any obvious sense classifiable as moral philosophy. Wittgenstein is indeed mainly concerned with the philosophy of logic and of semantics, with questions concerning the status of linguistic rules, the paradoxes of putatively private languages, the foundations of mathematics and so on. The danger is that, reared predominantly as we are in a scientistic culture and philosophical tradition which associates discourse about these matters with a certain kind of value-free 'detachment', we are apt to read our own predispositions in this regard into Wittgenstein's writings, even though everything we know about the man and much that he himself said about his work suggests that this is not the way to read him.

1.3 The *Tractatus*

Wittgenstein's account of semantic necessity and of the relation of language to the world, as he gives it in the *Tractatus*, may be trisected into three interlocking doctrines: there is a metaphysical doctrine which constitutes his atomist ontology, a logico-semantic doctrine which includes his logical atomism and picture-theory of the proposition, and a religio-ethical doctrine which concerns the extra-linguistic and extra-mundane status of moral and aesthetic values. Of these, Wittgenstein thought the third doctrine the most important and said as much in a letter to Ludwig von Ficker:

> . . . the point of the book is ethical . . . For the ethical is delimited from within, as it were, by my book; and I'm convinced that, *strictly* speaking, it can ONLY be delimited in this way. In brief, I think: All of that which *many* are *babbling* today, I have defined in my book by remaining silent about it.[52]

How seriously ought we to take this claim of Wittgenstein's that the *Tractatus* is chiefly concerned with ethics? The answer to this question will predetermine our whole method of interpretation here: for if we do take Wittgenstein at his word, then it will seem reasonable to treat the logico-semantic and metaphysical parts of the book as developing out of his conviction that moral and sacred values are inexpressible and not the other way

25

around. We shall then be disposed to think that the order in which Wittgenstein introduces his topics in the final published version of the *Tractatus* — starting with his atomistic ontology, going on to set forth the picture-theory and culminating with the terse remarks about value and unsayability — cannot be a reliable guide to the real meaning of the work, and that the best way to get at that meaning is to emulate Marx's method with the Hegelian dialectic by treating the *Tractatus* like an edifice which is 'standing on its head' and needs to be turned 'right side up again'.[53]

It is fair to state that neither Wittgenstein's claim nor the mode of interpretation it suggests are uncontentious. From Russell's introduction onwards, commentators have generally treated the *Tractatus* as a work primarily concerned with the philosophy of logic and of language, and have taken the so-called 'mystical' sections to be almost incidental appendages. The justification for so doing turns on the relative sparseness of the treatment accorded to the ethical topic in comparison with the extensive discussions of logical and ontological matters, and the paucity of argument with which the thesis of the ineffability of ethics is supported. These considerations have moved Hacker[54] to protest that the ineffability thesis hangs on no more than the bare assertion of the non-contingency of the ethical, and that ethical pseudo-propositions, while not being senseless tautologies or contradictions, are not in any obvious way classifiable as formal concepts either. If they were formal concepts, he argues, it would be clear why Wittgenstein treats them as pseudo-propositions, but, equally, in that case, they would incorporate variables taking a range of objects of a given category as their values, and the *Tractatus* is silent about what the substitution instances of such variables might be. If I have understood him, Hacker's objection comes down to the complaint that Wittgenstein neglects to treat such issues as the question of what would stand to the concept of ethical value as red stands to the concept of colour, as we should expect him to do if his remark in the letter to von Ficker is to be taken seriously.

This view is objectionable on two counts: firstly, it disregards an author's view of his own work without sufficient justification for so doing. Of course a philosopher is not always the best judge of the import of what he has written, and if it were possible to treat Wittgenstein's avowals to von Ficker as a mere aberration, we might — given the post-war circumstances, his probable mental state and his difficulties in finding a publisher — feel safe in ignoring them. The fact is, however (as Hacker admits) that Wittgenstein not only never disavowed the ethical doctrine of his first great work, even after revising his views on so much else in it, but continued to defend versions of it — notably, in the 'Lecture on ethics', prepared for delivery at Cambridge between September 1929, and December 1930. If, moreover, we take proper account of what has already been observed (1.24) about the centrality of Wittgenstein's ethical concerns to his intellectual life, we shall only find it possible to ignore Wittgenstein's own statement of his chief purpose in the *Tractatus* at the cost of regarding his letter to von Ficker as 'either self-deluding or disingenuous',[55] and that is not a judgement which is either conducive to understanding him or warranted by his stature. Secondly, it is no argument against the interpretation at issue to say that if the main point of the *Tractatus* were indeed an ethical one, we should anticipate (what is absent) a discussion of possible instantiations of the concept of the ethical. This, after all, is precisely what Wittgenstein warns us *not* to expect. Genuine ethical value belongs (as we shall see) to the realm of the unsayable. Such mention of it as Wittgenstein permits himself is not intended to be part of some theoretical explanation of how things are in the world, although, of course, if it were, we should be entitled to expect the explanation to be fleshed out in the way Hacker expects this. I conclude, therefore, that the remarks about ethics are pivotal to an understanding of the *Tractatus* and will at once proceed to a discussion of them.

1.31 Ethics

Wittgenstein's attitude to ethics may cautiously be characterised as Romantic. By this I mean that he not only displayed an ardent, yet scrupulously reverential, posture towards moral, religious and aesthetic matters, regarding them as belonging to an essentially unworldly domain, but that he tended to identify these three things with one another in his mind. 'Ethics and aesthetics', he remarks parenthetically, 'are one and the same' (TLP, 6.421). The stance is familiar enough to render it comprehensible, even to those of us who may not wish to emulate it: the joyful hush of the picture-gallery is equated with the solemn stillness of the place of worship and with the awe-filled silence which appropriately greets displays of stupendous virtue. At its worst, this sort of romanticism becomes the merely vulgar replacement of moral principle by moral posturing. At its best, it or something very like it is to be found in Wordsworth's poetry and in the philosophy of Wittgenstein's heroes Kant, Kierkegaard and Augustine. In company with them, the Wittgenstein of the *Tractatus* is wedded to a transcendentalism which sets genuinely ethical values apart from, and even in opposition to, the goals and goal-orientated activities which are the objects of mundane concerns. On this view, no set of facts or factual consequences can serve as the basis for any value-judgement and arithmetising calculations of the relative worthwhileness of likely upshots are simply beside the point. This is the thrust of the distinction Wittgenstein makes in his 'Lecture on ethics' between 'absolute' and 'relative' value. There he says that 'although all statements of relative value can be shown to be mere statements of facts, no statement of fact can ever be or imply a judgement of absolute value.'[56]

When Wittgenstein speaks of ethical values in the *Tractatus*, he uses the term 'value' to mean what he intended by the term 'absolute value' in the 'Lecture on ethics'. In the *Tractatus* conception, what might be called the problematics of meaning and morality are brought together and are seen as resolving one another. Ethical value is what makes sense of the world, but these values can no more become part of the world they make sense of than a hand can grasp itself. Wittgenstein puts this by saying:

> The sense of the world must lie outside the world. In the world everything is as it is, and everything happens as it does happen: *in* it no value exists . . . If there is any value that does have value it must lie outside the whole sphere of what happens and is the case . . . It must lie outside the world. (TLP, 6.41, original emphasis)

These seemingly dark sayings are really in complete accord with the logical and ontological discussions which precede them. In these the world was said to be a totality, not of things, but of facts (1.1), which are of course contingent arrangements which might have been otherwise. However, the possibility of configurations of this sort — which is just the possibility of there being fact-stating propositions — cannot itself arise out of necessities which are merely contingent, but must be rooted in the kind of absolute determinacy which we associate with formal logic or with transcendent values. Thus, it seemed to follow that it was 'impossible for there to be propositions of ethics. Propositions can express nothing that is higher' (TLP, 6.42). It is clear where this must lead. Propositions cannot express what is higher, being capable only of expressing truths or falsehoods about what is lower or worldly; but if they cannot do so, then ethical values in Wittgenstein's sense are inexpressible *tout court*. 'It is clear', he says, 'that ethics cannot be put into words.' (TLP, 6.421)

However, if '*The limits of my language* are the limits of my world' (TLP, 5.6, original emphasis), and if the sense of the world (and thus of language) in the form of absolute values is beyond the limits Wittgenstein sets himself to describe from within, how can these values constitute the meaning of language and world? How, if ethics cannot be put into words, can ethical values confer on words the meanings they have? What, furthermore, is the status of the remarks about ethics, God, and aesthetics that occur in the 'mystical' sections of the *Tractatus*? The Wittgensteinian answer to these questions bring to the fore two of the most elusive notions in his philosophy — the saying/showing distinction and the idea of an elucidation. He says of things that cannot be verbalised: 'They *make themselves manifest (Dies zeigt sich)*. They are what is mystical.' (TLP, 6.522, original emphasis) Earlier, in dealing with the impossibility of speaking about the will *qua* subject of ethical attributes and with the totally transforming effect which good or bad exercises of the will must have, not on the world, but on its limits, he concludes: 'The world of the happy man is a different one from that of the unhappy man.' (6.43) What this must mean is not, of course, that the happy man *enjoys* his life in a hedonistic sense in a way that the unhappy man does not. Were this the meaning, we could set about comparing the relative advantages and disadvantages of the two lives in terms of some sort of felicific *calculus*, because we would be dealing with some *facts* about the lives in question, not with a totality. Rather, the meaning must be that the life of a truly good man *shows* or makes manifest the values which make it possible, just as the life of an evil person manifests the absence of such values. Of such life-worlds it is not only otiose but nonsensical to advance the opinion (save for condemnatory, commendatory or 'prescriptive' purposes) that they are good or evil: for what is in question here is not praise, blame or prescription, but a life which is archetypical in that it represents a standard in terms of which relativising judgements are possible.

The lives of Buddha, Socrates and Jesus are standards in this way, setting the measure by which our efforts at value-preservation may be guided. However, the fact that they are standards is not, strictly speaking, explicable in words which are not mere retellings of the lives in question and descriptions of our attempts to model ourselves on them, any more than the fact that such-and-such a piece of metal is the standard for a unit of measurement is explicable apart from our pointing to it and explaining that our measuring practices are carried out in accord with it. We point or make verbal gestures at the great paradigms of happy or unhappy moral existences in order to draw attention to the values we live or fail to live by. Such verbal gesturings are what Wittgenstein means by elucidations. They are nonsensical, not in being senseless or empty of factual content as contradictions or tautologies are, but in being in a profound sense attempts to say the unsayable. More specifically, genuine propositions have bi-polar truth-possibilities, since the states of affairs they represent may or may not hold — i.e. genuine propositions are always possibly true or possibly false — while tautologies which include all logical truths are always true and contradictions are always false. Elucidations fall into none of these categories, yet they are (Wittgenstein thinks) the very stuff of which the philosophical attempt to apprehend the necessity which makes meaning in both its moral and linguistic senses possible is constituted. 'My propositions', he says, 'serve as elucidations in the following way: anyone who understands me eventually recognises them as nonsensical, when he has used them — as steps — to climb up beyond them'. (6.54)

It is interesting that Wittgenstein uses the term 'elucidation' at just two other places in the *Tractatus* and that he does so in highly significant contexts. He firstly employs it in the crucial discussion of atomic names which he regards as primitive signs, impervious to further definitional analysis. The meanings of such signs, he says, 'can be explained by means of elucidations (*Erläuterungen*)', and these latter, he adds, are sentences that already contain the primitive signs, 'So they can only be understood if the meanings of those signs are already known' (3.263). The next use of the term occurs in the course of the discussion of the nature and purpose of philosophy, in which he insists on its character as an activity and on its being radically distinguished from science. There he says that 'A philosophical work consists essentially of elucidations.' (4.112) The fact that the third use of the term is so closely associated with his ethical doctrine seems to me to constitute further evidence for the centrality of this doctrine to a right understanding of the whole of the *Tractatus* and to a proper grasp of the Wittgensteinian conception of semantic necessity in general.

1.32 Semantics

The chief tenet of the Tractarian philosophical semantics may be summarised in one sentence: semantic necessity is logical necessity. As pictures portray what they do in virtue of their pictorial form, so propositions are linguistic pictures of reality, and are such in virtue of their logical form. This form is an essence, concealed beneath the surface grammar of language and made manifest by dint of analysis. The enabling tool for this analysis is the notation of modern function-theoretic logic, made possible by the researches of Frege and Russell.

Wittgenstein's debt to Russell and Frege should not, however, prevent us from distinguishing his brand of logicism from theirs. He did not share their conviction that ordinary natural language was logically deficient and, *a fortiori*, he could not join them in thinking that the new logical notation embodied an 'improved' logic which ought to be regarded as an ideal language. Humankind, he thought, was capable of constructing languages which could express every sense, although it was not humanly possible to gather immediately from everyday language what its logic was (TLP, 4.002). In fact, all the propositions of everyday language were in perfect logical order as they stood (TLP, 5.5563). Logic was thought of by Wittgenstein, nonetheless, as constituting the most general condition for any possibility of representation: for logical form was what any picture of whatever form had to have 'in common with reality in order to be able to depict it' (TLP, 2.18). All pictures are logical pictures, although all pictures are not, for example, spatial pictures (TLP, 2.182). This is certainly logicism, albeit of a more refined and persuasive sort than the Fregean or Russellian varieties, for it treats all language (and hence all the world, which is equivalent to the limits of language) as determined by logic in the last resort. There is to be no no-man's-land between sense and nonsense, and no account of the possibility of representation which does not fall under the law of excluded middle.

The Tractarian philosophy of meaning, then, which brings the referential account of how meaning is possible to an unparalleled pitch of rigour and elegance, begins as a general doctrine of pictorial representation. We make pictures of facts for ourselves (TLP, 2.1). These represent situations in logical space, being models of reality that may be laid against it like a ruler. There will be some identity between a picture and what it depicts, else it could not be a picture of that which it pictures. This common element is pictorial form, which cannot itself be pictured, only displayed (TLP, 2.11–2.172).

For Wittgenstein, propositions are just such pictures or models of reality as we imagine it (TLP, 4.01). At first sight, this may seem implausible; but neither do musical notations or alphabets at first seem to be pictures of what they represent, although they are so, 'even in the ordinary sense' (TLP, 4.011). An obvious case of a proposition picturing a real state of affairs would seem to be some such sentence as 'my pen lies to the left of my pencil'. Unobvious cases are dealt with by the Leibnizian-sounding proposal that language has a hidden logical structure or depth-grammar which the surface-grammar of ordinary language tends to disguise. This structure can be rendered perspicuous by an appropriate logical notation. It is easy to see how the new quantifier logic lends credence to this view. Ordinary-language words, like 'nobody' and 'somebody', give quantifiers the spurious appearance of proper names, while the word 'exists' makes them seem to be predicates. Such ambiguities can result in confusions for both the formal and the philosophical logician. Thus, the word 'is' does treble duty as copula, identity-sign and existential quantifier; and formal concepts, such as 'object', 'number' and 'concept' itself, which are really signs of variables, appear to be genuine concepts that may be treated as the values of such variables. An adequate logical symbolism is, therefore, a valuable prophylactic against muddles which can result from inattentive use of everyday expressions. Yet Wittgenstein clearly viewed the possibilities offered by the new logical script in a far more exalted light. For him the introduction of any new device into the symbolism of logic was 'necessarily a momentous event' (TLP, 5.452); for logic was 'the great mirror' of the world (TLP, 5.511), and was 'transcendental' (TLP, 6.13), just like ethics.

In these tones of mystical fervour, in this mirror-imagery and talk of depths and surfaces, we may scent a danger to the security of the precepts segregating philosophy from natural science which will have dire consequences for the Tractarian system as a whole: for Wittgenstein is clearly disposed to treat the symbolism of logic as if it were a highly refined optical tool of natural science, useful for penetrating beneath the superficialities which appearances offer to unaided vision, so as to reveal the pristine simplicity of a uniform ultimate arrangement. Thus, despite the prohibition on regarding philosophy as one of the natural sciences or, indeed, as any sort of 'body of doctrine' (TLP, 4.111–4.112), we find language being subjected to the kind of reductive analysis we ordinarily associate with scientific procedures.

In accordance with this programme, the *Tractatus* set out to reduce the propositions of ordinary language to their simplest elements. The final products of logical analysis are not such as we encounter in everyday discourse. Propositions in natural language incorporate complex concept-words which are analysable into their characteristic marks. They also contain names of complexes such as are reducible to definite descriptions, analysable in their turn by the method pioneered by Russell into quantifiers and concept-words. Beneath these complexities, however, Wittgenstein discerned the 'elementary' proposition which was to explain the isomorphisism between language and reality. These are composite, being comprised of function and argument. A genuine elementary proposition asserts that a given state of affairs obtains or does not obtain, thus bisecting logical space, and will exhibit complete logical independence in respect of all and any other elementary propositions. The test of such independence is particularly stringent: 'It is a sign of a proposition's being elementary that there can be no elementary proposition contradicting it.' (TLP, 4.211)

Elementary propositions consist of names in immediate combination (TLP, 4.22–4.221). These atomic names occur only in the nexus of elementary propositions, which stand to them in the relation of function to argument (TLP, 4.23–4.24). They are governed by the rules of logical syntax which determine their combinatorial possibilities. They have no sense (*Sinn*), only reference (*Bedeutung*), and this just is the simple object in reality for which a given simple name must stand. Thus, the meaning of a name is its bearer, and to grasp that meaning is to understand the logical form of a name and to know the object for which it stands. Now the form of a simple name is what is common to it and other names of the same logic-syntactical category — i.e. the rule-governed possibilities of names combining, represented by the variable of which those names are values. These variables are not genuine, but only formal, concepts, like 'number', 'sound' or 'colour'. However, that 'red' is a colour or 'two' a number is not something that can be *said* in a proposition, properly so called, but only *shown* by the logical behaviour of which the name in question is capable. What expresses itself in language cannot be expressed by means of language (TLP, 4.121). The meanings of simple names can only be elucidated, and such elucidations are not comprehensible unless the meanings of these primitive signs are already known (TLP, 3.263). Thus, what can be shown cannot be said (TLP, 4.1212).

In attempting to provide a synopsis of the account of language and logic given in the *Tractatus*, it is difficult to avoid giving the impression that we are dealing with a wholly serialised explanation in which the analysis of the elementary proposition is followed by the introduction of the logical operators, so that we can get on with the story of how compound propositions are put together out of their irreducible elements. The account we are being offered is far more organic and fundamentalist than that: for Wittgenstein's thought is that in being given the concept of the elementary proposition we are, at the same moment, being given the concepts of all possible forms of combination of such propositions such as are expressed by complex propositions, joined up by the various logical operators and quantifiers. This point is obscured if, like Kenny, we say that Wittgenstein has 'invented' a[57] new formal device in devising the truth tables for the propositional calculus, but fail to appreciate that what has been invented is not a 'decision procedure',[58] but a *notation*. The importance of this is brought out by reflecting on the essential bipolarity of the concept of a proposition as we have so far been discussing it — i.e. its essential connection with the concepts of truth and falsity. Every elementary proposition is true or false. For every set n of such propositions there are just 2^n truth-possibilities. Thus, for a pair of propositions, 'p' and 'q', there are four possibilities, TT (when both are true), FT, TF and FF. The T/F notation allows us to represent possible truth functions without recourse to the logical connectives, as the schema Wittgenstein sets out (TLP, 5.101) elegantly shows. Thus, for example, 'q.p' is expressed by TFFF (p,q)', 'p v q' by 'TFFF (p,q)' and so on. All possible forms of propositional combination are therefore implicit in the notion of the elementary proposition, given its essential link with truth and falsity and with negation.

The T/F schema, then, seemed to Wittgenstein to be not merely a device to enable one to *decide* which truth-possibilities were presupposed by a given proposition, but a symbolism which could penetrate the very heart of the proposition's inner structure. More than this, it could lucidly reveal the essential difference between genuine propositions and pseudo-propositions. The latter exhibited no bi-polarity. A senseless contradiction of the form 'p . not-p' would display only Fs, while an equally senseless tautology of the form 'not (p . not-p)' would express only Ts. Tautologies and contradictions are not, however, nonsensical in the way that elucidations were seen to be. 'They are part of the symbolism, just as "O" is part of the symbolism of arithmetic.' (TLP, 4.4611) Tautologies are the propositions of logic (TLP, 6.1). It is the mark of such propositions that their truth may be recognised from the symbol alone, a fact which 'contains in itself the whole philosophy of logic' (TLP, 6.113). The fact that the propositions of logic are tautologies *shows* the formal properties of language and world (TLP, 6.12). Thus, although they are contentless, in the sense of being void of subject-matter, the propositions of logic represent the structure of reality. Their tie to the world consists in their presupposing that elementary propositions do have sense and that the names of which the latter are concatenated all have referents. Whether a proposition belongs to logic can be *calculated* by calculating the logical properties of the symbol which expresses it, 'and this is what we do when we "prove" a logical proposition. For without bothering about sense or meaning, we construct the logical propositions out of others using only *rules that deal with signs*' (TLP, 6.126, original emphasis). Of course, the calculations that are in question here are the operations we perform using the propositional and predicate calculi, and there will be a certain emptiness about them inasmuch as a proof that a proposition is a proposition of logic must have a tautology as first premiss, and such a premiss must be capable of *showing* that it is indeed tautological without further proof.

Two critical comments are in order at this point. Firstly, the explanation the *Tractatus* gives of how truth-operations on elementary propositions generate the totality of all propositions which, Wittgenstein says, is language (TLP, 4.001), incited the thought that there must be an occult 'generative grammar' which must yield an infinite set of sentences. This idea, which seems to be at the back of Chomskyian linguistics, rests on the presupposition that any given language, be it Afrikaans, Xhosa or English, is comprised of an infinite number of sentences, and there is no more reason to assume this than there is to assume that an infinite number of moves are possible in chess, because the status of some pieces are basic in determining what moves other pieces can make.

Secondly, the rules of logical syntax which are supposed to form the ultimate foundation of meaningful discourse have the structure of a *calculus*. The calculus-model was, as we shall see, progressively abandoned by Wittgenstein as his own criticism of the *Tractatus* developed, and was finally replaced by the language-game conception. However, its pivotal role in the Tractarian theory of meaning is, in any case, anomalous: for if, as I have argued (1.3), Wittgenstein's claim that the main point of the book is ethical is a claim we ought to take seriously, then absolute moral values, which lend themselves to no sort of calculating operations (1.31), are also supposed to be foundational in conferring sense on language. In other words, the ethics of the *Tractatus* seems to be at odds with its syntax and semantics. If this is so, it could clearly be used as a further argument against the position that ethics is central to the Wittgensteinian treatment of meaning; for it suggests that he took little account of what he had said about values when he got down to the business of showing how language works. I shall deal with this objection later by showing that although there is indeed an anomaly, the recognition of it contributes to a deeper understanding of the breakdown and reconstruction of Wittgenstein's philosophy of language in a way which re-emphasises the importance of ethics.

1.33 Ontology

The logico-semantic doctrines of the *Tractatus* are both historically and logically antecedent to its ontology. The fact that Wittgenstein decided to situate his theses about the substance of the world at the beginning of the book had the effect, which he could not have intended, of partially concealing the dependence of those theses on his views concerning logic and the nature of the proposition. There is indeed an isolated reference to 'simple objects' in a *Notebook* entry for September 1914 (NB, p. 3); but mention of the 'simples' does not occur with any regularity until the following year, and they are not discussed in the 'Notes on logic' of September 1913, in which, moreover, he says specifically that philosophy consists of logic and metaphysics, but that the former is the basis of philosophy (NB, p. 93). In the notes Wittgenstein dictated to Moore in Norway during April 1914, he says only that the 'simples' in a proposition are names of 'simples' in reality (NB, p. 111). The truth is that the requirement of absolute determinacy of sense, which is basic to the philosophical semantics of the *Tractatus*, creates the demand for absolute definiteness of denotation, which the metaphysical atomism of the book's opening pronouncements is designed to satisfy.

We can see that this is so by reminding ourselves of an essential feature of Wittgenstein's account of the proposition. This is the peculiarity that while elementary propositions have *Sinn* but not *Bedeutung*, the atomic names they express have *Bedeutung* but not *Sinn*. The latter are like points, the former like arrows (TLP, 3.144). It follows that there can be no empty atomic names. If such a name has meaning, then the meaning it has is just the object it denotes, so if there are to be simple names, there must be simple objects corresponding to them, and there must be such names, because 'The requirement that simple signs be possible is the requirement that sense be determinate.' (TLP, 3.23)

In accordance with this requirement, then, the *Tractatus* sketches a metaphysical picture of reality which dovetails neatly with its logical atomism and with its account of the elementary proposition. The world is all that is the case, but it is the totality, not of things, but of facts (TLP, 1–1.1). Facts are exactly isomorphic with the propositions that state them. The world divides into facts (TLP, 1.2), i.e. it divides into what is and what is not the case in a way which matches the bi-polarity of propositions. Simple objects are the ultimate constituents of the totality of things, and can enter into combination to produce states of affairs, it being essential to the nature of such objects that they should be possible constituents of states of affairs (TLP, 2–2.011). Given their combinatorial possibilities, the totality of simple objects determines all possible states of affairs, and the actual world is the realised combination of objects. However, as simple names are distinguished from the elementary propositions that express them, so simple objects must be distinguished clearly from facts. A fact is not merely a complex of simple objects. The fact that 'aRb' is distinct from the complex which consists in a's standing in the relation of R to b, although the latter may be a constituent of the former.

As simple names are unanalysable, so atomic objects are indecomposible. Corresponding to the logical form of its name, each object has internal properties which are its combinatorial possibilities with other objects. It also has external properties which are the properties it has of being combined with whatever other objects it actually is combined with, such as would be described by a true elementary proposition. Just as, in accord with Frege's dictum,[59] a name has meaning only in the nexus of a proposition (TLP, 3.3, 3.314 and 4.23), so objects occur only in combination.

The requirement that elementary propositions be logically independent of one another is matched by the stipulation that the atomic states of affairs into which objects enter be conceived of as logically independent of all other states of affairs, so that the existence or non-existence of a given state of affairs licenses no inference as to whether any other state of affairs does or does not obtain. Objects cannot be composite, because they constitute the substance of the world. If the world had no substance, then whether a proposition had sense would depend on whether another proposition were true, in which case we could sketch no picture of the world (true or false) (TLP, 2.021–2.0212). We might try to complete this part of the argument by adding that we *can* sketch pictures of the world (true or false) in virtue of the genuine propositions in our language, and that we are able to do this is what the picture-theory of the proposition explains, *ergo* there must be simple objects of the sort Wittgenstein says there are.

Yet even after the role of the simple objects in supporting the picture-theory has been understood, it is impossible not to feel a deep and suspicion-tinged curiosity as to what exactly these objects are supposed to be. Wittgenstein is characteristically laconic on the point. Specks in the visual field, he tells us, must have some colour, notes must have *some* pitch, objects of the sense of touch *some* degree of hardness (TLP, 2.0131). His 1915 notes offer as examples points of the visual space, patches in our visual field and even the appearance of stars (NB, pp. 45 and 64). Are we to take it then, that the simples are objects of acquaintance, as the Hintikkas[60] think? I cannot enter into the interesting and often subtle reasons given by the Hintikkas for thinking as they do about the simples. I can, however, venture a word of warning concerning the direction their thinking might point to, and suggest an alternative.

As I understand them, the Hintikkas assimilate Wittgenstein's thought about the simple objects to Russell's ideas concerning concrete objects of acquaintance as Russell expressed them in the book he wrote in 1913, entitled *Theory of knowledge*, and which he left largely unpublished. On the Hintikkas' interpretation, Wittgenstein refused (as Russell did not) to countenance logical forms as objects of acquaintance, thinking that the work of accounting for the logical form of complex propositions could be done by the class of regular, concrete objects of acquaintance, which Russell included in his classification of such objects. Now if we construe Wittgenstein's atomism along such lines, according to the ontology of the *Tractatus* the kind of importance that the Hintikkas accord to it, we shall be tempted to fall into the old mistake of thinking of it as a work of *epistemology*. Theory of knowledge, Wittgenstein thought, was the philosophy of psychology, and he conceded that with his method there was a danger of getting 'entangled in unessential psychological investigations' as previous philosophers had done (TLP, 4.1121). However, previous epistemological investigation begins with a problematic which the *Tractatus* eliminates. Empiricist-based theory of knowledge assumes a dualism which segregates knowledge from its object, conceptual schemes from their content and thoughts from things. For Wittgenstein, as has been said (1.11), language and world form a single inseparable reality. Facts form a whole with the propositions which represent them, since what both have in common is an unsayable logical form which shows itself in them. Simple objects, like atomic names, have logical form — i.e. combinatorial possibilities. It would be wrong to say in a technical tone of voice, however, that we are 'acquainted' with this form, as if other degrees of knowing were in question here. It is not as if, in speaking of having 'knowledge by acquaintance' of the metaphysical simples, we can hope to settle some doubt about our knowledge of the external world. The doubts that such talk is supposed to settle would be products of a scheme/content dualism, and such a dualism is absent from the Tractarian account.

The question as to the precise nature of the simple objects is, however, a salutory one. It reminds us of how the notion of 'logical form' saturates Wittgenstein's world-picture at every point. This is a partial justification, of course, for describing the *Tractatus* as a treatise on philosophical logic. This description is even harmless, provided we do not forget that logic, for

Wittgenstein, is like ethics in being transcendental. It is striking that Wittgenstein gives no independent proof of the existence of his ontological atoms. The logico-semantic postulates of the *Tractatus* cannot be cited as constituting such a proof, because, as we have seen, it was Wittgenstein's account of language which generated the need for the sort of ontology he gives us. To avoid circularity, he would have to provide evidence for the existence of the atoms which did not rely on the rest of his system, and this he fails to do.

So what are the metaphysical atoms doing in the account we have been examining? They seem to have no justification other than that they *complete* this account of the unity of language and world. However, would Wittgenstein have thought that they needed any justification other than this? He would, at this point, sound a warning against 'expecting an explanation, whereas the solution of the difficulty is a description' (Z, para. 314); for his aim was precisely to describe, not explain, the fusion of world and language. The doctrine of the atoms lends a kind of perfect symmetry to this description. This perfection mirrors the perfection of the absolute values which make sense of language and world in making them whole. The dogma of the atoms is not a logician's or an ontologist's, but a moral absolutist's dogma.

1.4 Limits and limitations

The *Tractatus* is a book about limits — the limits of a Whole, whose dual aspects are language and the world. It is an attempt to describe the limits of this Whole by working, as it were, from the inside outwards. Because language and the world are aspects of a single reality, which is in no way dualistically conceived, it seems likely that any error in the description occurring, say, at the level of semantics will have consequences for the ontology, and vice versa. Conceptual damage in any one area of the description will be difficult to contain, and a flaw in any part of the account will infect the entirety. This, as we know, is pretty much the story of the *Tractatus*'s demise. In trying to describe the limits of the sayable in a fashion which would do justice to the illimitable realm of absolute values which lay beyond it, Wittgenstein had written a book in which no mistake could count as venial.

Wittgenstein's own discovery of the mistake in question is a matter of history. It was the result of a re-examination of the notorious colour-exclusion problem (TLP, 6.3751), which had been introduced to exemplify the logicist claim that: 'Just as the only necessity that exists is *logical* necessity, so too the only impossibility that exists is *logical* impossibility.' (TLP, 6.375, original emphases) He had argued that the logical structure of colour eliminated the possibility of the simultaneous presence of two colours at the same point in the visual field. The grounds for this argument were that the assertion of such co-presence, being contradictory, violated the rule that the logical product of two elementary propositions could be neither tautologous nor contradictory.

Intrinsic to this argument is a programme for the reductive analysis of colour predications like 'x is red' or 'x is blue'. As they stand, these sentences are not elementary propositions in the Tractarian sense, because they are capable of contradicting one another, and thus of failing to satisfy the test that 'It is a sign of a proposition's being elementary that there can be no elementary proposition contradicting it.' (TLP, 4.211) Analysis, Wittgenstein thought, would reduce the degrees of colour-properties into the logical product of single statements of quantity, adding to each the clause, 'and nothing else'. By this method, he hoped to show the logical impossibility of a single visual speck's being, say, red and blue simultaneously, while also preserving the logical independence of elementary propositions. This would be done by saying some such thing as that the colour red contained all degrees of its own colour and no degree of the colour blue, and vice versa. This formulation purportedly demonstrates that the presence of R at t1, t2 . . . and at p1, p2 . . . excludes, but does not contradict, B's presence at those times and places.

As Wittgenstein came to see, however, all this move achieves is to push the problem a step further back. Colour predications contain statements of degree, so that numbers inevitably occur in them. In his 'Remarks on logical form' — the paper which signals the tentative beginnings of his retreat from his earlier positions — Wittgenstein notes that this circumstance is 'not merely a feature of special symbolism, but an essential and consequently unavoidable feature of the representation'.[61] If numbers enter into the above-described formulation, however, then it must fail as an analysis of statements of degree: for analysis of a statement like 'x is red' can only yield one of two unhelpful results. On the one hand, it may demonstrate that the degrees of vividity into which 'x is red' may be analysed are identical. In that event, the *logical* product will be no more than that specific degree of vividity, since the logical operation of conjunction does not do the work of the arithmetical 'plus' sign. On the other hand, the result may be that the degrees are not identical, so that one degree excludes another and we again confront the original problem.

Wittgenstein returned to the issue in the *Philosophical remarks*, there concluding that if different degrees of colour were mutually exclusive, elementary propositions could be contradictory (PR, VIII, para. 76). So, at last, he abandoned the requirement that elementary propositions had to be logically independent. That he should have clung to this doctrine for so long is, as Pears notices,[62] not explained by pointing out that it dovetails with other Tractarian positions, such as the position that no *de re* necessities are determinants of specific types of things, and the related assertion that the truth-table for the logical product of two elementary propositions can always be completed. A better explanation seems to lie in Wittgenstein's conception of analysis and in his ideas about objects. His model of logical analysis was that of a systematic dismemberment of language into its putatively ultimate constituents, while objects were thought of as simple particulars. This way of thinking made it seem inevitable that expressions denoting the objects could not produce contradictions in which they occur, because what they denote is simple without remainder.

It is unsurprising that Wittgenstein chose altogether to abandon, rather than to modify, the stringent requirement for logical independence; for the intrusion of numbers into elementary propositions dealing with colour, pitch and suchlike predications necessitated treating the notation rules for the propositional calculus as defective. In the truth-tables, as we saw (1.32), Wittgenstein believed himself to have found a notational device which would perspicuously display the possibilities of existence or non-existence of states of affairs by representing the truth-possibilities of elementary propositions in a descending bi-polar sequence, reading TT, FT, TF and FF for any two propositions p and q. However, when predications concerning degrees of a property, such as redness, are involved, the TT possibility will be an ill-formed line on the truth-table.

In his paper on logical form, Wittgenstein held that a perfect notation with rules excluding malformations of this sort would have to await 'the ultimate analysis of the phenomena in question'.[63] In the light of the entirely logicist view of necessity which the introduction of the topic of colour-exclusion was supposed to instantiate in the *Tractatus*, this suggestion, if it really does imply some empirical investigation of contingent 'phenomena', seems uncharacteristic, and it is not to be wondered at that Wittgenstein failed to follow it up. The more natural conclusion would be that his conception of logic and necessity had broadened and become more pliable, so that he was now beginning to think that propositions were not discrete bi-valent rulers to lay against reality, but rather members of syntactically connected propositional systems (*systemsatz*), and this was the conclusion — forerunner of the language-game conceit — which he in fact later drew.

Once the dogma of the logical independence of elementary propositions is discarded, the collapse of other salient features of the Tractarian system was inevitable. When they are no longer portrayed as being logically discrete, the very idea of 'elementary' propositions, supposedly more 'basic' than the sentential units of natural discourse, seems redundant, because it can no longer play the role assigned to it in securing determinacy of sense. The same holds for the atomic names which elementary propositions were supposed to express. Once the simple names are eradicated, there is no case for retaining the simple metaphysical objects which those names were supposed to denote. In this way, the activity of critical destruction, once begun, inevitably spreads inwards from the sphere of logic and semantics into the realm of atomist ontology. What appears to have escaped damage is the mystical doctrine, concerning what lies beyond the boundaries of language and world — the doctrine that the sense of the Whole must lie outside it in a limitless domain of inexpressible absolute value. Let us see if this is so.

1.41 Limits transgressed

We have already noticed (1.32) that Wittgenstein does two things in the *Tractatus* which do not seem to accord with its spirit: despite his own prohibitions on assimilating philosophy to science, he himself imitates scientific procedures by treating the devices of logical notation as instruments for penetrating beneath the appearances of language to its hidden and supposedly uniform depths, and he finds within those depths a logical structure which operates like a calculus, although he held that the sense of the world lay outside it in a domain of absolute value which could not be subject to calculation.

These two matters are connected via their bearing on the distinction between 'saying' and 'showing'. As I tried to bring out in my discussion of the ethics of the *Tractatus* (1.31), the values to whose transcendent status Wittgenstein alludes there manifest or show themselves in the world. There cannot be propositions concerning them as there can about accidental happenings in the world, events which might have turned out otherwise, the possibilities and possible upshots of which can be the subject of calculation. There can, therefore, be no *theory* of ethics, if by this is meant an explanation of why these values manifest themselves as they do. Requests for such explanations have about them the kind of pointlessness that attaches to questions as to why Socrates drank the hemlock, or why Paul suffered for the truth of the Gospel. However, logic, too, is said to be transcendental, and logical form, which is that in virtue of which propositions have sense, shows itself in language. Thus, there can be no *theory* of logical form any more than there can be a theory of absolute ethical values. Yet Wittgenstein certainly does offer us a theory of meaning which seeks to go beyond the film on the surface of our ordinary discourse, although that is supposed to be in perfect logical order. He tells a story of hidden, yet more fundamental, elementary propositions and atomic names, and this story is supposed to explain away the ambiguities of everyday speech. The irony is that in the telling of this story, intractable paradoxes are generated concerning the alleged logical independence of these special elements, inviting the conclusion that the colour-exclusion problem is but a symptom of a more profound scientistic malaise.

Wittgenstein's logical essentialism, moreover, obscures the connection he postulates between the transcendental status of logic and of ethics. In the latter case we can get at his meaning by drawing on lived examples. He prevents us from doing this with logic by focusing on a structure which is beneath and beyond the ordinary language which connects with the forms of life we know and can use as examples in moral argument. This fault he tried to remedy in the *Philosophical investigations*.

1.5 The *Philosophical investigations*

I have already remarked on the distortions engendered by the myth of the 'two Wittgensteins', and on the need to recognise certain unifying tendencies within the diversity of his thought (1.1). It is, moreover, entirely feasible that the whole corpus of Wittgenstein's published work to date exhibits not merely initial, middle and final phases of development, but other distinctive stages as well. However, this does nothing to gainsay the fact that what distinguishes the *Tractatus* from the writings which followed it constitutes a veritable revolution in the thought of a philosopher of genius, and that this revolutionary transformation is epitomised, and to some extent completed by, the *Philosophical investigations*. This revolution concerns Wittgenstein's quest for a correct account of semantic necessity, and consists in his abandonment of logicist essentialism in favour of the perspectives afforded by an approach which (as we shall see) is at once historicist, anthropocentric and materialist. The marks of this sea change are a set of radical stylistic and conceptual innovations. These include the introduction of an interlocutor into the discourse, the admission of hazy-edged, cluster-prone concepts into the argument, and, of course, the emergence of the notions 'language-game', 'family-resemblance' and 'form of life'. The chief doctrinal fruit of this revolution is a semantics which relates meaning to use. Its chief slogan is the maxim 'to imagine a language means to imagine a form of life.' (PI, i, para. 19)

1.51 Cartography and clustered concepts

The impression of diffuseness which the *Investigations* easily produces, especially when it is compared with the *Tractatus*, is misleading if it encourages the belief that order and clarity were ideals which Wittgenstein abandoned in his maturity. In his introduction to the *Investigations*, he reports specifically on his unsuccessful attempts to impose a 'natural', unbroken and linear order on his thoughts and concludes that his inability to achieve this was 'connected with the very nature of the investigation' (PI, p. ix). Instead, the end-result of his labours was such as could best be described in cartographic terms:

> The philosophical remarks in this book are, as it were, a
> number of sketches of landscapes which were made in the

course of these long and involved journeyings. The same or almost the same points were always being approached afresh from different directions, and new sketches made. Very many of these were badly drawn or uncharacteristic, marked by all the defects of a weak draughtsman. And when they were rejected a number of tolerable ones were left, which now had to be arranged and sometimes cut down, so that if you looked at them you could get a picture of the landscape. (ibid.)

Now if this method was, as Wittgenstein avers, forced on him by the very nature of his enterprise, then it seems to follow that there was something about the enterprise which had been misunderstood, or incompletely understood when he wrote the *Tractatus*: for the object of both books is the very same — namely, to give a *philosophical* account of the necessity which makes language possible — and the propositions of his first great work certainly are ordered in the way in which Wittgenstein tried and failed to order them in his last.

I have tried to explain the manner in and extent to which Wittgenstein's own transgressions of his Tractarian prohibitions on scientistic theorising in philosophic work were responsible for the disintegration of the flawed elements in the Tractarian structure (1.41). I now wish to suggest that his likening of his endeavour to a cartographer's project, and of the vast field of language to a map-like surface, are indications of a determination to avoid past mistakes and to adhere to the anti-theoretic postulates of the *Tractatus* (TLP, 4.111–4.113) with increased zeal. Wittgenstein had always believed that language, in so far as it was a proper object of philosophical interest, was an affair of surfaces, a realm in which everything lay open to view. 'Words', he had written as far back as 1915, 'are like the film on deep water.' (NB, p. 52). Yet as we saw, the Tractarian explorations are by no means confined to the surface of language. Wittgenstein's scientism, despite his own strictures, consisted precisely in an effort to emulate the physicists he had idolised and penetrate beneath linguistic appearances in search of a hidden logical essence. The *Blue Book* dictations go some distance towards recognising this; for Wittgenstein says therein:

Our craving for generality has another main source: our preoccupation with the method of science. I mean the method of reducing the explanation of natural phenomena to the smallest number of primitive natural laws . . . Philosophers constantly see the method of science before their eyes, and are irresistibly tempted to ask and answer questions in the way science does. This tendency is the real source of metaphysics . . . (BB, p. 18).

It is significant that scientific or pseudo-scientific modes of analysis are eschewed even more vigorously and in more wide-ranging terms in the *Investigations* than was the case in the *Tractatus*. In his last book, Wittgenstein appears to be giving the word *Wissenschaft* the very broad application which it naturally has in German. He inveighs not merely against one or another mode of theorising in philosophy, but against the introduction of any sort of theory whatsoever: 'And we may not advance any kind of theory. There must not be anything hypothetical in our considerations. We must do away with all *explanation*, and description alone must take its place.' (PI, i, para. 109, original emphasis) Philosophy done in this anti-theoretical spirit 'may in no way interfere with the actual use of language; it can in the end only describe it' (PI, i, para. 124).

Philosophical discourse, then, which recognises itself for what it is, will limit itself to a descriptive scrutiny of language, conceived as a map-like surface, comprised of an irregular network of rule-governed structures, which we will learn to call 'language-games'. Moreover, the verbal tools for carrying out this survey must not be construed as precision-instruments. They will for the most part be like the idea of a 'game', concepts 'with blurred edges' (PI, i, para. 71). These fuzzy concepts are what we need in order to gain an overview of language, rather than a privileged insight into its supposed inner mechanisms. Both the use of such concepts and the descriptive ends they are supposed to serve are products of the recognition that philosophy is, in important ways, far more like practice than it is like theory, an activity carried on in response to theoretical pictures of reality, but distinct from the pictures themselves. The distinction is notoriously difficult to draw accurately, but it resembles that which Marxists have traditionally drawn between historical materialism (a theory) and dialectical materialism (a philosophy).

Clearly, philosophy done in this spirit and with this conception of its field of enquiry will not facilitate a neatly sequential development of key concepts. Instead — in a way entirely characteristic of both the Hegelian and Marxist dialectical philosophies — concepts in the *Investigations* tend to form clusters, such that the full understanding of any one term of art will depend on a comprehension of several others. Thus, understanding the notion of a language-game depends to a significant extent on having grasped Wittgenstein's account of rules and rule-following, and vice versa, while understanding the notion of a life-form presupposes a hold on his ideas about game-playing and rule-following, conceived as lived practices. The point is of some importance, because there is an understandable temptation in interpreting Wittgenstein's later work to stratify his concepts and search for one that is 'basic'. If over-indulged, this urge can lead the commentator to misconstrue the application of these ideas, which are not designed to serve as lynch-pins in some grand explanatory system, but are rather intended as therapeutic devices for exposing and resolving perplexities of different (although specifically philosophical) sorts. This is not to say that all attempts to assign priorities to elements in the Wittgensteinian account are misplaced. Indeed, the theory to be introduced in the next chapter precisely involves according special importance to language-games of a particular kind. My contention here is rather that the *Philosophical investigations* — somewhat like its own portrayal of language — is a maze with many exits and entrances, often connected by intricately overlapping pathways. There is, therefore, no single univocally correct mode of access to it or route through it. The choice of these will often be dictated by the pressures of specific puzzlements. 'There is not', says Wittgenstein, '*a* philosophical method, though there are indeed methods, like different therapies.' (PI, i, para. 133, original emphasis)

1.52 The 'Augustinian' theory

In the opening sections of the *Investigations*, Wittgenstein begins a critical re-examination of the dominant topics of referentialist semantics — naming, ostension, and assertion — which had been ascendant themes in the account of semantic necessity given in the *Tractatus*. A carefully selected quotation from the description of language-learning given by Augustine in the *Confessions* is made to serve as a model of all theories which take as their major premiss the dictum that the meaning of a word is the object for which it stands. The fact that the passage quoted (from Book I,

Chapter 8) certainly does not do justice to Augustine's views on language should not lead us to conclude, as Kenny does,[64] that Wittgenstein is carelessly misrepresenting a philosopher he greatly admired. His intention, surely, is not to saddle Augustine with the responsibility for perpetuating a naïve denotationalist theory. Why should Wittgenstein have wished to do this, when he must have realised that in some respects Augustine's full opinion of the matter approaches his own? It is far more probable that, in selecting the passage, Wittgenstein simply wished to put before us ideas which might occur to any intelligent and reflective person, who was moved to wonder at the fact of our possession of the power to communicate as we do. Augustine's words, Wittgenstein says, 'give us a particular picture of the essence of human language' (PI, i, para. 1), and it is clear that he thought that anybody, including the author of the *Tractatus*, might easily succumb to the influence of this picture and be captivated by it.

Because we find in these early paragraphs critical references to the denotationalist theories of Russell, Frege and the early Wittgenstein himself, it is easy to see the discussion simply as an attack on previous reference theories and so to miss the subtlety of Wittgenstein's treatment of the Augustinian paradigm. However, Wittgenstein is not chiefly concerned merely to demolish this paradigm. Augustine, he says, 'does describe a system of communication; only not everything we call language is this system' (PI, i, para. 3). Moreover, in proposing the definition 'The meaning of a word is its use in the language', he adds at once, 'And the *meaning* of a name is sometimes explained by pointing to its *bearer*.' (PI, i, para. 43, original emphases) Far more important than his criticism of some conclusions implicit in the Augustinian picture is Wittgenstein's suggestion that by staring too fixedly at it we are led to ask the wrong kinds of questions — questions which cannot satisfy our real needs. We are led to wonder about the mysterious way in which names seem to be tied to extra-linguistic objects, instead of asking about the use to which expressions are put and about the surroundings in which they have the uses which in fact they have. The trouble with talk about 'meanings' and 'meant objects', Wittgenstein wants to say, is less that such talk invites reification of meaning, although it does, than that it fails to address the issue of how meaningful language is possible at all. The defect in the Augustinian picture lies not so much in the picture itself, but in calling it the whole picture.

1.53 Use in a context

In attempting to throw the real and complex nature of semantic necessity into relief, Wittgenstein underscores the role played by observable, purposive human practices in determining the meaning of linguistic expressions. To know the meaning of a word is to understand not just what object it is used to denote (for it may denote no object), but the use or uses to which it may, for communicative purposes, effectively be put. The word 'meaning' is used wrongly if it is used to signify something that 'corresponds' with a word. Such a use of 'meaning' confuses the meaning of a name with its bearer. 'When Mr N.N. dies one says that the bearer of the name dies, not that the meaning dies. And it would be nonsensical to say that, for if the name ceased to have meaning it would make no sense to say "Mr N.N. is dead".' (TLP, i, para. 40)

Inevitably, a shift in the focus of the investigation away from the immediate relation of meanings to meant objects and towards the uses to which expressions can be put involves a concomitant shift of attention towards the contexts in which signing practices are actualised. For it is only context — i.e. the surroundings in which a speech-act is embedded, including all manner of other practices which form its setting — which tells us the kind of use to which an expression is being put, or indeed, whether it is being given any application whatsoever. Thus, Wittgenstein held that whether a given sign is a word or a proposition depends on the situation in which it is uttered or written. If A must describe complexes of coloured squares to B and uses the word 'R' by itself, we may say that the word is a proposition. However, if he is memorising words or teaching someone else their use, we will not say that they are propositions (PI, i, para. 49).

With the advantage of hindsight, it is easy to see how the notion of use-in-a-context serves as a prophylactic against the errors which may be engendered by the spell of the Augustinian picture. That picture ties meanings to objects, yet it is not obvious how the bond is effected, so long as linguistic expressions and the objects they denote are thought of as being everyday expressions and parts of everyday experience. It needs almost no argument to show that an ordinary mortal and mutable cat on a mat is not the *meaning* of the word 'cat'. While the usefulness of the picture itself remains unquestioned, however, the impulse to connect meanings to objects continues unchecked. The next fatal step is to postulate, on the one hand, a realm of hidden primitive expressions accessible only through logical analysis which do the denoting, and, on the other, a domain of atomic objects which are what the primitive expressions supposedly denote. What needs to be done, and what the focus on uses and their contexts does, is to check the impulse towards microscopic analysis before it starts and to substitute for it an urge to describe the macrocosm of human behaviour and lived situations which is already concretely before us. It is possibly no accident that Strawson, in the 1950 paper which criticised Russell's theory of descriptions, invokes the idea of a 'context of utterance', by which he means 'at least the time, the place, the situation, the identity of the speaker, the subjects which form the immediate focus of interest, and the personal histories of both the speaker and those he is addressing'.[65] For the metaphysics which underpins Russell's atomism has its origins in the very same picture which the Wittgensteinian notion of contexts of use is designed to combat.

1.54 Language-games

Wittgenstein's most famous terminological innovation — the 'language-game' conceit — has as its chief function the role of assisting the process of describing language by providing a highly flexible way of specifying contexts in which signing activity takes place. Language-games, we may say, are structured contexts of use in which meanings find expression. The immediate predecessor of this device made its debut in Wittgenstein's so-called 'middle period' with the introduction in the *Philosophical remarks* of the notion of the *Satzsystem*, more complex and pliant offspring of the clear-cut and rigid Tractarian calculus. The *Satzsystem*, although it too is a kind of calculus, does not require the relations of exclusion obtaining between its member propositions to depend solely on bi-polar truth-functions, but rather on the rules dictated by the semantic features of concept-words. Thus, in a system dealing with, say, numbers, it will make no sense to speak of 'the weight of the number 5', although it will make perfect sense to speak of something weighing five tons. The *Satzsystem* is, therefore, a transitional device, designed, on the one hand, to retain what seemed worth preserving in the old conception of language, and, on the other, to cope with new dimensions of complexity and indefiniteness which Wittgenstein's evolving perspectives on his subject-matter had begun to reveal.

The language-game simile made its first public appearance in the *Blue Book* dictations of 1933–4. There it was used to draw attention to the simple forms of language with which children first learn to use words, so that these forms of speech should be recognisable as 'forms of language not separated by a break from our more complicated ones' (BB, p. 17). In the *Brown Book*, Wittgenstein speaks simply of language-games as being 'systems of communication' (BB, p. 81), well-exemplified by what became the builders' language game of the *Investigations* (PI, i, para. 2). In the latter work, however, he supplies a list of activities which he is prepared to call 'language-games' which ranges extensively over such practices as giving and obeying orders, forming hypotheses, play-acting, translation, joke-telling and praying (PI, i, para. 23). In supplying this list, Wittgenstein indicates that he is using the term 'language-game' so as to emphasise that the speaking of a language 'is part of an activity, or a form of life' (ibid.). This list, and the connection with life-forms it seeks to establish, should serve as a warning against conferring on the term 'language-game' a narrower and more reified sort of precision than its inventor intended. Churchill is right, I think, in ascribing the urge to do this to forgetfulness of the concept's relativity to particular investigative aims.[66] Sometimes it suits Wittgenstein's purpose to use the term in an heuristic way in order to drive home specific points, and then it is often true that the games to which he draws our attention are very simple, contrived and highly structured. In these cases, the phrase 'rule-governed structure' is an apt description of what these language-games are. However, there are other cases — colour identification (e.g. ROC 284, OC 524–531 and PI, ii, p. 226), imagining (Z, 625), lying (PI, i, para. 249) and even the language-game with the word 'game' (PI, i, para. 71) — where the operations envisaged are just too complex and intermixed with changing human contexts to allow us to define these games purely in terms of the rules that govern them. It is, I think, the prevalence of examples of these more complex kinds of practices in the later writings which has persuaded the Hintikkas[67] that Wittgenstein, in his last phase, accorded language-games in themselves a kind of primacy over the rules which were supposed to govern them.

There is no need, however, to commit ourselves to viewing this matter in terms of phases in Wittgenstein's development. What seems clear is that 'language-game' is a term of art, deployable at various levels of abstraction and for various purposes, some of which draw our attention to sets of highly-structured and explicit sets of rules, while others seem more intimately related to the forms of life of our actual or possible experience. In general, the account of meaning, given with their assistance in the *Investigations*, comes to this: An expression will have the meaning or use it does have only in the setting of a language-game, just as a chess-piece has the powers of potential deployment it does have only in the setting of the game called 'chess'. To explain a game is to do no more or less than to describe its rules (which is not, of course, to say that the rules will always be obvious or easy to describe). There will thus be no more or less to the phenomena of understanding and meaning than grasping the import of and acting in compliance with the rules of a given language-game. In response to any challenge to justify one's belief that a given expression 'x' has such-and-such a meaning, it will always suffice to reply that one understands the language-game in which 'x' has meaning, where this reply can be supported by a practical demonstration of the competence claimed. Such competence may, however, not be easy to demonstrate in all instances, and may entail the ability to play a large number of related language-games, or even most of the games comprising a given language.

The language-game figure can facilitate accounts of this sort precisely because the rich variety of its associations enables it to converge on and blend with the subject-matter it is being used to describe. Some games are simply slices of linguistic behaviour. This attribute of the language-game conceit is germane to topics towards which I am moving.

1.55 Family resemblance

Like other games, language-games present a wide spectrum of divergence, but they also display many areas of overlap and similarity. The acute philosophical observer will notice that no single feature captures such unity as survives through the differences. Wittgenstein, therefore, can think of no better characterisation of the similarities thus displayed than 'family-resemblances', and so resolves to say that 'games' form a family (PI, i, para. 67). He also speaks of language as being 'a family of structures' (PI, i, para. 108). The central idea here is that as shadings of colouring, build, temperament and so on, all co-operate in marking individuals as members of one family or ancestral line, so too the multiplicity of the modes of similarity and dissimilarity between language-games allows them often to blend and often to differ. Wittgenstein's use of the expression in other places shows that he thought of it as an apt description, not only of the totality of language-games, but also of more localised instances of speech, action and propositional attitudes. He says there is 'an endless variety' of actions and words having the 'family likeness' we call 'trying to copy' (BB, p. 33). A family of groups of activities and experiences is said to constitute attitudes of observation (BB, p. 152), while the activity of alluding to someone is said not to consist of a 'family' of mental and other processes (Z, 26). It is noteworthy, moreover, that when Wittgenstein is discussing Frazer's treatment of the European fire-festivals, he says of these rituals much the same thing as he says of the relations holding between game-types in the *Investigations*: 'Besides these similarities, what seems to me to be most striking is the dissimilarity of all these rites. It is the multiplicity of faces with common features which continually emerges here and there.' (RFGB, p. 74)

The deep thought behind this choice of imagery is a social and historicist one. The family is, first and foremost, a human social unit, bound to other units of its kind by ties of kinship which often manifest themselves as irregular and indistinct. Philosophical semantics is comparable to a kind of descriptive anthropology, which is forbidden to simplify and universalise these complex relationships as structuralist anthropology attempted to do with its subject-matter. Kinship relations and the phenomena which display them change, not just as physical objects change, but as historical institutions do. It is in being akin to them that our language is comparable 'to an ancient city: a maze of little streets and squares, of old and new houses, and of houses with additions from various periods; and this surrounded by a multitude of new boroughs . . .' (PI, i, para. 18). To imagine a language, then, is to imagine a history which is our own human history, governed by necessities which are of an historical sort. It is in this sense that 'to imagine a language means to imagine a form of life' (PI, i, para. 19).

1.56 Life-forms

The above quoted sentence is among the best known of the

Wittgensteinian aphorisms, introducing as it does a conception which informs and transforms the whole of the later philosophy of language. In so far as it is correct to speak of a revolution in Wittgenstein's thought, it is the introduction of this conception more than any other which signals the onset of that revolution, thus presenting a grave obstacle to attempts to link the transcendental subject of the *Tractatus* to the linguistic communities of the *Investigations* as Williams[68] tries to do. For the Tractarian subject is the creation of a special sort of neo-Kantian transcendental idealism, and, as Bolton[69] convincingly argues, to interpret form as life-form — i.e. to assert that humans are the sole agents of knowing, believing etc. — is to exclude all kinds of idealism, transcendental or otherwise, even when the term 'idealism' is given the reasonably broad compass that Bolton allows it. Are we, then, to say that Wittgensteinian philosophical semantics in its latter phase ought to be characterised as materialist? That depends on how the term 'materialist' is understood. If the adjective is construed in its eighteenth-century mechanist setting, then it certainly does not fit Wittgenstein's employment of the expression '*lebensform*'. For, as Baker and Hacker[70] point out, his use of the phrase is most likely to have been influenced by Spengler's talk of a 'culture language' in *The Decline of the West*, and the 1934–5 dictations in fact equates use in a language with a culture (BB, p. 134). To speak of a people's culture may certainly include reference to what might be called their 'material culture' — the tools they use, the food they eat, their manner of procuring it and so on. However, the word 'culture' is also and more generally used to denote the spiritual, artistic and intellectual life of a community, so if life-forms are indeed associated with cultural life, and if the expression 'form of life' as Wittgenstein uses it is to be construed in a materialist sense, then the sort of materialism involved must be of a different variety than its eighteenth-century predecessor.

The sense in which materialism enters into consideration here can best be explicated by noting other places in the *Investigations* and elsewhere where Wittgenstein talks about life-forms. He makes it clear that forms of life are linked to language-games, inasmuch as both pertain to *activity* (PI, i, para. 23). It is at the level of the life-form, which goes beyond mere opinion, that human beings agree in the language they use (PI, i, para. 241). Such things as the 'phenomena of hope' are modes of the complex form of life which has mastered the use of language (PI, ii,

p. 174). Forms of life are to be thought of as 'given' (PI, ii, p. 226). 'Comfortable' certainty is said to be akin, not to hastiness or superficiality, but a form of life, although Wittgenstein appends to this idea the reservation that it is ill-formulated and probably badly thought (OC, 357–358). Concepts are to be thought of as standing in the middle of our life, and our life is said to be permeated by the rule-governed nature of our language (ROC, III, 302–303).

Now these stray remarks give the impression that life-forms are, in a sense, more fundamental than the opinions and concepts which are expressed in language inasmuch as they are necessary conditions of it. For although there is also a sense in which language is *rule*-governed, and although its rule-governed nature interpenetrates with the forms of life that use it, the latter constitute a pervasive setting or field of activity which must be present whenever language-using takes place. It seems, moreover, incontestable that, if anything ought to be called 'mental' or 'spiritual' or 'ideal', it is the concepts or opinions which language expresses, and such things, on Wittgenstein's showing, depend for their expression on there being forms of life, settings of lived activity, which are not 'mental' or 'spiritual' in the fairly obvious sense that opinions and concepts are. Nor are these forms 'ideal' in the way that the logical form of the *Tractatus* period clearly was. At the same time, 'form of life', in Wittgenstein's phraseology, does not simply denote a biological species, although biological considerations may very well enter into a full description of some or other life-form. This is because the forms of life that are of interest in the *Investigations* are those, and only those, forms capable of mastering the use of language and falling within the range of our own imaginative grasp. The point of saying 'If a lion could talk, we could not understand him' (PI, ii, p. 223), is to drive home the thought that there is no family resemblance between the forms of life possible to speaking beings and the lives of animals (or angels for that matter), and hence no sense in speculating about what it would be like to be an animal or an angel or on the possibility that they may have what we have in having a language. Thus, the sense in which Wittgenstein's life-forms are material instances is one which converges with what Pears[71] rightly calls his 'anthropocentrism'. The title of the *Lebensform* concept to be regarded as a materialist notion rests on its accessibility to the publicisable disclosures of human experience and imagination. In other words, we can know a form of life as objectively as we can know any other material phenomenon, although what we have in the former case is not knowledge of an external object but self-knowledge. A form of life, then, is a knowable instance of material human existence, a 'slice' of our lives, our culture, our history, and capable of just those modalities of joy, terror, grief and so forth of which only human beings are capable. Life-forms are also material in being subject, in the last instance, and despite the spiritual capacities and powers which distinguish them from the rest of material reality, to those natural regularities which govern all matter. We shall return to this point, and examine it in greater detail shortly.

Wittgenstein is at pains to emphasise that 'language' in its full sense means human language; that animals do not talk, and that such uses of language as commanding, questioning, recounting and chatting are 'a part of *our* natural history' (PI, i, para. 25, my emphasis). However, this ought not to lead us to think that, because all forms of life are accessible to human imagination in virtue of being themselves human forms, they are all easily accessible. Family resemblances between one social formation and another may be indistinct and difficult to trace. The way of life of a given community may be so much at variance with the norms of another as to make each seem 'bestial' to the other, and this is particularly likely to be the case when moral forms of life are very different. Such differences will entail difficulties in communication, particularly with respect to discerning what rules inform a group's playing of its language-games or even whether rule-guided activity is taking place at all.

1.57 Rule-following

Wittgenstein studies have recently concentrated on the topics of rules and rule-following, which are certainly a major concern of an extensive discussion in the *Investigations* (PI, i, paras 139–242). Some of this secondary literature, however, betrays, through an over-intense propensity to try to 'pin down' the notions of a rule and of what it is to be guided by one, the marks of a failure to take seriously the tendency already mentioned (1.51) of key-concepts in the *Investigations* to blur at the edges, blend with one another and form concept-clusters such that understanding of any given notion presupposes understanding of all other concepts within the cluster. When the notion of a rule is cut free of its moorings in the surrounding concepts of the 'language-game', 'family-resemblance' and 'form of life', reflection on such matters as the correct explanation, justification and anticipation of action in accordance with a rule tends to produce precisely those bizarre forms of mental cramp which the Wittgensteinian therapy was supposed to eradicate. Thus, Kripke[72] and Wright[73] take Wittgenstein to be propounding a special sort of 'rule-scepticism' in his discussion of these questions, the solution to which is alleged to lie in taking a 'communitarian' view of the whole issue — i.e. the view that the very idea of following a rule depends on the existence of a rule-following community.

Both the idea that Wittgenstein propounds rule-scepticism and the community view of rule-following have been extensively criticised by Baker and Hacker,[74] and I cannot take space to deal with the ramifications of the debate here. A few remarks are, nonetheless, in order, and must suffice. Firstly, the story (certainly as Kripke tells it) of how Wittgenstein supposedly invented a new form of philosophical scepticism relies for its plot on a passage presenting us with the following predicament:

> This was our paradox; no course of action could be determined by a rule, because every course of action could be made out to accord with the rule. The answer was: if everything can be made out to accord with the rule, then it can also be made out to conflict with it. And so there could be neither accord nor conflict here. (PI, i, sec. 201)

This paradox would be exemplified by a pupil who, having apparently understood instructions on how to write the series of even integers, continues after '1000' in some eccentric way, but gives an interpretation of the rule he was set to follow which is on all fours with his performance. The very fact that what is presented to us here is a *paradox* — a proposal which precisely conceals an absurdity — is evidence that we are not being asked to take seriously some new form of scepticism, but are rather confronted with a conceptual confusion which a wisely directed clarification of concepts can be expected to dissipate. Indeed, in the very next sentence in the passage just quoted, Wittgenstein points out that this paradox evidences a 'misunderstanding', which can be seen from the fact that one interpretation of the rule after another is displayed serially as if they each offered momentary contentment. He goes on, as we should expect, to point out that there is a way of grasping a rule which is noninterpretative, but which is shown in our compliance or failure to comply with the rule in question. Now this compliance or failure to comply is a *practice*, internally related to whatever rule is in question, which *shows* whether the rule has been understood or misunderstood, obeyed or disobeyed. The chimera of rule-scepticism can only get its grip when this is forgotten, as it will be if the network of reminders in the form of the notions of language-games and the life-forms — the live human signing practices — to which they are tied are left out of account in considering the concept of a rule.

Secondly, according to Kripke, Wittgenstein offers us a 'sceptical solution' to scepticism about rules. This is said to involve the repudiation of the idea that sense is given by truth-conditions, and its replacement by the doctrine that sense is given by assertability-conditions which are tied to acceptance by a community. The assertion-conditions for someone's meaning W by 'W' are his inclination to use 'W' in the way he does, and that the rest of his community use it in the same way. Wright, too, has recourse to communal decree in this regard, when he says that nobody can unilaterally 'make sense of the idea of correct employment of language save by reference to the authority of securable communal assent . . .'[75] However, appeals to communal concensus surely fail to provide either an accurate account of Wittgenstein's own view of rule-following or an independent explanation of how our own rule-guided behaviour is in fact possible. Wittgenstein says explicitly that it is possible for someone to encourage himself, give himself orders, obey, blame and punish himself, to ask himself questions and answer them (PI, i, 243). There is no suggestion that we could not (as we clearly can) imagine a person, considered in isolation, speaking or acting in a rule-guided fashion, or that in imagining this, we are, by some occult process of initiation, admitting him to our community. The notions of community membership, communal agreement and social contract are helpless to explain our mastery of or failure to master rules for communication, because what was puzzling about the communicative capacities of a solitary individual in a 'state of nature' is no less so if we imagine a community in that state. We learn to follow rules by training, drill, example and explanation, and this is indeed an initiation of sorts; but it is not an initiation into membership of a community, but into a network of practices governed by normative regularities. For such training to take place, agreement must certainly be presupposed, but this is not agreement between members of a community; it is agreement in linguistic usage, in definitions, judgements and in form of life.

Thirdly, exponents of the communitarian interpretation in fact risk obscuring that feature of Wittgenstein's account which, I suspect, they are most anxious to emphasise. This is that language, for Wittgenstein is, in being our own human language, the language of social creatures. However, language is not for Wittgenstein, as it is for Locke, 'the great instrument and common tie of society',[76] a merely supplementary function of the condition of human nature, enabling individuals to form social units. It would be strange indeed if Wittgenstein had devoted his whole life as a philosopher to reflecting on the nature of language, and a good part of it attacking the kind of referentialist and ideational semantics that Locke advocated, only to produce a Lockean conception of the relation of language to society. The conception of this relation which he in fact produced is one wherein our natural history as social beings is inseparable from our nature as speaking beings. The latter is not the instrument, but the expression of, the former, and no natural state precedes our capacity to regulate our behaviour in a normative fashion.

At all events, these debates concerning rule-scepticism and the communitarian 'solution' to it should not be allowed to obscure the main point to emerge from the rule-following considerations in the *Investigations*. This concerns the nature of the internal relationship holding between a rule and its application. That relationship is best characterised as what Marxists are accustomed to call 'a unity of theory and practice'. These two terms may be taken as descriptions of two components which emerge as essential to rule-following, whether the rules in question are strictly depth-grammatical, like the rule prescribing that 'How heavy is red?' is a nonsensical question, or alogarithmic, like rules for addition. In all such cases there will be, firstly, a theoretical component, consisting of the understanding or conceptual grasp of whatever rule is in question; and secondly, a practical component made up of the series of purposive acts whereby that understanding is evidenced. In order to follow the rule, 'add two', say, someone must, firstly, understand the language-games in which 'add' and 'two' have meaning; and secondly, be able to evidence his understanding by continuing the series of additions accordingly — a demonstration which might also constitute his explanation of the rule.

Notice that theory forms a union with practice here in at least the sense that no intervening mental process mediates between the two stages of rule-following, and this is part of what is meant by saying that understanding a rule is internally connected with actions done in accordance with it. Wittgenstein goes so far as to say that in so far as there are mental processes which are characteristic of understanding, understanding is not a mental process (PI, i, 154). At the same time, to unite theory and practice is not to identify them, and the two stages of rule-following must not be conflated. It is logically possible for someone to understand a rule without giving any practical proofs that he has done so, just as it is possible for practices which would usually be evidence that a rule has been understood to deceive us in a given case. What we must guard against is falling into the sceptical trap of asking for further demonstrations and explanations when all the evidence we could have that a rule is being followed is before our eyes.

1.58 Privacy

Wittgenstein's famous private-language argument follows on from and relies directly on his discussion of rule-following. Its target is the Lockean ideational version of referentialism, according to which names refer to ideas or sensations within discrete consciousnesses. On this account it ought strictly to be possible for a subject to give a secret name to any of his sensations whenever he experienced it, and so to construct a language which was 'private', not merely in the sense that someone spoke it to himself, but in being an esoteric system of signs which was opaque (logically speaking) to anyone other than its inventor. Since Locke's semantics and epistemology are influenced by Descartes' assumption that the mind is better known than the body, it is also possible to see Wittgenstein's arguments against the possibility of a private language as being anti-Cartesian in intent, although we must not lose sight of the fact that the *Investigations* is chiefly concerned with language, not with epistemology.

Attention to this distinction preserves for us the full deep-thrusting subtlety of the critique offered here (PI, i, 243–315) by preventing us from thinking that it is no more than an attempted response to scepticism and solipsism carried on within the familiar framework of epistemological discourse as we have known it since the seventeenth century. Wittgenstein's attack goes well beyond these confines. He aims to do nothing less than disabuse our minds from the spell of a misleading picture, rooted deep in the grammar of the language-games we play (or think we can play) with sensation-words and with the very idea of language itself. Wittgenstein is not, as Pitcher[77] seems to have thought in an exposition effectively criticised by Donagan,[78] and as the imaginary interlocutor of the *Investigations* suspects, 'a behaviourist in disguise' (PI, i, 307). He is content to leave undisturbed some of our best cherished Cartesian intuitions about our introspectible states by allowing sensations to be 'private' (in the broad sense), non-dispositional accompaniments of behaviour which naturally expresses them. We may, on this view, invent for our own purposes our own secret names for sensations which appear, as it were, in the recesses of our subjectivity. What we may not do is devise signs for such experiences which are essentially and in principle opaque to the minds of others. We may not, in other words, imagine a language which is private, not in the sense of being the creation of a speaker who, as a matter of fact, invented it in complete solitude, but in the sense that its expressions could not in any circumstances be understood by anyone other than its inventor.

A private language, for Wittgenstein, is one in which the individual words which comprise it refer to what can only be known to the speaker. They refer to his immediate private sensations, so that another person will be unable to understand the language (PI, i, 243). Thus, the objects to which the words in a putative private language refer are private in a double sense. They are, firstly, epistemically private in that only the speaker can know what they are and when they occur; and secondly, private in the sense of 'belonging' to or being 'owned' by the speaker and only the speaker of the language in question. Sensations appear to be the most obvious candidates for satisfying these two conditions, and the sensation of being in pain is what Wittgenstein mainly fixes on in discussing privacy. I cannot have your pains; you cannot have mine. I alone can know the what and when of my aches and agonies; you alone are privy to the temper and timing of yours. From these simple premisses, a determined sceptic purports to extract the alarming conclusion that a private language is in principle unintelligible to others: for when I have a sensation and name it, only I, given my non-transferable knowledge and possession of that sensation, can know what the name I give to it means. It seems, then, that the only person I can talk to is myself. The sceptic has only to insinuate that perhaps this is what we are all really doing, and the transition to solipsism, if not accomplished, seems readily accomplishable.

Wittgenstein's argumentative strategy is to forestall the very possibility of making the initial moves which will set this scenario in motion. He denies that the speaker of a 'private language could understand the words he invents — i.e. he denies that the attachment of a 'name' to a private referent is a genuine move in any playable language-game. He seeks to show that what is called 'naming' in this case is a dead ritual, a meaningless ceremony, bereft of any real rules or techniques for the application of rules, and shorn of the lived context which must accompany all signing practices.

This point is established with the aid of vivid examples, accompanied by subtle therapeutic counter-arguments. Even in a situation in which humans exhibited no observable pain-behaviour, we might imagine a child prodigy inventing for itself a name for the sensation of toothache: but, Wittgenstein responds, the child would not be understood when he used his name. What does it mean in this case to say that he has 'named' his pain? In saying that he gave a name to his sensation we are forgetting that 'a great deal of stage-setting in the language is presupposed if the mere act of naming is to make sense' (PI, i, 257). The lesson here is that pain-behaviour enters into the *grammar* of pain-naming. Such behaviour ought not to be treated merely as the outward sign of an inner state, but as internally connected to everything else that goes with giving a name to a sensation. Certainly, the behaviour which expresses pain is not the sensation of pain, and grimaces, shrieks and the like can be used to deceive; but they cannot always or usually be so employed if the language-games we play with pain are to continue, any more than Hamlet can be performed *as a matter of course* amidst scenery and in costumes appropriate to Ali Baba and the Forty Thieves.

Wittgenstein goes on to explore the possibility that someone could diarise recurrences of a particular sensation by associating it with the sign 'S' and writing this 'sign' in a calendar on each day that it recurs. The diarist is reminded by Wittgenstein that no definition of 'S' can be formulated. The notion that the sign can be given a kind of ostensive definition by concentrating attention on it and so pointing to it inwardly, is met by an ironic question as to what this 'ceremony' is for. The diarist's desperate reply that by concentrated attention he impresses on himself the connection between sign and sensation evokes the response that in the case before us there is no criterion of correctness. 'One would like to say that whatever is going to seem right to me is right. And that only means that here we can't talk about "right".' (PI, i, 258)

The point of this and ensuing moves in the dialogue is to get the diarist to see that the solipsistic picture which lurks behind his attempts to imagine a private language is a picture which deprives him of any independent criterial rule with which to make intelligible his talk of 'correctness' and 'incorrectness'. His case is not that of someone who calls up a mental image of a railway timetable in order to check up on his memory of a departure-time. For that mental image is itself checkable against the timetable of which it is an image and to which the public has access. Rather, the diarist is like someone who buys several copies of the morning paper to assure himself of the truth of what is said in it (PI, i, 265). The conceptual articulations which make ordinary sensation-talk intelligible and allow diary-keeping to remain within the realm of rational activity have been severed in the private diarist's story. He is the fly, who must be shown the way out of the fly-bottle (PI, i, 309).

Now the private-language argument's immediate purpose is not to show that language is a social product or that men are social creatures, any more than the discussion of rule-following which preceded it is intended to prove that language is made possible by communal consensus. What it does set out to do, however, is to break the spell of a misleading picture of what language users are, which has traditionally served the interests of idealist philosophies of mind and individualistic social philosophies. Descartes' angelism — i.e. his view of the human person as a *res cogitans*, an essentially intellectual being — is an example of the former philosophical tendency. Locke's individualism in political philosophy is an example of the second. To the extent that it succeeds in destroying a picture useful to these traditions, Wittgenstein's argument is hospitable to historicism and materialism, and contributes to the construction of an historico-materialist account of semantic necessity.

1.59 Material regularities

The two-pronged assault on the angelistic conception of language-users as discrete embodied spiritual essences, and on the individualistic picture of them as autonomous creatures with pre-social natural origins, is intended to restore to us a more familiar image of the speaking being as a bodily, rather than embodied agent, and as a social, rather than merely socialisable actor on the linguistic stage. From this it follows that even such regions of language as the 'languages' of logic and mathematics must, in a qualified way, depend not only on the normative regularities embodied in human praxis, but also on the natural regularities which stabilise the material world. The qualification may be expressed by saying that grammatical norms are relatively autonomous with respect to the consistencies of brute nature. Grammatical correctness and mathematical truths are indeed causally reliant on material reality being and remaining as it is, but they are not causally *determined* by it in the way that the rules for success in, say, carpentry or cookery are. At the same time, we could not calculate and correct one another as we do and always have done, if the physics of our universe did not prevent the random appearance and disappearance of everyday objects, the unexplained expansion and contraction of our measuring instruments and so on.

His appreciation of the relation between these two aspects of semantic necessity enables Wittgenstein to avoid the implausibility of saying such things as that the certainty of mathematics is based on the reliability of ink and paper, while recognising that calculation with paper and ink which was subject to queer changes would be impossible (PI, ii, p. 226). He counters talk about the 'inexorability' of logic, not by supposing that inferences belong to the order of physical causation, but by drawing attention to the fact that the word 'inexorable' is used in various ways, and that there correspond to our laws of logic 'very general facts of daily experience' which make simple demonstrations of those laws possible (RFM, i, 118). It is not the laws in themselves which are inexorable, but we who are inexorably strict in applying and interpreting them. As the examples afforded by the behaviour of young children (and some adults) show, no external necessity compels us to be always on our strictest best behaviour in this regard. However, our capacity to devise, understand, apply or misapply these cannons is a bequest of our material surroundings and neurological make-up.

This way of describing the interplay between nature and convention can be made to seem so much in harmony with our commonsensical intuitions that we are apt to forget the many stubborn obstacles that Wittgenstein has had to clear away before presenting it to us. In particular, the many guises that logicism and vulgar materialism are capable of assuming have all had to undergo exposure via the critiques of the Augustinian and Cartesian pictures before the dialectical connections between the conceptual and material realms can be seen aright.

1.6 Grammar and necessity

We are now in some position to take stock, and to try to give a synoptic answer to the question concerning the nature of the Wittgensteinian view of semantic necessity with which this chapter began. It now appears that Wittgenstein's philosophy of language expresses a movement from the logical essentialist dogma that the necessity which ultimately governs language is a purely logical necessity in the direction of a perspective which sees language as possessed of no essence of any kind, but as being reliant for its continued existence and coherence on a combination of natural and normative regularities of various sorts. The abandonment of logicism, however, is by no means equivalent to the abolition of logic. Instead, the undifferentiated purity of the Tractarian notion of logical form has been supplanted by a vision of language as a vast variety of logico-grammatical possibilities. Language in the *Investigations* is a tapestry of language-games. To describe a language-game is to describe its grammar and the grammatical behaviour consistent with playing it correctly, and 'everything descriptive of a language-game is part of logic' (OC, 56).

It is important to be clear about how this new notion of logical grammar stands in respect of other notions and distinctions in philosophical logic. In particular, it is not the case, as Canfield[79] imagines, that the Wittgensteinian notion of a grammatical remark coincides with the usual notion of an analytic truth: for as Baker and Hacker[80] explain, Wittgenstein did not hold that every grammatical proposition was a type-sentence, either instancing or being reducible to a law of logic. The analytic/synthetic distinction is framed in terms of such type-sentences; but whether an expression is a grammatical proposition depends not only on its form, but also on the roles it plays on occasions when it is uttered — i.e. on the *use* to which it is put. Giving an ostensive definition by reference to samples would be an instance of a Wittgensteinian proposition of grammar, yet it is hard to see how this could be called an analytic truth. It is true that such classical examples of analytic truths as '2 + 2 = 4' and '"Batchelor 'means' unmarried male"' are also grammatical propositions in Wittgenstein's sense. It is also evident, however, that the circumstance that the word ABOVE has five letters is a truth of grammar for Wittgenstein (PI, i, 160), whereas an orthodox believer in the viability of the analytic/synthetic distinction would have to classify it as an arbitrary orthographic convention.

1.7 Conclusion

The new conception of logic is a natural accompaniment of the transition from the idealist account of semantic necessity which typifies the Tractarian period to the materialist perspective which the *Investigations* open up. In the latter case, although the limits of my language still mean the limits of my world (TLP, 5.6), it is also true that the material world sets limits on the conceptual possibilities governing language. The natural stabilities governing our existence leave us free to invent new mathematical systems, to develop improved logical notations and to create all manner of new language-games. We make our own languages, but we do not make them just as we please, and we cannot conceive of a language in contexts in which a radical breakdown of the material order is supposed to have occurred. In this sense, our freedom depends on the recognition of material necessity — a necessity which is not just a matter of physics, but of our biological and neurological make-up as well. Within these confinements, however, we are free to construct regularised signing practices in accordance with our own social nature — the normative regularities which make language-learning and linguistic instruction possible. The dialectical interaction between these natural and normative restraints is what Wittgenstein's notion of a use-orientated grammar is designed to mediate. That he could have arrived so remarkably at a dialectical and materialist vision of language is certainly explicable in terms of the tensions between Kantian, empiricist and dialectical tendencies in his philosophical background already discussed. What is absent from the mature account of semantic necessity, however, is the moral dimension which was seen to have played such an essential part in the formation of the Tractarian approach to the problem of semantic necessity, and which constitutes a concern which Wittgenstein never repudiated. The arguments of the next chapter are designed to fill this lacuna.

Notes

1. In referring to Wittgenstein's works, I have for convenience adopted the practice of placing references to the relevant page or paragraph numbers in the text, accompanied by the initial letters of the title. Full details of the titles thus referred to are given in the list of abbreviations.

2. Baker and Hacker report that the idea of publishing both texts in a single volume arose in the context of a rereading of the *Tractatus* together with Nicholas Bachtin in 1943 and not in 1941, as the Preface to the *Investigations* suggests. They also observe that when Wittgenstein reopened publishing negotiations with Cambridge University Press in late 1943, the Syndics agreed to his condition that the two works should be published together in this way. See G.P. Baker and P.M.S. Hacker, *Wittgenstein understanding and meaning* (Basil Blackwell, Oxford, 1980), p. 21. Bachtin's possible influence on Wittgenstein during this period is of considerable interest, but remains obscure. Fania Pascal writes of Wittgenstein's friendship with this 'fiery communist' in her 'Personal memoir' in *Ludwig Wittgenstein: personal recollections* (Basil Blackwell, Oxford, 1981), p. 28. For a more detailed discussion of the relationship, see T. Eagleton, 'Wittgenstein's friends', *New Left Review*, no. 135 (1982), esp. pp. 74–6. Bachtin's brother, Mikhail, a Marxist philosopher and aesthetician, published in 1929 a work entitled *Marxism and the philosophy of language*.

3. G.E.M. Anscombe, *An introduction to Wittgenstein's Tractatus* (Hutchinson, London, 1959), original emphasis.

4. A. Kenny, *The legacy of Wittgenstein* (Basil Blackwell, Oxford, 1984), p. 13.

5. A. Kenny, *Wittgenstein* (Penguin, Harmondsworth, 1973), p. 226. In a later commentary, Kenny continues to maintain this position, citing as further evidence the survival of the thesis of the bipolarity of the proposition which, he says, is a 'crucial element' of the picture theory. See A. Kenny, *The legacy of Wittgenstein*, p. 22.

6. E. Stenius, *Wittgenstein's 'Tractatus'* (Basil Blackwell, Oxford, 1960), pp. 61–112. See also E. Stenius, 'The picture theory and Wittgenstein's later attitude to it' in Irving Block (ed.), *Perspectives on the philosophy of Wittgenstein* (Basil Blackwell, Oxford, 1981), pp. 110–39.

7. P.M.S. Hacker, 'The rise and fall of the picture theory' in Block (ed.), *Perspectives*, pp. 89–109. Hacker's subsequent abandonment of the view that the *Tractatus* propounds a form of realism — a view he also adopted in the first edition of his *Insight and illusion* — has not altered his opinion on this point. See P.M.S. Hacker. *Insight and illusion*. 2nd edn

(Oxford University Press, Oxford, 1986), pp. 61–2. I am grateful to Dr Hacker for allowing me to read this edition in proof.

8. A. Holiday, 'Wittgenstein's silence: philosophy, ritual and the limits of language', *Language and communication*, vol. 5, no. 2 (1985), pp. 133–42.

9. M.O'C. Drury, 'Letters to a student of philosophy', *Philosophical Investigations*, vol. 6, no. 2 (April 1983), p. 82.

10. D. Lee (ed.), *Wittgenstein's Lectures, Cambridge 1930–1932* (Basil Blackwell, Oxford, 1980), pp. 73f.

11. I. Kant, *Critique of pure reason*, J.M.D. Meiklejohn (trans.) (Dent, London, 1943), p. 3.

12. G.H. Von Wright, 'A biographical sketch' in N. Malcolm, *Ludwig Wittgenstein: a memoir* (Oxford University Press, London, 1966), p. 5.

13. G.W.F. Hegel, *Hegel's philosophy of nature*, A.V. Miller (trans.) (Clarendon Press, Oxford, 1970), p. 41, original emphasis.

14. Ibid., p. 6.

15. For a fuller discussion of the reaction which includes Helmholtz's account of it, see W.C.D. Dampier-Whetham, *A history of science* (Cambridge University Press, Cambridge), 1930, pp. 312–15.

16. P. Barker, 'Hertz and Wittgenstein', in *Studies in History and Philosophy of Science*, vol. 11, no. 3 (September 1980), pp. 243–56.

17. H. Hertz, *The principles of mechanics*, D.E. Jones and J.T. Walley (trans.) (Dover Publications, New York), 1956, p. 45.

18. Ibid., p. 1.

19. L. Boltzman, *Theoretical physics and philosophical problems*, Brian McGuinness (ed.) (D. Reidel, Dordrecht and Boston, 1974), p. 155.

20. Cf. E. Broda, *Ludwig Boltzman* (Ox Bow Press, Connecticut, 1983), p. 97.

21. L. Boltzman, 'Theories as representations' in A. Danto and S. Morgenbesser (eds) *Philosophy of science* (Meridian Books, New York), 1960, p. 247.

22. W. Mays, 'Wittgenstein in Manchester' in *Language, logic and philosophy*, Proceedings of the 4th International Wittgenstein Symposium (Kirchberg/Wechsel, Austria, 1979), p. 172.

23. See A. Janik and S. Toulmin, *Wittgenstein's Vienna* (Weidenfeld and Nicolson, London, 1973).

24. M. Dummett, 'Wittgenstein's philosophy of mathematics' in G. Pitcher (ed.), *Wittgenstein: the philosophical investigations* (Macmillan, London, 1966), p. 425.

25. I. Kant, *Prolegomena to any future metaphysics*, P.G. Lucas (trans.) (Manchester University Press, Manchester, 1953), p. 9.

26. Anscombe, *An introduction*, p. 12.

27. B. Russell, *The principles of mathematics* (Allen and Unwin, London, 1903), pp. 456–61.

28. Ibid., p. 490.

29. Ibid., pp. 53–65, 73 and 502.

30. B. Russell, 'On denoting' in *Logic and knowledge*, R.C. Marsh (ed.) (Allen and Unwin, London, 1956), p. 48.

31. See Hacker, *Insight and illusion*, pp. 134–45, for a full and illuminating discussion of the issue.

32. Rush Rhees, 'Postscript' in *Ludwig Wittgenstein: personal recollections* (Basil Blackwell, Oxford, 1981), p. 231.

33. C. Taylor, 'The opening arguments of the *Phenomenology*' in Alasdair MacIntyre (ed.) *Hegel: a collection of critical essays* (University of Notre Dame Press, Notre Dame and London, 1972), pp. 151–87. See also Taylor's *Hegel* (Cambridge University Press, London, New York and Melbourne, 1975), especially pp. 143f., 305 and 567.

34. S. Lovibond, *Realism and imagination in ethics* (Basil Blackwell, Oxford, 1983). Lovibond finds the Wittgensteinian insight that obedience to a linguistic rule consists in conformity to a practice 'strongly reminiscent of the Hegelian concept of Sittlichkeit or "concrete ethics" ' — p. 63. She also finds in Hegel's *Phenomenology* an anticipation of Wittgenstein's employment in *On certainty* of the notion of trust as underpinning the possibility of language: pp. 155–7.

35. M.O'C. Drury, 'Conversations with Wittgenstein' in Rhees (ed.), *Ludwig Wittgenstein: personal recollections*, p. 141.

36. J. Moran, 'Wittgenstein and Russia', *New Left Review*, no. 73 (1972), p. 93.

37. Ibid., p. 91.

38. P. Sraffa, *Production of commodities by means of commodities* (Cambridge University Press, Cambridge, 1960), pp. 93–5.

39. A. Gramsci, *Selections from political writings* 1921–1926, Quintin Hoare (trans. and ed.) (Lawrence and Wishart, London, 1978), p. 218.

40. Ibid., p. 233.

41. By I. Steedman, in his *Marx after Sraffa* (New Left Books, London), 1977.

42. N. Malcolm, *Ludwig Wittgenstein: a memoir* (Oxford University Press, London, New York and Toronto, 1958), p. 69.

43. Gramsci, *Selections*, p. 483n.

44. D. Rubenstein, *Marx and Wittgenstein* (Routledge and Kegan Paul, London, Boston and Henley, 1981), p. 3 and pp. 185–9.

45. S.M. Easton, *Humanist Marxism and Wittgensteinian social philosophy* (Manchester University Press, Manchester, 1983), p. 28.

46. Ibid., p. 29.

47. Rubenstein, *Marx and Wittgenstein*, p. 169.

48. Easton, *Humanist Marxism*, p. 3.

49. Malcolm, *Ludwig Wittgenstein*, p. 39.

50. Rush Rhees (ed.), *Recollections of Wittgenstein* (Oxford University Press, Oxford, 1984), p. 79.

51. A. Janik, 'Wittgenstein, Ficker and *Der Brenner*' in C.G. Luckhardt (ed.), *Wittgenstein sources and perspectives* (Harvester Press, Sussex, 1979), p. 167.

52. L. Wittgenstein, 'Letters to Ludwig von Ficker', B. Gillette (trans.) and A. Janik (ed.) in C.G. Luckhardt (ed.), *Wittgenstein sources and perspectives*, pp. 94–5, original emphasis. Wittgenstein seems to be making a similar point in his reply to Russell's comments on the MS of the *Tractatus* when he says:

> . . . You haven't really got hold of my main contention, to which the whole business of logical propositions is only a corollary. The main point is the theory of what can be expressed by propositions

... and what cannot be expressed by propositions, but only shown; which I believe is the cardinal problem of philosophy (quoted in Anscombe, *An introduction*, p. 161).

53. K. Marx, *Capital*, vol. i, afterword to the second German edition, S. Moore and E. Aveling (trans.) (Lawrence and Wishart, London, 1954), p. 29.

54. Hacker, *Insight and illusion*, 2nd edn, pp. 105–6.

55. Hacker, *Insight and illusion*, 1st edn (Clarendon Press, Oxford, 1972), p. 83. The phrase has been dropped from the 2nd edition because (so Dr Hacker informs me) he had come to think it arrogant (personal communications, 1984). The argument on this point, however, is substantively the same in both editions.

56. L. Wittgenstein, 'Wittgenstein's Lecture on ethics', *Philosophical Review*, vol. lxxiv (1965), p. 6.

57. A. Kenny, *Wittgenstein* (Penguin, Harmondsworth, 1973), p. 29.

58. Ibid., p. 34.

59. G. Frege, *Begriffschrift* in P. Geach and M. Black (eds), *Translations from the philosophical writings of Gottlob Frege* (Basil Blackwell, Oxford, 1952), p. 14; and G. Frege, *The foundations of arithmetic*, J.L. Austin (trans.) (Basil Blackwell, Oxford, 1950), p. 71.

60. M.B. Hintikka and J. Hintikka, *Investigating Wittgenstein* (Basil Blackwell, Oxford, 1986), esp. Chapter 3, pp. 45–86.

61. L. Wittgenstein, 'Some remarks on logical form', *Proceedings of the Aristotelian Society*, supp. vol. ix (1929), p. 166.

62. D. Pears, 'The logical independence of elementary propositions' in Block, *Perspectives*, p. 75.

63. Wittgenstein, 'Some remarks', p. 171.

64. Kenny, *The legacy of Wittgenstein*, pp. 10–11.

65. P.F. Strawson, 'On referring' in *Logico-linguistic papers* (Methuen, London, 1971), p. 19. The paper first appeared in *Mind*, vol. lix (1950).

66. J. Churchill, 'The coherence of the concept "language-game" ', *Philosphical Investigations*, vol. 6, no. 4 (1983), p. 257.

67. Hintikka and Hintikka, *Investigating Wittgenstein*, pp. 196 f.

68. B. Williams, 'Wittgenstein and idealism' in G. Vesey (ed.), *Understanding Wittgenstein*, Royal Institute of Philosophy Lectures, vol. 7 (Macmillan, London, 1974), pp. 76–95.

69. D. Bolton, 'Life-form and idealism' in G. Vesey (ed.), *Idealism past and present*, Royal Institute of Philosophy Lectures, Series 13 (Press Syndicate, University of Cambridge, 1982), pp. 269–84. For another criticism of Williams's interpretation see N. Malcolm, 'Wittgenstein and idealism' in Vesey (ed.), *Understanding Wittgenstein*, pp. 249–68.

70. G.P. Baker and P.M.S. Hacker, *Wittgenstein understanding and meaning* (Basil Blackwell, Oxford, 1980), pp. 136–7.

71. D. Pears *Wittgenstein* (Fontana/Collins, 1971), esp. pp. 168 f.

72. S.A. Kripke, *Wittgenstein on rules and private language: an elementary exposition* (Basil Blackwell, Oxford, 1982).

73. C. Wright, *Wittgenstein on the foundations of mathematics* (Duckworth, London, 1980), esp. Chapters I and XII.

74. G.P. Baker and P.M.S. Hacker, *Scepticism, rules and language* (Basil Blackwell, Oxford, 1984).

75. Wright, *Wittgenstein on the foundations*, p. 220.

76. J. Locke, *An essay concerning human understanding*, vol. II, A. Campbell Fraser (ed.) (Dover, New York, 1959), p. 3.

77. G. Pitcher, *The philosophy of Wittgenstein* (Englewood Cliffs, New Jersey, 1964), Chapter 12.

78. A. Donagan, 'Wittgenstein on sensation' in G. Pitcher (ed.), *Wittgenstein: The Philosophical Investigations* (Doubleday, Garden City, New Jersey, 1968), pp. 324–51.

79. J. Canfield, *Wittgenstein language and world* (University of Massachusetts Press, Amherst, 1981), p. 209.

80. G.P. Baker and P.M.S. Hacker, *Wittgenstein rules, grammar and necessity* (Basil Blackwell, Oxford, 1985), pp. 267–9.

2

Semantic Necessity
as Moral Necessity

2.0 Introduction

We began our exploration with a question (which we also attributed to the Tractarian Wittgenstein), and which we styled 'the problem of semantic necessity'. We wanted to understand the nature of the necessities that make language possible, and so we asked what were the necessary conditions for the very possibility of language, setting our question against the backdrop of the evolving portrayals of language which Wittgenstein left us. A result of this exercise, which flows especially from our examination of the *Investigations*, is to alert us to the danger of giving the question too Socratic a shape. We are to beware of asking, with respect to semantic necessity, the same sort of questions Plato's Socrates asked with respect to such things as virtue, justice, knowledge and beauty. We ought not to expect the kind of univocal answers as classical antiquity's greatest essentialist expected to the questions he asked. The great lesson of the later Wittgensteinian semantics is surely that there is no single necessity governing language, but a variety of necessities, both natural and normative, and thus nothing that could be called *the* problem of semantic necessity. We may say, if we like, that semantic necessity has turned out to be not a logical, but a practical sort of necessity. Saying this, however, will at once invite the reminder that no common factor unites our language-using practices, so that 'practice' here is merely a convenient label, covering all the many different things we do in communicating with one another.

Yet these counsels may fail to assuage our perplexity: for we may still be bemused at the very fact that all this vast multiplicity of language-games and this rich diversity of practices should, despite all their variety, exhibit the kind of coherence we expect of a language that is to serve as a fully viable means of communication. Thus, we may be moved to ask 'What kind of necessity gives language its coherence?', which is simply a rather different form of the question 'How is language possible?' or 'What is semantic necessity?'. Nor need such questions be accompanied by essentialist expectations. We need anticipate no discovery of anything uniform concealed beneath the appearances to which we still faithfully attend. It seems entirely possible to keep to the linguistic surface, contenting ourselves with trying to discern among the shadings of resemblance which, in their various ways, connect the language-games to one another, some pattern of concentricity which would give us an answer of the kind we seem to want. Should such a pattern emerge and should we discover at the centre of the surface of the language-map a core-cluster of games which could arguably fulfil the function of conferring coherence on the whole, there is no reason to assume that the games comprising this core will be undifferentiated with respect to one another, even if the family-resemblance between them is especially marked in certain respects.

Enthusiasts for Wittgenstein's later philosophy will perhaps complain that this project is inconsistent with the therapeutic, non-theoretic style of philosophising which was one of his chief bequests. They may hold that a continued quest for the sources of semantic necessity is itself the result of the kind of conceptual confusion which the post-Tractarian writings sought to disentangle. I am not convinced by this sort of objection.

It is by no means self-evident that to enquire into the nature of a specifically semantic necessity is to ask what Wittgenstein would have called an 'idle' question. This certainly does not follow from the circumstance that logicist essentialist solutions to the question are exposed as chimerical by the arguments of the *Investigations*. To think otherwise is surely to miss an aspect of the ironic dimension of his work, to which attention was drawn much earlier on (1.1): for it is precisely by restoring to us the full complexity and seemingly arbitrary character of grammar that the anti-essentialist critique reawakens our sense of wonder at our ability to understand and be understood within the linguistic communities to which we belong. It is just at the moment when, through careful attention to a number of painstakingly constructed elucidations, we have liberated ourselves from various explanatory myths — concealed sentential structures or generative rules, secreted in the recesses of the cerebral cortex — that our best philosophical instincts ought to give us pause for reflection at the how and why of the integrity our very public and material signing practices achieve through the diffusion of games which constitute a single language.

In response, therefore, to Wittgenstein's hope that the semantics of the *Investigations* would stimulate some of us to thoughts of our own (PI, p. x), my course in this chapter will be to employ certain features of the notion of a language-game in order to show that certain of such games — which will turn out to be bound up with moral aspects of our form of life — are essential to the coherence of any imaginable language. My argument for this position will assume a grasp of much of the material already covered. In particular, it will assume the linkage between the notions of a language-game and a life-form.

2.1 Games and core-games

The *Investigations* gives us a cartographic overview of language. It is a collection of *Landschaftskizzen* (PI, p. ix), yielding an holistic *in-breadth* portrayal of the linguistic landscape which supplants the cross-sectional conceptual diagram of language *in-depth*, supplied in the *Tractatus*. In the new dispensation, we are to think of the field of language as a curious map, the surface of which is constantly changing, as in those films of the Earth's surface, taken by artificial satellites. This mapped surface is comprised of a bewildering meshwork of sub-divisions, whose irregular and interlocking boundaries are continually shifting. These sub-divisions are Wittgenstein's language-games. Our task is to account for the internal coherence through change and diversity of this multiplicity of games, and to do so in a fashion which scrupulously respects the integrity of the surface we are considering and leaves it intact. We must try to pick out which of these games or game-clusters is essential to the coherence of the whole, without lapsing into a modified version of Tractarian essentialism. We must search for a linguistic core, but avoid stratification, and our project must be subject to the cannon that in imagining a coherent language, we are imagining not abstract structures, but a form of life.

Clearly this enterprise of identifying core-language-games

stands in need of some preliminary justification. We must begin by conceding that, considered with respect to each other, individual language-games can display no hierarchy. As we saw previously (1.55), no single feature is common to the myriad sorts of speaking practices we call 'language-games'. Rather, they are united by various sorts and degrees of family-resemblance. There can be no principle whereby, relative to their internal properties, we can assign priorities between language-games, because resemblance is a symmetrical relation. If A resembles B, then they are equally like or unlike each other, although either may be more or less like C than it is like the other member of the original pair.

If, on the other hand, we ask instead how it is that in imagining a cluster of language-games and material practices, we are also imagining a life-form, we will feel the need of the notions of 'core' and 'periphery'. The reasons for this have to do with the fact that in imagining a cluster of such games and practices, rich enough to be properly described as a language or a part thereof, we are always presupposing a mode of agreement which goes to the heart of the form of life to which that language belongs. Such agreement is possible only in forms of life to which human beings and only human beings have access, and it is a conceptual matter that a form of life cannot be a human form unless the integrity of the persons, who speak the language to one another, is somehow sustained. No language-learning or coherent communication by means of language will be feasible unless a modicum of sincerity on the part of those who use and teach the use of the language can be assumed. This in turn presumes that the notion of moral accountability and the value of trust are somehow preserved by the speakers. The collection of normative regularities, in the form of repeatable actions and utterances, whereby such value-preservation is achieved, are what I call 'core-language-games', which perform the essential function of enshrining, as it were, the norms internal to our form of life which make agreement within it possible.

The perception that these core-games are as essential to such agreement as are the natural regularities, which constitute the backdrop that material reality provides for our speaking practices, may be enhanced by reflecting on how a form of life radically different from ours might communicate. Our languages and life-worlds are characterised by the perpetual possibility of discrepancies intervening to sever the usual bond between what a sign seems to mean and the real intentions of the signaller. This possibility of disagreement or disunity between theory and practice is the source of the possibility that we may be misunderstanding or deceiving one another when we speak, or that our ways of meaning may have puzzling ironic dimensions.

However, we might easily imagine a form of life to which none of this applied. There might be creatures so constituted that their only mode of communication consisted of changing colour. As blushing in our case normally indicates embarrassment and turning pale is a sign of fear, so they can convey a far wider spectrum of emotions, desires and intentions to one another by correspondingly various changes of colour. They might, for instance, indicate desires for different types of nutriment by turning various shades of green. Different shades of red with them could indicate different sorts of danger, and so on. However, although the form of communication available to these animals may accord with the natural regularities governing their lives, the question of agreement or disagreement between what their signals apparently mean and what they really mean does not even arise, for they convey their messages as spontaneously as we blush or turn pale. No question of sincerity or insincerity can be at issue here, and hence there is no need to seek out among their signals a value-preserving core, which keeps their system of signals intact.

A moral to be drawn from the comparison between alien life-forms and our own is that agreement in language and life-form is *natural* to the latter in a way that it is not to the former, and this observation is germane to my contention that there is no conflict between the quest for core-language-games and the idea that language-games are unified only by family resemblances. For while the family resemblance trope negatively inhibits our craving for generality by preventing us from assuming that some common feature must ground the likenesses between games, its positive contribution is to help us to see that the resemblance that games bear to one another is a function of our finding it *natural* to classify and assimilate them to one another in the way we do. Here, of course, 'natural' means 'natural to the human form of life', and it is perfectly natural for us to classify things in a way which prioritises them. Indeed, as I shall now try to show, the assignment of priorities is inevitable in the case of language-games.

2.11 Playing seriously

Contentious and uncontentious connotations accompany the language-game conceit. Uncontentiously, it is associated with rules (since most games are rule-governed), with family resemblance (since the form of unity in diversity which games exhibit is best captured by this concept) and with human *praxis*, since all games are either played by people or playable by them. More controversially, the notion suggests play, theatre, mime, mimicry and convergent degrees of seriousness and unseriousness. Wittgenstein did not make extensive use of these latter associations, and commentators have generally been cautious in exploring their possibilities. Thus, Baker and Hacker warily conclude: 'We are moving in the realm of analogy: language is not a game, nor typically are the activities into which its use is woven.'[1] They are of course right. Language is not *a* game, nor does the Wittgensteinian account treat it as such. It is regarded as a collectivity of games with a richly varied membership. Many of these are bound up with what would usually be regarded as game-playing activities, but most of them are not. Most of us do not spend most of our time telling jokes, guessing riddles, play-acting or otherwise recreating ourselves.

This, however, does not diminish the fact that the notions of seriousness and unseriousness or their cognates inevitably enter into descriptions of game-playing, and that 'serious', like such words as 'big', 'small', 'good' and 'evil', is a gradeable adjective. We accuse one another of taking certain games too seriously and of not taking others seriously enough, just as we can form judgements about the degrees of seriousness appropriate to the various regions of our discourse. Unless he is a professional entertainer, only an eccentric will seriously devote his life to joke-telling, but in any numerate society, all adults are well-advised to take seriously the language of elementary arithmetic. Indeed, it is a mark of someone's having learned a language thoroughly that he displays a certain *savoir-faire* in evincing the appropriate degree of seriousness in the various language-games he plays, and that he knows which speakers to take seriously and on what occasions. The tests of such expertise will vary (sometimes markedly) from language to language, and from culture to culture. What passes for a harmless jest in one linguistic and cultural setting may be a deadly insult in another: the babble of a lunatic may be read by the inhabitant of a shamanistic culture as a spiritual revelation which must be decoded in accordance with special interpretative rules and techniques.

No simple rule-of-thumb is available to enable us to tell over all cases whether an agent is according a game the degree of seriousness proper to the playing of it. Grave demeanour and the appearance of slow deliberation in the application of rules will be reliable guides in some instances, but not in others. Chess, bridge, poker and patience are all conducive to sincere displays of fervent attention by those who play them, but the first three require to be taken with great seriousness only by professionals, and the last is a recreation pure and simple. On the other hand, there are activities — calculation, colour identification and telling the time are examples — which competent performers carry out almost mechanically, and this is just because misperformances in these cases can have such serious consequences that we aim to teach novices correctly to apply the rules of these language-games automatically and without much need of reflection. Not only are outward signs of putatively 'serious' inner states of concentrated attention and the like unreliable indications that a player is playing with the requisite sort of seriousness, there is in fact no single 'inner state' which would adequately match the various levels of seriousness that different language-games require.

What is quite undeniable, however, is that there can be no question of serious play, and *a fortiori*, none of correct or incorrect discriminations between degrees of seriousness, where *the point* of a game has been altogether misunderstood or completely disregarded. This holds even for cases in which, although the point of a game depends on what must be done so as to win it, a player deliberately sets out to lose: for here, the player must grasp the game's point in order to achieve his aim, and it might even be said that what counts as 'defeat' for everyone else counts as 'victory' for him. It is possible to play a very interesting version of chess in which the object is not to checkmate ones opponent, but to be placed in that position one's self. Although it is a moot point whether this game is the game of chess, it depends on the rules and object of the game everybody else calls 'chess' being thoroughly understood. Similarly, deliberate misreporting on states of affairs presupposes not ignorance, but full awareness of the point of the statement-making language-game. There are also games in which winning and losing are not in question, where rules are invented on an *ad hoc* basis and where rule-governedness is a minimal consideration. Frolicking, prattle and babbling are examples of these. The point of the first might be explained in terms of getting unfettered exercise to get rid of excess energy; the object of the second could be to allay nervousness; and we might do the third in order to mock what we took to be a barbarian tongue. Anyone might seriously engage in these activities with such projects seriously in mind; but there are no *pointless* activities that we should want to call 'game-playing', and, hence, no game-playing activities which are devoid of any sort or degree of seriousness. The frolics of fox cubs, the prattlings of parrots and the babblings of babies have no genuine counterpart in the foibles of freshmen, the pattering of party-goers or the mockery of pseudo-mimics. The latter admit of some sort of purposiveness, whereas the former do not.

It seems, then, that in the point of any language-game we have an objective determinant of the degree of seriousness appropriate to the playing of it. Subjective attitudes associated with serious behaviour — attentiveness, calmness, grave thoughts and the like — and the expression these find in the form of judicious speech-acts are subordinate to the set of objective conditions which this factor supplies. These objective conditions are tinged with subjectivity only in a rather special sense which does not damage their title to be thought of as objective. The point of a language-game is the point that speakers of the language in question give it, inasmuch as the life-form unique to the players interpenetrates the games they play, and in so far as the grammar of the game which contributes to its having the point it does is founded on regular patterns of human conduct. However, as we saw in examining the private-language argument (1.58), no language-game is constructable by a speaking subject such that no other subject could in principle gain access to it. There are, therefore, no games with points which are in principle unpublicisable, and it is in this sense that the point of any game can be said to belong to the realm of objectively knowable things.

Thus, to say of a language-game that there is very little (or a great deal) of point to it is to make an objective evaluation concerning the degree of seriousness due to it, and to do this is to make a judgement about the game's relative efficacy and importance in sustaining the whole linguistic network to which it belongs and in preserving the form of life which uses that language. For a game has the point it has in virtue of its internal connections with other games, and a sufficiently wide overview of these connections will show that unless certain games had point, others would be pointless. Few if any games of skill or chance would survive the demise of the language-games we play with words like 'victory', 'defeat', 'success' and 'failure'. Grammatical jokes would cease to entertain us, were there not overarching language-games in which the usual rules of grammar are standardly employed. The former are merely novel reminders of the correct modes of discourse which the latter have institutionalised. Furthermore, not only is it true that colour identification or arithmetic as we now play them would lose their point if the neuro-physiological aspects of our life-form were such that only some of us saw grass as green and none of us could count beyond 2, it is also true that our life-form would not be as it is if radically different ways of telling colours and of counting were customary with us. By this I do not mean that our physical and psychological make-up would alter or atrophy from disuse (although it might): I mean rather that a hypothetical observer from outside the mode of life we call our own would describe it differently from what might have been the case had the potential contained in our natural make-up not gone unrealised or been frustrated by the way we had gone on identifying colours and doing arithmetic.

The possibility which this whole discussion of serious play opens up is that of using the gradations of seriousness evidenced throughout the field of language as an index determining the hierarchical arrangement of the language games we play with respect to their relative importance in ensuring the coherence of the entire field. I shall try to show that at the apex, so to speak, of this hierarchy are certain language-game-clusters, the rules of which are constitutive of our own human form of life, because the necessity they embody is a moral necessity.

What I shall try to establish, via the criteria of the imaginative possibility of language retaining its coherence in their absence, is that these core-games must pertain to the preservation of that sphere of religio-ethical value which, in the Tractarian picture, belonged to the realm of the unsayable. Three sorts of core-game will be distinguished and discussed — namely:

(1) games in which truth-telling is evaluatively distinguished from the telling of deliberate falsehoods,

(2) games in which justice and fairness are distinguished from injustice and unfairness, and

(3) games which give ritualised expression to religious belief, awe or wonder.

2.12 Counterfeit core-games

Before any imaginative experimentation begins, something more needs to be said to justify the selection of the above-mentioned sorts of language-games as fit subjects for tests, designed to establish their indispensability to the field of meaningful discourse. (Something must also be said about what we take ourselves to be doing in conducting thought-experiments with imaginary languages, and we will examine this question in the next section.) For not only is there

(1) no evidence that truth-telling, just-dealing and the ritualised expression of religious reverence are the only game-clusters which fulfil the function I attribute to them, but

(2) nothing has been done to distinguish language-games which genuinely fulfil this function and those which merely give a bogus appearance of doing so.

I see no need to deny (1). There may very well be core-language-games other than the ones I have listed. If the language-games I have seized upon turn out to have the role and status I claim for them, that will be enough to show the linkage between moral and semantic necessity which I am anxious to establish. To claim that a moral necessity governs language is perfectly compatible with the claim that other kinds of necessity determine its possibilities as well. To distinguish, as we have already done, between the limits set by brute-natural regularities on the one hand, and normative regularities on the other, is precisely to allow for this plurality. The problem presented by (2) is more serious: for there are sorts of intentional action which, although the point of doing them makes the doing of them a serious affair and they do seem to have a role of importance in supporting forms of life, do not seem to me to be genuine, but only counterfeit examples of the kind of life-preserving practice. I have in mind in speaking of core-games.

Compare, for instance, the activity of force-feeding a prisoner with that of extending an invitation to dine. In the former case, we are, as we are not in the latter, using an abnormal method to sustain life in someone who has either lost the will to live or deliberately chooses to endanger his life. Invitations to dine are embedded in a background of civilised normality which is absent in the force-feeding case. Even in surroundings of extreme poverty, the speech-acts whereby we ask others to share food with us are expressions of a way of life we already enjoy with a certain fullness, and signal an anticipation of its continuity. Such invitations are celebrations of our enjoyment of the institutions of friendship and courtesy. They are also a means of preserving the virtues of kindness and generosity, and are not just ways of keeping ourselves alive. That careerists, snobs and social climbers give dinner parties out of baser motives gainsays none of this: for it is only because the issuing of invitations and other ceremonials of hospitality are paradigmatically preservative of certain values that they can successfully serve ignoble ends. Perverters of the institution are obliged to treat abuses of hospitality as seriously as those who practise it in good faith.

Political history provides a fund of examples of counterfeit-core-games of a sort Marx made much of in the famous opening passage of his *Eighteenth Brumaire*.[2] These are propagandistic attempts to relive through re-enactment an historical period which is irrevocably dead or dying. Thus, in South Africa in the 1930s, Malan's Nationalists and the Afrikaner Broederbond attempted to revive the spirit of the Greak Trek of the 1830s by organising a nation-wide *Eeufees* or *Tweede Trek* — a vast pageant, complete with ox waggons, in which thousands of Afrikaner families in traditional costumary participated. However, the object of this exercise betrayed its artificiality, for the Broederbond's aim in organising the festival was the restoration of rural pioneering, ethical and religious values which had been extinguished by industrialisation and urban poverty. The contextual conditions within which this particular communal form of life could be sustained by normal expedients had been eroded by objective historical processes, just as, in the example of the force-fed prisoner, the setting in terms of which his life would normally have been preserved has been erased. In neither case are the life-preserving activities altogether lacking in efficacy. His captors may well succeed in keeping their prisoner clinically alive for a considerable time, and the *Tweede Trek* celebrations did, as a matter of historical fact, succeed in re-awakening national sentiment of a particular sort among Afrikaner poor Whites. In both cases, however, the quality of what is preserved or revived is notably diminished, and the expedients whereby even this was achieved cannot be repeated indefinitely.

A genuine core-game, then, will be free of the defects which characterise the bogus variety. It will be inextricably bound up with many facets of the life-form it sustains, so that the practice of it will be the norm, not an exceptional event. The usualness of its occurrence in social life will not detract from the seriousness with which even those who deviate from the values it preserves are compelled to treat it. Finally, a true core-game does not diminish the quality or richness of the form of life to which it contributes. In imagining such a game, we will inevitably be drawn into imagining a fully-developed social *Lebensform*. As the discussion progresses, it will become apparent that the game-clusters which concern us satisfy these criteria.

2.2 Imaginary languages

At this point, some remarks are in order concerning the favourite Wittgensteinian activity of imagining a language. These are intended to meet some of the needs of those who, seeing nothing obvious about the assimilation of semantic necessity to moral necessity, may feel they are being 'railroaded' into according the sorts of language-game singled out in these pages the same pride of place I give to them. It will already be evident that the argumentative strategy to be employed in justification of my claims respecting the status of language-games having a value-sustaining function will take the form of a transcendental argument wherein the project of constructing a possible language in which these games are absent is shown to collapse into self-stultification. This procedure, it will be said, may do no more than create the illusion that language depends on moral necessity, if it is used selectively to test only those language-games which would support that thesis by passing the test. Might we not reach quite different conclusions by deciding to place, say, mathematical language-games at the centre of the language-map and trying the same type of thought-experiment?

Difficulties of this sort are best met by distinguishing, in the first place, between the activity of constructing a genuinely imaginative picture of a possible language to serve as material for a viable thought-experiment, and that of merely fantasising about language in a way which yields portrayals which are not congruent with the natural context assumed or the form of life imagined. Thus, a genuine image of a possible language in the context of the natural regularities familiar to us, the words and sentences of which are supposed to be spoken by humans, will obviously not be an image which includes the possibility of regular and sanctioned instances of violations of the rules of valid deductive inference. In a possible world in which the fundamental things are as they are with us, an image which pretends to include such things as the squaring of the circle, sanctioned instances of self-contradiction or arithmetical forms in which $2 + 2 = 5$, is not merely an idle picture which can do no conceptual work: it is not a picture of a language at all. A man may give reasons (even bad ones) for lying, acting unjustly or refusing to reverence what his fellows reverence. However, unless his understanding of the terms involved is different or defective, he cannot begin to give reasons for affirming 'both p and not-p' or talking about 'square circles'. To insist on this is not to say merely that a language from which the ground rules of elementary inference had been subtracted would fall into incoherence in the way that I contend it would, if value-preserving core-games were to become extinct. It is to make the different point that the project of constructing a human and humanly imaginable language cannot get off the ground if it is supposed that elementary regions of logic and mathematics are other than they are with us. A form of life radically unlike ours might communicate without our kind of basic logical geography, but we can neither hope to understand such communication or imagine what form it would take.

2.21 Imaginary linguists

Any genuine imaginative construct of a community of competent speakers must conform to our deepest intuitions as to what constitutes a human community, however superficially bizarre we choose to make the behaviour of its inhabitants appear. We cannot people our possible worlds entirely with amnesiacs, future-blind pyschopaths or autistics. Our imaginary linguists must have a recollectable history, just as we do. They must have expectations of a future and a capacity to envisage that future as a consequence of past concerns.

These attributes dovetail with the assumption that the world that the imaginary linguists inhabit, and whose features and furniture are topics of their language, exhibits in general the same sorts of natural regularities that our world displays. Preternatural and supernatural events, if they happen at all, must be the exception and not the rule, or else the rules of the language we purport to imagine will resemble the rules of our language so little as to make the exercise pointless. Moreover, just as we can imagine possible languages, so also must the users of the languages we imagine be imagined as being at least not constitutionally incapable of imagining the forms of expression to which we have access, otherwise it will follow that actual and fictive worlds are mutually opaque.

This last proviso needs clarification. There are, after all, modal logics which are developed on the strength of the supposition that the accessibility relation between possible worlds is not symmetrical. We believe ourselves able to imagine the life of, say, a seventeenth-century Trappist monk; but does our right to assume this depend on believing that the monk can imagine our twentieth-century life? Before we can imagine the language of a pre-mathematical people, must we imagine them as able to imagine what mathematics is like?

The caveat that actual and fictional language-users must have comparable imaginative capacities is not meant to exclude such examples. That the monk and the cave-man lack the intellectual equipment which would give them access to conceptual refinements available to us will not prevent us from constructing imaginary languages appropriate to what we know of their circumstances. What will prevent it is the notion that an innate incapacity permanently obstructs the fictional linguist's access to our linguistic domain: for to assume this sort of deficiency is to postulate a form of life qualitatively distinct from ours.

To this constraint we must add another concerning the patterns of change to which imaginary linguists and their language may cogently be supposed to conform. If opaqueness is to be avoided, then supernormality is to be eschewed as strongly, and for the same reason, as subnormality. We must not assume that the language of our fictive accounts has had an evolution incongruously different from the language in which those accounts are given. By this I mean that we cannot tell stories about the growth of a language and the development of its users in which the major stages in the evolution of our own natural language are left out or impossibly juxtaposed. Such stories must be ruled out because not only are they not narratives native to our own life-form, but also because, by doing violence to our recognition of the fact that certain language-games must be part of a society's repertoire before others can be added to it, they do violence to such dim notions of semantic necessity as we already possess; and it is precisely these which we strive to clarify through our thought-experiments. This is why we cannot imagine a language which began with set-theory or the differential calculus, or one which had mathematical language-games at its core, in the sense that these were to be thought of as central to its survival as a coherent whole.

2.22 *An objection turned*

It will be said that this whole attempt (2.2–2.21) to lay down in advance what is and what is not a legitimate exercise of the philosopher's imagination with respect to possible languages amounts to the requirement that we never do more than recollect what our own human languages are really like, and that this restriction robs the activity of imagining a language of its chief advantage. For the great merit of this activity seemed to be that it permitted a kind of free variation over a range of possibilities which the bare description of brute facts did not permit. If we are to lose this advantage, why not stop all pretence that we are creatively employing our imaginations, and confine ourselves to the duller security of bald factual description?

The answer here is that, although the proposal is indeed that we confine ourselves to what is humanly imaginable for human speakers, this does not render the exercise as barren as the objection insinuates. For we are committed to the adage that to imagine a language is to imagine the life-form which uses it — i.e. our own human form of life — and we are not brute facts to ourselves and do not know ourselves as we know brute facts — even psychological, sociological or historical brute facts, such as our intelligence quotients, the status of marriage as an institution in the regions we inhabit or the fact that Van Riebeck landed at Cape Town in 1652. We are not transparent to ourselves in the way that inanimate objects and even other life-forms are transparent to us, and this means that the linguistic possibilities available to us cannot be set within finalistic limits, although it does not mean that we can set no limits on them at all. There is clearly no single, ready-made rule-of-thumb to enable us sharply to differentiate at the start between sober imaginings and mere reverie. However, from the fact that unadorned observation of human affairs reveals instances of moral decline, it seems safe to assume that we can go on to imagine episodes culminating in the complete breakdown of certain moral norms in order to see whether a point must be reached at which the link between language and life-form is severed. This will be the point at which we say, not only 'We can't live like that', but also 'We can't talk if we live like that.'

I conclude, then, that when all considerations distinguishing genuine imaginative exploration from fantasy are taken into account, and given that we must assume the existence of core-games so long as we wish to employ the language-game analogy, it is perfectly in order to use the imagination to test the claim that value-preservation secures linguistic coherence.

2.3 Truth-telling

In the actual world of everyday experience which is the starting point for all imaginative constructions of possible worlds, all competent language-users will be proficient at a cluster of language-games, designed to preserve the virtue of truthfulness. We are at pains to familiarise children with these games from a relatively early age, sometimes for lofty reasons, sometimes simply because we know that however they turn out as moral beings, they must come to terms with these games in order to find their feet as worldlings. Thus, we praise truth-telling (in most circumstances), condemn and sometimes punish lying, and teach children how, and under what circumstances, to do likewise. The argument which follows is designed to show that, in the total absence of such language-games, language itself is unimaginable. Although I shall not present this argument in a strictly sequential fashion, its skeletal form is as follows:

(1) There can be no fully-developed language in which assertion-making by means of statements is not a prevalent speaking practice.
(2) Truth-telling, considered as an established moral norm, is an essential condition for the making of meaningful statements.
(3) Even in the case of impoverished semi-languages, consisting only of commands, there is an important analogue with truth-telling.
(4) Truth-telling is dependent on the satisfaction of sincerity conditions.

(5) 'Sincerity' is essentially not merely a psychological, but a moral notion. Therefore

(6) The necessity governing language is a moral necessity.

2.31 Trust and sincerity

The importance of premisses (4) and (5) in the above outline is obvious. A sincere speaker is a trustworthy speaker, even though the reliability of what he says may in some instances be jeopardised by ignorance of a non-culpable sort on his part. Moreover, the assumption that most speakers are trustworthy most of the time is one all speakers must make if discourse is not to collapse into confusion. On this showing, there will be some overlap between statement-making and promising. An assertion-maker is like a player of the promising game in that players of both language-games are taken to have entered into an agreement of a special sort to speak sincerely and to trust one another to speak in this way. 'Trust' and 'sincerity', therefore, serve as bridge-concepts, linking the notions of truthfulness and moral necessity.

The link would be damaged, however, if sincerity were not itself treated as being primarily a moral notion. Indeed, Searle, in both his early philosophy of language and his more recent philosophy of mind, fails to give the term the specifically ethical gloss which I give to it. Thus, an insincere promise is for him a promise nonetheless,[3] and not, as I should describe it, a 'false promise'. For Searle, moreover, 'a lie or other insincere speech act consists in performing a speech act, and thereby expressing an Intentional state, where one does not have the Intentional state that one expresses.'[4]

Leaving aside the infelicity of talking about 'expressing' a 'state' that one does not have, this way of putting matters makes it clear that Searle thinks it of only secondary importance that lying and breach of promise are offences against a *moral* code of conduct. The reason he thinks this is that 'sincerity' is to him primarily not a moral but a *psychological* notion. For although he allows that the intention to make a statement commits the speaker to making a true statement, he nonetheless defines a 'sincerity condition' as 'a level of the psychological state expressed in the performance of the [speech] act'.[5] Searle treats 'sincerity' like this because philosophical semantics is for him no more than a branch of the philosophy of mind. Now I do not wish to launch a full-scale assault on this individualistic and psychologistic way of proceeding at this point. I hope that some of the rest of what I have to say in this and subsequent chapters, taken with what has already been said about the historicist character of Wittgenstein's later philosophy, will help to explain why I think that if the philosophy of meaning is a branch of anything, it is a branch of the philosophy of history. What I do want to contest is Searle's right to reduce the meaning of 'sincere' to something purely, or even primarily, psychological, although I do not quarrel with his construal of it as a descriptive term.

To say of someone that he is sincere or insincere is always to make a judgement about him which is tied to judgements (and sometimes to recommendations) as to whether he is trustworthy or treacherous. I cannot think of someone as incorrigibly insincere without thinking him liable to treachery, nor can I judge him to be consistently sincere without thinking him trustworthy, although I may find it imprudent, for reasons extrinsic to my judgement that he is sincere, actually to rely on his ability to do the actions he promises to perform or to convey information as accurately as, *ceteris paribus*, he would have done. This last caveat is merely intended to cover cases of non-culpable ignorance or inability, such as reports on colours by a colourblind person, who is unaware of his disability, or promises to perform athletic feats by someone, who does not know that his heart is weak. Such instances do not alter the moral light in which another person stands for me, nor do they enter into moral appraisals of character which I may impart to others for purposes of advising courses of action (although we need not always be making moral judgements for such purposes, as prescriptivists seem to think).

Now, I take it that words like 'trust', 'trustworthy' and 'treacherous', when applied to human relationships, are such as uncontentiously do belong to the moral realms of our discourse, and the fact that there is an unavoidable connection between pronouncing on someone's sincerity and estimating his trustworthiness seems to me to show that our talk about sincerity is primarily moral talk. This is not to deny that there are conversational contexts in which speculations of a psychological sort may be conducted concerning whether someone means what he says or will do as he has promised, and that these are contexts in which we may, in a rather artificial way, suspend our admiration or check our indignation at the subject's behaviour. However, not only are these not the usual contexts in which we discuss sincerity, they derive their interest and purpose from the more usual contexts of moral appraisal. When we are occupied with the latter, we are not making estimates of the state of anyone's brain or psyche, for we are then relating the application of the concepts in question to what someone is expected to do or has done, rather than to what he may think or have thought.

The point at which psychologistic talk about sincerity seems unavoidably bound up with the language of morals is in the case of *akrasia*. It is here that the image of Intentional states being frustrated and denied expression as the result of a kind of psychic malfunction can get a grip. This is especially so if the philosophical doctrine involved avoids, as Searle's[6] 'biological naturalism' tries to do, the worst difficulties of Cartesian dualism by treating mental states as being the results of material conditions, which also turn out to constitute the medium or structure in which such states are realised. Thus, somewhat as the molecular structure of water is both the cause of water's wetness and the medium in which that wetness is realised, so mammalian neurological structure is both the cause and the medium of the realisation of mental states. Equipped with this attractive method of exit from the dualistic impasse, we may not feel embarrassed in treating the akratic as the victim of a psycho-neurological malaise, and so we may find it easier to say that he does sincerely mean to do as he promises, but is simply prevented from putting his intentions into effect by his affliction. There is a strong temptation to claim that the alcoholic, compulsive gambler or whatever 'gives every appearance' of meaning what he says when he vows to reform, but this is a mistake. Even if there is a thorough-going concordance between Intentional state and speech act, this does not show the sincerity of the speech act even at the level of the appearances. Certainly, on individual occasions, the akratic may seem entirely sincere. However, when the sum-total of his promises and failures to live up to them are reviewed, this way of putting the case is seen to be misleading: for what the appearances really disclose (and there is no need to go beyond them in order to see this) is that the akratic is incapable, morally speaking, of sincerity and is therefore unworthy of trust.

These things will be true of the akratic, even if he manages to convince himself that he means what he says at the moment when he is saying it, in the way that some actors are said to 'enter in' to their roles and to 'become' the characters they portray. As the actor's resumption of his everyday persona when he comes off stage shows that he does not genuinely believe himself to be Hamlet, so the akratic's persistent breaches of his word show that he is insincere. Neither can the akratic escape moral censure by pleading that his will unaccountably failed him in a case where he has broken his word only once, for it will always be open to us to wonder at his likely behaviour if his trustworthiness were to be put to the test in exactly similar circumstances over and again. It is true that we often feel inclined to say of the akratic that he simply does not know enough about himself to be sincere or trustworthy. In saying this, however, we are nonetheless making a kind of moral judgement. The ignorance in question is not of a non-culpable sort, as it would be if what was involved was lack of knowledge or understanding about some aspect of his neuro-logical or psychological make-up. I can plead ignorance of such matters without (except in special cases) feeling that I ought to know more about them. However, if someone persistently breaks his word or seems likely to do so, because he knows too little about himself to be sure of ever keeping it, then it will not do for him to say: 'I know that I know very little about myself, but I'm not interested in knowing more.' In such a case, it will be entirely proper to think that he ought to want to know himself better then he does.

It is not an accident of usage which inclines us to speak of insincerity and lack of integrity in the same breath. Rather, what we mean by a lack of personal integrity is that the unity in action between someone's promises and his subsequent behaviour has broken down, so that we can no longer find our feet with him as a moral being. The linguistic consequences of this must now be more fully examined.

2.32 A condition on conventions

Wittgenstein had argued that if language was to be a means of communication, there had to be agreement, not only in defini-tions, but also in judgements. He says:

> This seems to abolish logic, but does not do so — It is one thing to describe methods of measurement, and another to obtain and state results of measurement. But what we call 'measuring' is partly determined by a certain constancy in

results of measurement (PI, i, para. 242).

Responding earlier to the interlocutor's allegation that he is making human agreement the arbiter of truth and falsity, he replies: 'It is what human beings *say* that is true and false; and they agree in the *language* they use. That is not agreement in opinions but in form of life.' (PI, i, para. 241, original emphases)

Reflecting on the complexity of the notion of 'agreement' being employed here and the variety of ways we might fail to achieve it, Winch concludes that 'the notion of a society in which there is a language but in which truth-telling is not regarded as the norm is a self-contradictory one.[7] This means that the absence of the norm in question would have the same consequences for language as the absence of those natural regularities on which such language-games as counting, classifying and measuring depend for their existence. Winch argues further that the very conception of a distinction between true and false statements — and therefore the conception of statements *simpliciter* — could not precede general adherence to the truth-telling norm.[8] By this reasoning, adherence to the norm is not itself conventional, but the condition of there being any conventions whatsoever.

Now if Winch is correct (as I shall try to show he is) in holding that we cannot postulate a society in which there is language but no standard of adherence to the rules of any truth-telling game, then the concept of 'agreement' which points to this position would seem to be of the very pre-logical and value-laden sort which ought to interest us. This would follow from its being the case that even the sorts of ordinary language on which the technical language of formal logic is parasitic are unimaginable in conditions in which the norms of truth-telling are absent from social life. In other words, if truth-telling games are core-games in the sense explained earlier (2.1–2.12), then this language-game-cluster provides a paradigmatic example of the kind of semantic necessity we are anxious to scrutinise, and we will have gone a good way towards establishing propositions (1) and (2) of the heads of argument given above (2.3).

Winch rather briefly considers and disposes of two ways in which it might seem possible to imagine a language-using society without the norm of truthfulness.[9] In one case it is supposed that what we call 'true' statements were always uttered instead of the statements we call 'false', and vice versa. In the second case, the supposition is that the incidence of 'true' and 'false' statements is statistically random. Winch's way with the first supposition is simply to point out that all it entails is that statements would have to be taken in the opposite sense from that which they now carry for us — i.e. locutions which we use to express true statements would express false statements in the suppositional world, while true statements would be expressed by locutions which, as things are, we use to express false statements. Thus, the supposed reversal of our normal speaking practices has a cancelling effect which preserves the content of the regularities involved in those practices, so that the norm of truthfulness is unaffected.

The supposition of random incidence, however, has more far-reaching implications, and is deserving of a fuller treatment than Winch gives it. He contents himself with the remark that in this case there could be no distinction between truth and falsity and thus, no communication, since communication requires that people's utterances be taken in certain specific ways by other people. This point has been well put by Davidson, who, noting that some forms of disagreement do more damage to understanding than others, remarks that 'disagreement about the truth of attributions of certain attitudes to a speaker by that same speaker may not be tolerable at all, or barely.'[10]

What needs emphasis here is that this scenario is one in which the very idea of playing a truth-telling game has become unthinkable and the notions of trust and sincerity, inasmuch as they are indispensable features of such language-games, have dropped out altogether. The full result of this breakdown is not only that, because nobody any longer understands the distinction between lying and telling the truth, statement-making between individuals becomes inconceivable. It will also be the case that no individual can be thought of as ascribing to himself such propositional attitudes as that he believes that p, desires p, hopes that p and so on: for such inner monologues depend on the public form of the conventions for making assertions still being current. The point is worth making because it underscores the fundamental character of the sort of agreement and disagreement at issue here, and invites questions as to whether a creature shorn of these capacities would be anything we should any longer want to call a human form of life. For both the inner life and the social life of the inhabitant of a community which lacks the possibility of making assertions are so impoverished that it seems a moot point whether we can place ourselves in his position.

Be that as it may, the form of communication available in this community is certainly a drastically underdeveloped one, even if it does deserve to be called a language, which was the claim made at (1) in the argument outlined earlier (2.3).

2.33 Imperatives

Now someone may say that he finds it entirely possible to imagine a society in which what we now call 'lying', understood as the deliberate misattribution of attitudes by speakers to themselves, is endemic but uncensured to the point where it goes unnoticed, but in which certain language-games other than statement-making are, nonetheless, playable. The idea here is that a society from which the truth-telling norm had vanished might retain a norm of unquestioning obedience to authority. This, the objection runs, might enable it to evolve a language which began with very primitive names, consisting only of commands and acts in accordance with these commands, like the language-game played by Wittgenstein's builders (PI, i, para. 2). However, once the possibility of playing such primitive games has been established, it might seem possible to construct more complex games on the same normative principle until something very different from our own natural language, but which, nonetheless, deserves to be called 'a language', emerges.

Notice that this proposal does not involve a denial of the conclusion (6) that the necessity governing language is a moral necessity, for its founding premiss is the existence of a moral norm of obedience. However, there are, in any case, two related considerations which count against it. Firstly, it is a necessary condition of our calling a speech act a 'command' that the person to whom it was issued should be capable of disobeying it. However, without the language-game of making assertions, which has been shown to depend on preservation of the truth-telling norm, we would not be able to distinguish misunderstanding a command from disobedience to it. We must, for example, be able to imagine the possibility of the apprentice in the builders' language-game saying something of the order of 'No, I'm not going to fetch it' when he hears the command 'Slab', even if we only imagine him saying this to himself. In other words, we have to write in the possibility of the ascription or self-ascription of propositional attitudes to situations in which the language-game of imperatives is thought of as playable, otherwise what we will be imagining will not be a linguistic transaction but an interaction between automatons.

Secondly, the proposal that a language, approximate to what we call 'language', could be erected from a foundation of primitive imperatives alone, will not pass the test posed by the fact that human language-acquisition is attained by instruction and example, unless a moral value closely analogous to truth-telling is presumed. For although there is a mimetic element in the way infants learn their mother tongue and adults learn new languages, their performances must go beyond parrot talk before we can say that the language has been learned. They must be able to apply, expand and effect liaisons between concepts in the language in situations removed from the models they began by imitating: for this guidance in the form of instruction is necessary, and with instruction goes the possibility of a misrepresentation of attitudes on the part of the instructor. Unless the instructor can be *trusted* not to mislead in this way, the pupil can have no way of knowing how he is to regulate his responses or what will count as a correct response. This is the analogue with truth-telling referred to in proposition (3) of my heads of argument.

These two counter-arguments reveal the fatal flaw in the case for the possibility of a language constructed from imperatives alone. That weakness consists in the admission that some moral value, in the form of the norm of obedience, is preserved by the creatures who are supposed to be the users of the language. It turns out that the language of imperative utterance, founded on this norm, cannot sustain itself in isolation from the language of assertion. This result is an interesting upshot of the dictum favoured by the Aristotelian and Thomist virtue-centred systems of ethics, according to which it is impossible to be virtuous by practising only one single virtue. Thus, courage and generosity must be balanced by prudence, and all three will require some measure of wisdom and charity. It would seem that not only do language-games tend to form clusters, but so too do the values which sustain them.

2.34 Truthfulness and moral necessity

I have already intimated (2.3–2.31) that with regard to truth-telling, the notion of 'sincerity' and 'trust' forge the link between semantic and moral necessity. Roughly, the thinking behind this contention runs as follows: 'in imagining a language we are always imagining a recognisably human life-form, and our form of life involves personhood and the preservation of personhood — a point already touched on (2.1). However, truth-telling, while being essential to the possibility of language, is inseparable from the trust–sincerity relation, and this is the very relation which preserves the integrity of personhood. The idea of a moral commitment seems apposite here — a kind of wager which is unusual in that the making of it seems unavoidable and inasmuch as it is prior to calculations as to loss or gain in the ordinary sense of those words.

This, I think, is what Winch is driving at when he stresses that liars are no less committed to the truth of their statements than are truth-tellers, arguing that this notion of commitment marks the distinction and the connection between the concepts of what words mean and what people mean by them and that meaningful statement-making is only possible in a society in which people are related by a common respect for truthfulness.[11] Putting the matter in terms of a commitment of this sort may help to bring out what was insisted on earlier (2.32) — i.e. the pre-conventional status which marks adherence to the norm of truthfulness. On this point at least, Winch would have to agree with Davidson when the latter remarks: 'Convention cannot connect what may always be secret — the intention to say what is true — with what must be public — making an assertion. There is no convention of sincerity.'[12]

Moral philosophers, trained within a particular tradition, may find this notion of moral necessity inconvenient, because it seems to lay too little emphasis on choices and decisions, as they understand these matters, and, hence, leaves too little room for praise, blame, approval and disapproval. When the deontologist, the utilitarian, consequentialist or prescriptivist thinks of ethical matters, he thinks of decisions to act well or badly and of choices between ends and between different conventions governing human behaviour. When he thinks of moral beings, he thinks of individual choosers, whose choices make them liars or honest persons. Choice and the capacity for choice are, for this sort of moral philosopher, factors which distinguish morally charged from morally neutral situations. He cannot believe that these factors can be present at a level of social life where pre-conventional semantic forces, akin to natural forces, are held to be dominant, and this is why he cannot think that truthfulness *qua* semantic necessity is linked to truthfulness *qua* moral virtue.

The sort of philosopher I have in mind, moreover, is liable to be firmly of the opinion that the language of moral argument, which he takes it to be his business to analyse, has chiefly to do with teaching or defending standards or conventions for judging the worth of actions, and that these activities cannot be pursued at a region of discourse where the concept of choice is unavailable. Typical of this line of thought is Hare's proclamation: 'To teach a person — or to decide on for oneself — a standard for judging the merits of objects of a certain class is to teach or decide on principles for choosing between objects of that class.'[13]

The way out of these difficulties is, firstly, to re-assert just as firmly that in likening the need for a language-using society to preserve the norm of truthfulness by sustaining the bonds of sincerity and trust that are essential to it to a natural necessity, we have in mind something which is natural, not to animals or physical objects, but to humans, who must preserve their language in preserving their personhood. It is this crucial qualification that makes the description 'blind necessity' inappropriate to the phenomenon we are considering. This distinction relies, of course, on an idea of the natural which was readily available to Aristotelian and Scholastic thought but which has been nudged out of our everyday usage by the stupendous advance over centuries in the so-called 'natural' sciences. The pre-modern notion not only permits us to distinguish what is natural to humans from what is brute-natural, but also has affinities with a broader construal of the adjective 'rational'. This opens up a perspective which lets us see how it is possible for humans to fall into a pre-rational state which is unnatural to them, although it would be natural to brutes.

Now it is possible to imagine this process of degeneration occurring, not indeed as the immediate result of individual choices for or against or between conventions relating to truthfulness, but rather as the outcome of a social history of corporate neglect of the value-preserving institutions in question, to which such choices could certainly contribute. We could imagine a society in which, as a result of growing inattention to the activities which vitiate the value, the notions of lying and truth-telling lost their meaning so that a sort of Tower of Babel situation ensued, with communication breaking down and the human rational character of the community being altogether lost.

Clearly, this catastrophe would have many of the same effects as a purely natural calamity might bring about, in terms of a drastic diminution of the life-form's capacities and powers, and a consequent loss of the quality of life it once enjoyed. However, much more than enjoyment is at stake here — for not only would it be the case that with the loss of their language these creatures would have lost the ability to preserve other moral values besides truthfulness; they have lost their happiness (in the sense of Aristotle's term *eudaimonia*) by their fall from a rational to a pre-rational state. This is a communal loss, to which all members of the community, present and future, must be subject. The individualism of Lockean epistemology and political theory, and of Mill's ethics, has been influential in making it difficult for modern moral philosophers to grasp this conception of historically transmitted communal culpability. We are apt to think it 'unfair' that the consequences of dereliction of a duty by some individual or group of individuals should be visited on others not directly associated with the immediate culprits, and we feel that it is, *a fortiori*, unjust that guilt should be transmitted beyond the immediate circle of wrongdoers.

The difficulty we experience in making sense of the biblical myth of The Fall is largely attributable to our habituation to these individualistic modes of thought. That this is so can be seen from the fact that the myth makes no sense as a moral tale if it is viewed solely through the conceptual lenses provided by the modern individualistic tradition, yet it made perfect sense to the semitic tribes who first recorded it, and can be made sense of by scholars, able to penetrate the conceptual framework which is the key to its meaning. It is no accident that two people, not a single individual, are guilty of yielding to the serpent's temptation, or that Adam's attempt to excuse his culpability by saying that Eve gave him the forbidden fruit does not count with Jehovah. Both the original deviation from the norm of obedience and its outcome are expressed in terms of corporate responsibility and communal guilt. That this guilt is of a different and far more serious order than anything that a purely individual choice might confer may be judged from the fact that subsequent breaches of the Talmudic code, like Cain's murder of Abel, are punished on an individual basis, although such breaches are treated as consequences of the original Fall. The cycle of such consequences cannot be broken, save by an event of equally cataclysmic importance, like the coming of a Messiah, which will undo the act

99

which first set the degenerative process in motion, and will redeem the entire community, past, present and future.

Reflection on the meaning of the story of The Fall may help to bring out what is also true of the imaginary case in which the truth-telling norm is obliterated from social life — viz. that once our individualistic presuppositions are adjusted, it is really the sheer scale of the social catastrophe under consideration that makes it hard for us to see that it is indeed also a moral catastrophe.

2.4 Justice

The function truth-telling performs in preserving the possibility of statement-making is a powerful inducement to treat this game-cluster as more 'fundamental' than any other sort of language-game, including other core-games. So too is the consideration Isenberg[14] emphasises to the effect that, whereas some reason is required to show why other impulses to perform other *prima facie* immoral acts should be restrained, the impulse to lie requires a reason for being discharged or acted on, not a reason why it should be restrained. Yet these other core-games will, on closer inspection, display a function no less indispensable to our ability to make assertions, give orders, ask questions or perform any other act in our linguistic repertoire. This is partly because the various sorts of core-games are in fact so intimately related that any attempt to serialise them in a hierarchy can only serve to obscure their many areas of overlap and internal connectedness. I propose to bring this out in discussing the role in sustaining the possibility of language of those language-games which function to preserve the value of justice or fair play in human society, and I shall provisionally define 'justice' on the model of Socrates' treatment of it in the first book of the *Republic* as rendering to every person what is due to them.[15] The language-games whereby this value is preserved include, of course, such activities as the construction of legal and moral codes of conduct and the criticism of such codes, as well as praising just actions and deploring those we think unjust.

By the definition of justice as giving each his due, which Polemarchus offers Socrates in the first book of *The Republic*,[16] a paradigmatic case of injustice will arise when something is done to someone which is clearly not his due. Outstanding instances of such injustice will occur when, as in cases of judicial murder, an action done with the aim of inflicting harm is directed at a person or persons known to be innocent of any fault. (This formulation avoids talk of 'undeserved punishment' and actual harm being done, because, at least on the Socratic treatment of the matter, it is doubtful whether unjust punishment is really punishment, just as it is doubtful whether an innocent man can be harmed.)

Following the same procedure as we adopted with truth-telling, we may now test the possibility of imagining a society of language-users in which the norm of just-dealing goes un-preserved. This will be a society in which, for instance, innocent people are randomly condemned by the courts for crimes they are known not to have committed, without any disapproval of the judges' conduct being expressed by any other member of the society. We may, if we like, imagine that the judges' behaviour *began* by being motivated by some utilitarian principle for maximising happiness, or that their misconduct originated as a way of maintaining the power of authority. What is crucial for our purposes, however, is that the end result should be such that no principle can be invoked to regularise judicial murders and the like, so that the norm of just-dealing has altogether vanished from the life of the society we are trying to imagine. In this respect, the case before us is different from that examined by Anscombe[17] in her famous polemic against consequentialism: for the case we need is more radical than hers, and must concern not only the establishment of the limiting conditions for the use of *moral* language, but the conditions for there being any language at all. We need, in other words, to see whether a moral cataclysm will result in a linguistic catastrophe.

It is important too to be very clear about this: the kind of social indifference to guilt or innocence that concerns me leaves untouched the various juridical forms which have waxed and waned through epochs of social change. A tribe of hunter–gatherers, say, might have forms of trial and punishment which seem barbarically harsh and even irrational to us — indeed, they might have practices whereby for the common good, as they conceive of it, the innocent are sacrificed — and yet maintain the prohibition against attempting to harm the innocent in other areas of their legal and moral life. Nor is the matter to which a given culture may attach its notions of guilt or innocence the focus of my concern. I should be content to allow that language could be sustained in a culture in which killing was never murder, but in which eating cabbages was punishable by death. What I should not admit is that language was possible in a society in which the notions of guilt and innocence had no application, and this would have to be the case in a society in which harmful actions were randomly directed at the innocent without attracting any censure or remark from any member of that society.

What appears to stand in the way of accepting this thesis is the fact that there are certain social contexts and certain contexts of linguistic use in which questions of guilt or innocence are not immediately at issue, and where, therefore, some language-games at least would seem to be playable whatever havoc reigned in the judicio-ethical system of a given society. Counting and colour-telling, it will be said, are important linguistic skills, but we do not call someone 'guilty' when he makes mistakes in learning or applying them. Nor, on the face of it, does there seem to be any reason to think that someone could not learn to apply the rules for playing such language-games just because he showed no ability to distinguish guilt from innocence or to see the harm in wishing to harm one who was known to have done no wrong. I shall now try to show that this objection results from a flawed appreciation of the notion of a linguistic rule, and of the consequences to the notion of rule-following which flow from the state of moral decline with respect to justice we are trying to imagine.

2.41 Moral blindness and rule-blindness

In discussing earlier the Wittgensteinian account of rule-following (1.57), I remarked that the main point to emerge from that account concerned the *internal connection* between a rule and its application, and that this connection was best characterised as a unity (although not as an identity) between the theory or understanding of a rule and the publicly observable practice whereby that understanding could be evidenced. It is the thought that attention to what is involved in following a rule will dissipate the fog surrounding the notion of internal connectedness, rather than the idea that language is governed by rules, which mainly contributes to the topic's importance. For such questions as 'How is language possible?' or 'What is semantic necessity?' can readily be made to assume the aliases, 'How is logic possible?', or 'What is an internal connection?' This is because of our conviction — which seems inescapable in the last resort — that language belongs only to rational life-forms, and hence only to creatures capable of forging logical connections and, *ipso facto*, only to creatures capable of understanding the following rules. A rule-blind community would be a speechless community, and a society which was incapable of learning or devising new rules would have to consist of persons who were unable to develop their own language or learn a new one. This must be true, regardless of whether we think that the definition of a language-game as a rule-governed structure admits of exceptions. Too large an expanse of the language-map is covered by a trace-work of rules, albeit of a highly diverse and often pliable kind, for it to be conceivable that a language recognisable as such, could exist without rules and the capacity to be guided by them.

Now the state of moral anarchy we have been considering with respect to justice has very special implications for our capacity to formulate and follow linguistic rules. The first warning of this is contained in the circumstance that the rules for the correct application of the words 'just' and 'unjust' differ markedly from the rules for applying secondary quality adjectives like 'hard' and 'red', and even from the rules governing adjectives which have an evaluative component, like 'appetising' or 'comfortable'. We learn how to correctly apply words like 'hard' and 'red', only by attending to hard and red objects, and we show that we have learned our lessons by using the words to pick out objects that are in fact hard or red. We learn how to apply such descriptions as 'appetising' by, *inter alia*, comparing our own and other people's reactions to edible substances. However, although there may be paradigmatic exemplars of a range of secondary qualities, such as the primary colours in our method of dividing up the spectrum, there are not ideal standards of these which can be the subject of rational criticism in terms of and in comparison with our actual classificatory practices. The same holds for our evaluations in those things which are genuinely matters of taste. There are prime examples, but not ideal standards of what is appetising or comfortable, and although judgements in such matters may vary surprisingly between and within societies, it is not rational criticism that accounts for this variation, but altered circumstances and changed habits resulting from changing experiences.

With 'justice' the case is different. It shares with many other value-laden terms, like 'truthfulness', 'reverence' and 'goodness' what Pitkin calls 'a tension between purpose and institutionalization'.[18] What this means is that our value-preserving institutions, the language-games we play and the activities we routinely observe in order to safeguard justice in our society, are orientated towards a goal or ideal standard of what constitutes justice. We may criticise our practices and institutions in terms of this standard or we may try to adapt the standard in conformity with current institutionalised practices. The interplay between these two polarities is the dynamic which produces changes in the rules for correctly describing actions as just or unjust. However, we cannot, without robbing the whole critical process of its point, tamper with either the standard or the institutions in any way we please. We may not (to take the case we have been considering) so alter the theory or practice of our ethics, politics or jurisprudence as to obliterate the distinction between an innocent person and a guilty one. For without that distinction, the word 'justice' is not merely given a different range of applications; it can have no application whatsoever, nor can its etymological siblings 'judgement' and 'justification'. The latter two expressions are conceptually tied to the notion of justice, and the fact of this bonding shows the true nature of the threat which a social universe void of justice (and not merely a universe which is very unjust) must pose to our rule-following capacities. For to act justly is always to exemplify a rule or standard in terms of which conduct is justifiable, and to be incapable of just actions is to be incapable of acting in accordance with, or justifying one's behaviour in terms of rules which, as we saw, have a very special status in the life of any society that uses language. It is to be incapable of unifying theory and practice, of making the right kind of connection between a rule and its application in this respect. However, the fact that 'justice' has a distinctive grammatical structure does not mean that other regions of language which do not have that structure will be immune from the consequences of its disappearance from the linguistic scene. The rules for the use of this word do not differ from the rules of other language-games as the rules for moving a pawn differ from the rules for moving a knight in chess. Rather, they differ somewhat as the rules for checkmate differ from all other rules in chess, in that their subtraction from the whole renders other language-games pointless or incoherent.

The full implications of this last point emerge more clearly once the example of a society in the state of moral anarchy is fleshed out. Until it is, we may be inclined to think that the inhabitants of this unfortunate community could carry on as usual with at least some of their activities, including their communicative activities, despite the arbitrary behaviour of the authorities and despite their own indifference to this behaviour and its consequences. This is not so, however. In a world in which no distinction is any longer possible between guilt and innocence, it would not be possible to distinguish harm-attracting activities from safe ones. There could be nothing like reasonable grounds for the supposition that such-and-such a language-game was a harmless one to play, or that this or that way of trying to act in accordance with a rule, though it did us no harm yesterday, would not be treated as treason tomorrow. The tyranny we are attempting to imagine is one in which people are in the grip of rulers who are not only uncommanded but irrational in a very radical sense of that word, and in such a situation the confidence needed to pass from a rule to its application would evaporate.

It is not fortuitous that justice should turn out to be like truthfulness in being a pre-conventional value. In both cases, preservation of the value turns on the existence of an unspoken bond of trust, spread throughout communities in which languages are spoken. This is why the conceptual anatomy of lying and injustice has a structure very like that of breach-of-promise. The liar, the unjust judge and those who lend active or tacit support to their actions are all traitors to a confidence which is the precondition of their treachery in being the precondition for all and any covenants and conventions between individual persons or groups of persons. This is, perhaps, one reason why social philosophers as disparate as Hobbes and Rousseau have been led to speak of a social contract, marking the division between 'civil society' and the 'state of nature'. It is as if, for such theorists, the notion of a social contract was a surrogate for the notion of trust. We must beware, however, for reasons already given in our discussion of rule-following and the communitarian misinterpretation of Wittgenstein on this point (1.57), of importing anything suggestive of a social concensus into our account. For as Cavell puts it:[19]

> The conventions which control the application of grammatical criteria are fixed not by customs or some particular concord or agreement which might, without disrupting the texture of our lives, be changed where convenience suggests a change . . . They are, rather, fixed by the nature of human life itself . . .

2.5 Rituals and reverence

Moral values are preserved for their own sake, not for the sake of sustaining language. Indeed, some of the strangeness of the proposal that value-preservation is a necessary condition for the possibility of language can be put down to our instinctive recognition of this fact. It makes no sense to say that when we speak and act in defence of such values as truthfulness and justice we do so in order to preserve our ability to speak. To say that would be to treat language itself as a value, a kind of ultimate end, for the sake of which other things are said and done. Language *per se* is not an end or a value in itself. It is rather an instrument which can be made to serve a rich variety of ends and is extremely valuable on that account. That X is a necessary condition for the possibility of Y does not entail that Y is done for the sake of X, and we do not speak for the sake of preserving our values any more than we live in order to eat.

What is true is that the preservation of moral values for their own sake is inconceivable unless the social activities and institutions whereby they are preserved are informed by the attitude we call 'reverence', which has natural affinities with the attitudes of respect, awe and wonder. These attitudes find their typical expression in ritual — that vast game-cluster which stretches from elementary gestures of courtesy and respect, such as bowing, hand-shaking and saluting, through anthem and hymn-singing to the most elaborate religious ceremonies. Thus, the idea of something being reverenced, through a signifying practice in which that reverence is publicly displayed, marks a point of convergence between the game-clusters surrounding truth-telling and justice and that species of language-game called 'ritual' which so interested Wittgenstein. The fact of this necessary association is an incentive for examining the case for treating ritual-games as core-games.

2.51 Ritual-games

Ritual resists easy definition. We may say, for the sake of having a rule-of-thumb formulation, that rituals are formal acts or procedures of a customary sort, usually (but by no means always) associated with solemnity and, often, with religious observance. The qualification is needed so as to include such frolicsome and even frivolous rites as maypole-dancing and mistletoe-kissing, although it is noteworthy that even these usually function as markers of some special occasion. Now these acts and procedures all undoubtedly have *uses*, and it is to these that an observer will be referred if he asks their meaning. In addition, these acts are embedded in the history, culture and life-circumstances of those who use them — i.e. in a form of life. It is the combination of these two considerations that inclines us to say that rituals are part of a people's language. However, what seems to mark ritual as a special case, and may even make us hesitate to call it part of language, is that it imparts no facts or information which could not have been conveyed just as well or better in another mode of discourse. There are signs and symbols, but no 'propositions' of ritual. We might put this by saying that rituals *show* rather than *say* whatever they are intended to express. This last thought may contain the germ of an insight into the real function within language of ritualistic behaviour. Such insight can be impeded by a culture-bound, scientistic perspective which sees religious rites (particularly alien ones) as the meaningless by-products of foreign or 'primitive' superstition. This view is mistaken in that it treats rituals as though they originate in erroneous explanatory hypotheses about the world's workings. Yet if their primary function is not to state facts, then the purpose of rituals cannot be to explain the world in the way that scientific and quasi-scientific theories try to do.

The reductionist prejudice in favour of explaining ritual in terms of faulty theories to which the participants are supposed to subscribe has, however, been sufficiently influential to provoke a counter-tradition among anthropologists. Thus, Durkheim protests: 'In reality, then, there are no religions which are false. All are true in their own fashion; all answer, though in different ways, to the given conditions of human existence.'[20] In his critique of Fraser's *Golden bough*, Wittgenstein gave a more precise expression to this sentiment. Complaining that Fraser's anthropology makes the magical and religious views of mankind look like errors, Wittgenstein says:

> No *opinion* serves as the foundation for a religious symbol. And only an opinion can involve error . . . Burning in effigy. Kissing the picture of one's beloved. That is *obviously not* based on the belief that it will have some specific effect on the object which the picture represents. (RFGB, p. 64, original emphases)

These remarks need to be qualified. In agreeing with them, I am not saying (what is false) that erroneous beliefs in, say, the existence of rain gods are no part of the cultures of which a given set of ritual practices are also part, or even that the participants in some or other rite may not themselves believe untrue things about the workings of nature. Nor do I intend to dismiss historical explanations which include reference to such mistaken beliefs solely on the grounds that we can have no knowledge of historical causation. Durkheim, although he asserts that it makes no sense to speak of religion beginning its existence at a given moment,[21] is not saying that historical explanation is impossible, and I think Cioffi quite right to deny that Wittgenstein is saying it either.[22]

The argument is, rather, that even a reliable account of the origin of some rite in, say, the practice of human sacrifice to appease angry gods or in cannibalism, cannot be telling the full story of the rite's present social and linguistic function. Such an account will do nothing to dispel the sense of awe, dread or reverence that the rite may inspire, for the practices and beliefs to which scholarship attributes the origin of the rite must themselves inspire those very same feelings. We have here to do with responses and disquietudes which seem to signal our arrival at an impasse at which explanation ends, and which are onmipresent in even our most articulate attempts to explain them away. Certainly, there will be important connections between particular ritual practices and certain world-pictures, accurate or not, which have, or may be taken by participants to have, explanatory power. However, the function of ritual is not to invent or explain such pictures, nor, in many cases, is comprehension of them a condition of participation, since even young children and infants may participate in baptism, funerals and sacred meals. We learn to participate or to officiate in such ceremonies as we learn to play any other language-game — by observation, instruction and drill. Ritual-games are unlike the general run of language-games, however, in that they seem (if we discount the view that they are based on misguided hypotheses as to their possible effects) to be played for their own sake. In this they resemble certain pastimes.

These peculiar features — absence of explanatory or informa-tion-bearing function, lack of any specific form of efficacy and a certain self-containedness of purpose — are not grounds for expelling ritualistic forms of behaviour from the realm of meaningful discourse. Like most language-games, ritual-games are rule-governed and their rules are learned as any rule of language is learned. Rituals are often dramatisations of events charged with significance, and these dramas are repeatable in a way in which the events themselves are not. Indeed, repetition is typical of ritual. Thus, the Christian Mass retells over and again the story of the Last Supper, the tribal dancers in a dry season repeat the movements which re-enact the longed-for return of the rains, and the lover regularly performs the reverent gesture towards the portrait which gives expression to an otherwise inexpressible yearning. Only in and through language are such things possible. The question is not whether rituals are part of our language, but what function they fulfil within it, and how important that function is.

2.52 Rituals and reasons

In her seminal study of the symbolism of pollution and purification rites, Douglas argues that:[23]

> The analysis of ritual symbolism cannot begin until we recognise ritual as an attempt to create and maintain a particular culture . . . The rituals enact the form of social relations and in giving these relations visible expression they enable people to know their own society . . .

If this claim can be shown to be correct, then the case for treating rituals as core-language-games is made. If the function of ritual within language is creatively to sustain the life-form which uses language, and if it performs that function by preserving values indispensable to the life-form, then it serves the same end as the game-clusters supporting the values of truth-telling and justice were seen to serve. Mention has already been made of the relevance of reverence to value-preservation and of the way ritual acts as a typical expressive medium for reverent attitudes. We have also said (2.1) that in imagining a language we presuppose a mode of deep-seated agreement which is only possible if the integrity of the persons who speak the language is sustained, and clearly this cannot be done unless reverence for persons and their rights to speak and be listened to is a prevailing norm.

Now it is true that many minor ritual acts, like throwing salt over one's shoulder or touching wood, are not expressions of reverence or anything much like it, but most fully developed ritual performances are concerned with it, or at least with attitudes akin to it. Solemn religious rites and even gay or joyful ones all express reverence, as do such secular celebrations as courtroom formalities, academic processions and military courtesies. However, ritual actions, unlike the ordinary speech-acts which perform an allied function, are not *reports* of inner states or felt emotions, as in 'I don't like Smith, but I can't help respecting him.' They are precisely *expressions* of reverent attitudes — i.e. signs or symbols which show or display reverence — such that it is irrelevant what feelings the performers are feeling at the time. (They may even be hired to perform the gestures or say the words which make up the pattern of the rite.) This expressive activity, moreover, very largely consists in establishing symbolic connections as well as lines of demarcation between loved, venerated or dreaded objects and the persons who love, venerate or dread them. This can be seen fairly easily in such familiar ritual acts as curtseying, bowing, genuflection and prostration. It can also be seen in the custom of carrying a bride over the threshold which segregates the sacred hearth from the public world beyond it, and in the custom among some Bronze Age peoples of using their burial grounds as boundaries as a warning marker against encroachment by other tribes.[24]

The drawing through ritualistic activity of these parameters constitutes what anthropologists have become used to calling the creation of 'ritual space'. Now this 'ritual space' makes an indispensable contribution to the creation of logical space — i.e. the space which defines the limits within which diverse kinds of reason-giving and reason-requiring expressions can function and the relations in which the varieties of reasonable behaviour stand to one another. To see how it does this, we must consider, as we did earlier (2.33), the role of instruction and imperative utterance in language-learning situations: for these are clearly contexts in which a pupil must often be required to act, not indeed unreasonably, but *without* reasons. Just as someone learning the first elements of geometry can make no progress if he insists on questioning the basic Euclidean axioms and keeps demanding that reasons be given in support of these before he will accept further instruction, nobody can become proficient in playing even quite mundane, but essential, language-games, unless he is prepared to acknowledge the authority of his instructors and act as they tell him to act for an initial period with implicit faith. What makes the pupil's acceptance of his tutor's authority in such cases not blind, but reasonable, is not a set of reasons as to why that authority ought to be treated as legitimate. Rather, it is the circumstance that the authority of the parent, language-teacher, speech-therapist or whatever *shows* itself in the full context of the learning situation to be something which must be respected or reverenced. This is not just a psychological, but a conceptual requirement, and it can be met precisely because there are ritualistic regions of our language in which reason-giving, statement-making and theorising are underplayed and the practices which show what is appropriate in a given case are exploited to the full. Thus, the priest-king's regalia shows, rather than says, that reverence is due to him and the priestly incantation is not the reason, but the sign that bread and wine have become objects of veneration. Such ceremonial language-games are centrepieces in a web of discourse, the strands of which reach out to our most basic intercourse with those who must be taught even simple language-games and those who are to be initiated into new languages or new developments in language. A society from which they were altogether absent would not be a society in which human signing-practices could be transmitted by instruction.

2.6 Conclusions

The above account of core-language-games is intended to redeem the promise made in the introduction to this essay. There I proposed to provide an answer to moral cynicism via a realist theory of ethics which would overcome the fact/value dichotomy, on which moral scepticism relies, by identifying moral with semantic reality, and do so in terms of the concept of power on which moral cynicism has relied since the time of Plato's Thrasymachus. If my attempt to resolve the enigmas connected with the notion of semantic necessity is rightly directed, then neither the sceptical nor the cynical positions can be sound ones. For the questions 'Is moral knowledge possible?' and 'Why should I behave morally?' are undeniably framed in the medium of language, and that medium has been shown to be unimaginable without, and to depend for its coherence upon, certain value-laden practices and moral certitudes. The cynic's questions therefore fail to square with the fact of his asking them. This is not to say that his position is, strictly speaking, self-contradictory, in the formal logician's sense. His position is, rather, anomalous in the deeper sense of being *de facto* undermining of the pre-logical core of language, on which the technical language of the science of valid inference must be parasitic.

The journey away from logicism towards a more historicist ambience brought us to a view of the ethical, intended to silence cynicism and still sceptical disquietudes by making the 'is' of semantic fact depend on the ethical 'ought'. However, the historicist approach to language, while freeing us from the fascinations of one sort of world-picture, entices us towards others no less problematic. The account of core-language-games, because it treats language as a field of explicitly social activity, cannot avoid settling accounts with a more general. theory of social explanation.

Notes

1. G.P. Baker and P.M.S. Hacker, *Wittgenstein understanding and meaning* (Basil Blackwell, Oxford, 1980), p. 80.

2. K. Marx, *The Eighteenth Brumaire of Louis Bonaparte* in K. Marx and F. Engels, *Collected Works*, vol. 2 (Lawrence and Wishart, London, 1979), pp. 103–4.

3. J. Searle, *Speech acts* (Cambridge University Press, Cambridge, 1969), p. 62.

4. J. Searle, *Intentionality* (Cambridge University Press, Cambridge, 1983), p. 10.

5. Searle, *Intentionality*, p. 164.

6. Ibid. pp. 264 ff.

7. P. Winch, *Ethics and action* (Routledge and Kegan Paul, London, 1972), p. 61.

8. Ibid., pp. 61–2.

9. Ibid., p. 62.

10. D. Davidson, 'Thought and talk' in *Inquiries into truth and interpretation* (Clarendon Press, Oxford, 1984), p. 169.

11. Winch, *Ethics and action*, pp. 65–6.

12. D. Davidson, 'Communication and convention' in Davidson, *Inquiries into truth*, p. 270.

13. R.M. Hare, *The language of morals* (Oxford University Press, London, 1952).

14. A. Isenberg, 'Deontology and the ethics of lying' in J.J. Thomson and G. Dworkin (eds), *Ethics* (Harper and Row, New York, 1968), pp. 178–9.

15. Plato, *The Republic*, Desmond Lee (trans.) (Penguin, Harmondsworth, 1974), 331e.

16. Ibid.

17. G.E.M. Anscombe, 'Modern moral philosophy', *Philosophy*, vol. XXXIII (1958), pp. 1–19.

18. H.F. Pitkin, *Wittgenstein and justice* (University of California Press, Berkeley, Los Angeles and London, 1972), p. 187.

19. S. Cavell, *The claim of reason* (Clarendon Press, Oxford, 1979), p. 110.

20. E. Durkheim, *The elementary forms of the religious life* (George Allen and Unwin, London, 1915), p. 3.

21. Ibid., p. 8.

22. F. Cioffi, 'Wittgenstein and the fire-festivals' in Irving Block (ed.), *Perspectives on the philosophy of Wittgenstein* (Basil Blackwell, Oxford, 1981), p. 215.

23. M. Douglas, *Purity and danger* (Routledge and Kegan Paul, London, 1966), p. 128.

24. I am grateful to Dr P. Mason for drawing my attention to this example.

3

Historical Necessity

3.0 Introduction

So far, I have outlined the main themes in Wittgensteinian philosophical semantics, underscoring certain concepts and using these to construct the theory that semantic necessity is moral necessity. I have argued that the preservation of a particular set of normative regularities is as essential to the very possibility of language as is the existence of regularity in nature. My ultimate intention is to graft that theory on to Karl Marx's theory of historical necessity, trying to show that his theory and my own are indispensable to one another. On my theory's side, the interdependence is a function of the historicist character of the later Wittgenstein's account of language. For if the slogan that to imagine a language is to imagine a *Lebensform* means (as it must) that language belongs inseparably to the human social process, than any account of semantic necessity must, at least, not conflict with and, at best, be on all fours with the most accurate and generalised explanation of the workings of that process. Equally, anything purporting to be an accurate general account of historical dynamics must be hospitable to a correct philosophy of language and meaning: for all history is, after all, the history of language-using creatures and becomes unimaginable if language is abstracted from it.

In the next chapter, I shall argue more fully the case for linking ethico-semantic with historical necessity by trying to show that language belongs among the productive forces which, Marx held, were the real determinants of social change. If that argument is sound, it will follow directly that the pre-logical moral core of language is intimately involved in determining not only the internal coherence of our discourse, but also the total social dynamic in which that discourse takes place.

In this chapter, however, I shall concentrate on briefly outlining the character and genesis of historical materialism, beginning, as I did in describing Wittgenstein's development, with some remarks on the nature of and relationships between the relevant texts. I shall go on to consider the conceptual background which influenced the direction Marx's enquiries ultimately took, trace the development of his theory of history to its mature expression in the *Preface* of 1859 and in *Capital*, and proceed to an account of its salient features. My treatment will focus on only one aspect of historical materialism, which I shall sometimes call Marx's theory of historical necessity. By this I mean the thesis that the development of society's material productive forces is primarily responsible for producing changes in the entire social formation. Such crucial features of Marxian thought as the theory of class struggle and the labour theory of value will, therefore, not be dealt with at all.

3.01 Marx and Wittgenstein

Two factors have dictated that historical materialism, and not some other body of social theory, is most compatible with the set of ideas about meaning and morality so far developed. Firstly, Marx's account of historical necessity is the most powerful general explanation of social change we presently possess. Although it does not pretend to encompass everything included in the adjective 'social', it does purport to explain more and to do so more rigorously than comparable theories do. The explanation it offers is rendered perspicuous by Marx's employment of a structural image — the base–superstructure model — to exhibit the relations said to obtain between the productive forces and the rest of the social whole. If these relations are as Marx said they were, then historical materialism offers just the sort of realist vision of human society which moral realism requires.

The second factor is the strikingly similar pattern of development Wittgenstein and Marx evince in thinking about their respective subject-matters. As I mentioned earlier (1.23), there is in both cases a movement away from an initial fascination with logicist essentialism (although the myth takes a different form in each instance) in the direction of materialism. Thus, Wittgenstein begins by thinking that language is governed by a hidden logical essence, disguised by the surface-grammar of ordinary discourse. He comes by degrees to abandon this view, attending ever more intently to linguistic practices which are open to view, and growing to the conviction that the possibility of language depends on the existence of certain material regularities in nature which enable us to regulate and systematise our own behaviour in a way compatible with the production of a coherent network of meaningful signs and symbols and rules for their use. In a comparable fashion, Marx is at first gripped by the notion that history is governed by a logical essence which its phenomenal form conceals. Here, of course, the logic in question is Hegelian and very different from the sort the Tractarian Wittgenstein had in mind. It is, nonetheless, an affair of concepts and internal connections which is supposed to determine, as an idea determines the mode of its expression, the socio-cultural fabric which cloaks it. Like Wittgenstein, moreover, Marx finds his attention diverted away from this occult essence and focused increasingly on the observable activities of live historical creatures and the material world they inhabit, until he comes to believe that a combination of material resources and entirely exoteric human productive capacities and powers determine the courses of the processes he investigates.

This parallel between Marxian and Wittgensteinian thought is important to my enterprise, for the possibly obvious reason that my account of moral powers is indebted to Wittgensteinian and Marxist concepts to a degree and in a fashion which would count against it were there no genuine affinities between them. Accordingly, I shall in what follows try to deepen the grounds for the comparison by interspersing my commentary on Marx with remarks designed to draw attention to points of contact with Wittgenstein's concerns, where these seem to exist. It is as well to emphasise, however, that there are many areas where such grounds do not exist. In many important and obvious ways, Marx and Wittgenstein are very different thinkers, with divergent, even antagonistic, approaches, positions and preoccupations. Marx was a journalist and political activist, at home in the turbulence of current events; Wittgenstein was an engineer, teacher and Cambridge professor who felt *de trop* in the turmoil of his times. Marx wrote voluminously about politics and economics, topics towards which Wittgenstein, despite his friendship with Sraffa, displayed no professional interest. There are also differences in their attitude towards science and the way they distinguished it from philosophy. As we saw (1.11), Wittgenstein believed he had initiated a new way of philosophising, designed to exclude scientific theorising from genuinely philosophical discourse. He saw himself primarily as a philosopher, striving to practise his craft within the cannons of that method. Marx, on the other hand, saw himself primarily as the founder of a new science, the discoverer of principles governing human history, comparable with the Darwinian principles governing natural history, and thought of his major work, *Capital*, as embodying truths discovered by the methods of the science he had founded.

At this point differences and similarities become difficult to disentangle. Both wrote (for the most part) in their mother tongue, and the German word *Wissenschaft* has a broader inclusion than does its English equivalent, 'science'. Yet in the *Tractatus*, Wittgenstein seems to want to give the word the more restrictive sense it has in English, for he speaks not of science *simpliciter*, but of natural sciences (*Naturwissenschaften*) when he wants to distinguish philosophy from science (TLP, 4.111). By the time we reach the *Investigations*, however, the definition of what is properly philosophical activity has grown much more restrictive so that any kind of theory or hypothesis and all explanation are excluded from it (PI, i, para. 109), although it does not follow that he would have been content to label all these activities as 'scientific'. Marx also distinguishes philosophical from scientific work — a distinction which the orthodox tradition preserves by classifying philosophical and scientific topics under the headings of dialectical and historical materialism respectively. However, Marx is by no means as scrupulous as Wittgenstein in segregating philosophical and scientific considerations in his writings. The latter are, moreover, informed by an explicitly acknowledged philosophical method which derives from Hegel. Furthermore, because he predates the positivistic tradition which was to influence adherents of his theories as famous as Bogdanov and Lunacharsky, Marx is less committed than was Wittgenstein to a conception of scientific discourse as value-free, although he left plenty of room for ambiguities to arise on this point. What does seem clear is that Marx was, in a sense in which the later Wittgenstein was not, in the business of explaining phenomena in terms of underlying forces, and it is this difference which crucially distinguishes their respective enterprises.

3.1 Marx's texts

In considering the character of Wittgenstein's texts (1.1), we noticed the possibility of reading his two major publications as ironic commentaries of one another, taking the form of a bi-directional lampoonery wherein new thoughts mocked old ones and old thoughts recurred to jibe at what presented itself as new. While it would be too much to claim that Marx uses precisely this technique, it is certainly true that his use of irony is, if anything, more pronounced than Wittgenstein's. Marxian irony reflects, moreover, a conviction which was certainly Wittgenstein's, that the object of his study was itself possessed of a disposition to deride and elude efforts to penetrate its nature or control its courses. History, Marx believed, concealed from its participants the true content and consequences of their actions, treating them like actors who understand neither the import of their parts nor the play in which they are performing. This belief emerges in the brilliantly ironic passage with which *The eighteenth Brumaire of Louis Bonaparte* opens:[1]

> Hegel remarks somewhere that all facts and personages of great importance in world history occur, as it were, twice. He forgot to add: the first time as tragedy, the second as farce . . . The tradition of all the dead generations weighs like a nightmare on the brain of the living. And just when they seem engaged in revolutionising themselves and things, in creating something that had never existed, precisely in such periods of revolutionary crisis they anxiously conjur up the spirits of the past to their service in order to present the scene of world history in this time-honoured mask and this borrowed language.

It is striking that in the *Brumaire*, Marx not only ascribes to history the same capacity to engender misleading pictures as Wittgenstein was to ascribe to language in the *Investigations*, but also compares the regressive behaviour of historical actors precisely to the behaviour of someone learning a language:

> In like manner, a beginner who has learned a new language always translates it back into his mother tongue, but he has assimilated the spirit of the new language and can freely express himself in it only when he finds his way in it without recalling the old and forgets his native tongue in the use of the new.[2]

Scholars have commented from various perspectives on Marx's use of irony. Van Leeuwen, for instance, sees a 'profound irony' in the analogy drawn in *Capital* between Dante's religious faith and bourgeois political economy's faith in the exchange value of commodities,[3] while Wolff has argued that Marx's irony is the '*necessary* literary device for the correct expression of the concrete relationship between reality and appearance'.[4] What seems most plausible is that, believing as he did that the appearance of historical events often concealed the forces which gave rise to them, Marx adopted a style best suited to cope with that state of affairs. The ironic mode of expression also gave him a necessary sense of distance from his subject-matter which by its very nature had to be thought of as an intimate condition of his nature which enveloped him at every point — just as a language does.

If one function of irony is to distance a writer from his topic, it can also serve, when employed as diligently as Marx employed it, to distance him, if not from his own currently held opinions, then at least from views he may once have held, and from orthodoxies which lay claim to his allegiance. This is important, because the trenchant tone which resounds so often in Marx's texts can foster the idea that his conclusions were dogmatic. Yet dogmatism, in the sense that Kant held finalistic metaphysics to be dogmatic, finds irony a subversive companion. Because irony depends on double *entendre* and on the unexpected being the case, it is the ideal stylistic tool for doing what classical German idealism after Kant called 'critical philosophy', and Marx as an heir to that tradition aspired precisely to produce critiques. Thus, in criticising his contemporaries and predecessors as vehemently as he does, Marx is often undermining Hegelian or neo-Hegelian and Fuerbachian positions with which he once sympathised, so that with him the habits of criticism and self-criticism go together. This is especially so in *The German ideology* and in the criticisms of Hegel's political philosophy. This same capacity for self-criticism is even more marked in Wittgenstein, who had not only felt the influence of 'critical philosophy' in its Kantian form, but had to undertake a life's work of self-criticism on discovering that his first and putatively final 'solution to all the problems' of philosophy harboured within itself the seeds of its own destruction.

Of course, differences co-exist with similarities in this respect in the texts of these two great ironists. Wittgenstein's self-critical method was designed to prevent what he saw as lapses into misplaced scientific theorising. Marx, although he began as a philosopher, became a theoretician, aspiring to construct a holistic explanation of the social dynamic. Yet both are enemies (as was Kant) of the kind of finalistic metaphysics which pretends to be a super-science — Wittgenstein because he held that it produced bad philosophy, and Marx because he believed it resulted in pseudo-science. Both saw irony and the critical method it informed as a weapon in the struggle against such metaphysics and as a safeguard against the bewitching deceptions of which appearances are capable. For Wittgenstein, the philosopher, however, there was no need to go beyond appearances in order to see language and world aright. For Marx, the theoretician, by contrast, illusory appearances were the product of the material reality which underlay them, and they could only be dissipated by a genuine insight into its nature.

3.11 Youth and maturity

It is interesting that the wish to trace a coherent progression in the self-critical movement of Marx's thought should confront the same false dualism as once infected Wittgenstein studies. The myth of the 'two Wittgensteins' parallels, to some extent, the story of the schism between the young and the mature Marx. Both misnomers betray a faulty understanding of the authors concerned, although they cannot be disposed of in quite the same way. It is not enough to say of Marx, what was true of Wittgenstein, that continuities co-exist with disjunctures within the full corpus of his texts. That judgement was licit when we confronted two major *philosophical* texts and the main object was to show that a reading which took the later book as being *solely* an innovative correction of its predecessor was inadequate. Neither the Tractarian nor the post-Tractarian Wittgenstein could consistently have claimed to have made further 'progress' in his later work, unless this was taken to mean that the *Investigations* was less contaminated by theory than the *Tractatus* had been. The main content of this philosophical project, moreover, is constant throughout the texts — to resolve the philosophical bemusement which the very possibility of language arouses.

Marx's case is rather different: here we face a plethora of texts, dealing with philosophy, politics and economics and culminating in a *magnum opus* which it would be absurd to treat as purely philosophical, even if it embodies the methodological fruit of past philosophisings. *Capital* is so obviously the fruit of a long theoretical endeavour, and not the start of an altogether fresh train of thought, that there must be a powerful inclination to conclude that the works preceding it contain positions which are progressively transcended, rather than abandoned in the later writings, and are thus preparatory to and formative of the mature theory of history. By the same lights, its seems reasonable to expect currents of thought, present in such early texts as the *Critique of Hegel's 'Philosophy of right'* of 1843 and the *Economic and philosophical manuscripts* of 1844, to be extant and even strengthened in intermediate works, like *The German ideology*, reaching their zenith in the period of maturity, i.e. roughly from 1859 onwards.

This seemingly sensible and straightforward approach has, however, to overcome the objection that it masks what have been called 'teleological' presuppositions. Thus, Althusser, in an essay designed to combat exegesis emphasising the 'humanism' of the young Marx, asks whether 'this uncertainty about the moment when Marx *passed on* to materialism, etc., is not related to the spontaneous and implicit use of an analytico-teleological theory'.[5] The same charge seems to be implicit in McLellan's thesis that: 'To consider Marx's development as progress towards a definite goal is to misunderstand its various stages by viewing them solely in terms of what they led up to.'[6]

Certainly, the dangers these commentators warn against are real enough. It is often a mistake to take a simple unilinear view of someone's development. The Marx of 1859 is assuredly a vastly different and more rigorous theoretician than the Marx of 1843. It is also true that blindness to such differences may be the result of the unconscious importation of Aristotelian or Hegelian teleology into our readings. However, from the fact that over-simplifications can sometimes be traced to metaphysical pre-suppositions, it by no means follows that they can always be so traced. Nor does it follow that, because it is wrong to read Marx's development solely in terms of a specific goal, it must be wrong to see it in such terms at all. The belief that all bad scholarship is the offspring of bad metaphysics leads to the implausible idea that philosophical therapy is the only medicine needed by erring scholars. Some relativists and relativising sociologists are fond of remarking that there are no ideologically 'innocent' readings of texts; but they have forgotten that the theory that all thought is theory-laden (whatever its merits or demerits) cannot function as an argument against a specific thought merely on the grounds that that thought is theory-laden. Equally, the theory that all ways of reading are burdened by some or other theory cannot function as an argument against a specific way of reading Marx purely on the grounds that that approach is theory-laden, quite apart from the consideration that the theory involved may be a good one.

It is a moot point whether Althusser's protest's against 'teleological' readings of Marx lapses into this sort of question-begging. What is certain is that he claims a privileged position for a theory of his own which he brings to the debate on how best to prioritise the texts in question: for he assumes a purportedly Marxist philosophy of science, according to which the opening up of new 'continents' of scientific knowledge, like the emergence of new historical epochs, are separated from one another by revolutionary breaks or 'ruptures'. The decision to read Marx exclusively in the light of this theory must be prompted by the supposition that he can only be understood on his own terms, and to suppose that is to prejudge the truth of what he said. Sadly, it is in something like this spirit that Althusser concludes his essay on 'Contradiction and overdetermination' with a plea that more light be shed on Marx, adding that this is 'the same thing' as shedding more Marxist light on Hegel.[7]

To point to these difficulties is not to detract from Althusser's contribution in drawing attention to the superior importance of Marx's later writings, especially *Capital*. His interventions supplied a necessary counter-balance to the tendency among some scholars in the 1960s to present Marx as being primarily a moralising humanist and to overemphasise the early writings of the young Marx in order to do this. However, his efforts to correct that tendency relied on the same schismatising techniques as his opponents had used. As even McLellan more thoughtfully remarks in a later study, 'Marx's thought is best viewed as a continuing meditation on central themes first explored in 1844.'[8]

Inattention to such continuities has the effect of radically separating Marx's ethical concerns from his preoccupations as a social scientist. The young Marx, on this reading, takes an almost exclusively ethical view of political economy, while the mature Marx treats it with that ammoral objectivity which positivism has taught us to associate with scientific realism. Not only does this dichotomy obstruct the attempt to develop a Marxist ethic, it also does violence to what is in the texts. Were Marx the moralist divorced from Marx the theoretician, we would not expect to find in the young Marx's polemics in the *Rheinische Zeitung* the coexistence, perceptively noticed by Hoffman,[9] between an ethical, universalist view of the state, typical of the young Marx, and a coercive, instrumentalist conception of politics which predominates in the mature theory of history.

The segregation of the earlier, ethical, from the later, theoretical, texts also fails to explain the moral fervour which inhabits the pages of *Capital*, especially when factory conditions and the division of labour come under scrutiny. Had Marx intended the theories of his maturity to conform to the hygienic requirements of positivist scientism, he could not, for instance, have written of the capitalist manufacturing process that it

> converts the labourer into a crippled monstrosity, by forcing his detail dexterity at the expense of a world of productive cababilities and instincts; just as in the States of La Plata they butcher a whole beast for the sake of his hide or his tallow.[10]

The genuine problems raised by this combination of zealous scientific enquiry and moral vision will seem absolutely intractable only to *a priori* empiricists, which Marx was not. Because he had not been trained in a tradition which took empiricism for granted, the amalgam of ethical and scientific interests which the full corpus of his texts present would not have seemed to him the puzzling phenomenon it does to those who, like Lukes, have found the classical Marxist view of morality paradoxical, ill-founded and illusory.[11]

I conclude that the reading of Marx's texts which most naturally suggests itself is also the most likely to lead to a correct appreciation of his theory of history, and is in any case less dangerous than bifurcating his texts. Accordingly, I shall assume that there is a progression in his thinking in which the final products are less creations *ab initio* than the result of his developing what seemed true in his earlier works and transcending positions which seemed to represent the truth less clearly.

3.2 The conceptual background

It is usual to remark that Marx's philosophy was made in Germany, his politics in France and his economics in Britain. This simple schema should not be taken too literally, for Marx's first wrestlings with the problems of political economy predate his departure for Paris in 1843. True, his first meeting with Engels, and such critical events as the composition of the *Economic and philosophical manuscripts*, involvement in the Communist League and researches into the anatomy of British capitalism all belong to other places and times; but the soil in which these implantations could germinate was prepared in Germany, and its conceptual chemistry comprised enough of the three elements — philosophy, politics and economics — to enable the theory of historical necessity to evolve as it did. The convictions that the problems posed by the pre-Hegelian forms of German idealism were soluble only by a philosophy which was both dialectical and historicist grew out of Marx's legal and philosophical studies in Bonn and Berlin. The notion that the criticism of religion was really a political affair and that political criticism was to be founded on a critique of economic systems was born of his experience as editor of the *Rheinische Zeitung*. In other words, the quest for a method which would facilitate investigations into the processes governing forms of social consciousness was impelled by his theoretical struggles with German philosophy and jurisprudence, while the search for a model which would portray the structure of the necessity governing these processes resulted from his practical struggles against Prussian censorship and other prevalent forms of economic and political repression.

What may be thought of as the first cycle of Marx's attempts to come to terms with the specifically philosophical components of his conceptual background was completed before he reached his twentieth year. By that age, his precocious intellect had carried his thinking through a pattern of metamorphoses which seems to duplicate the great moments in the history of classical German idealism, from Kant and Fichte, through Schelling, to Hegel. His reading during this period was, as it seems to have remained, encyclopedic, his intellectual zeal, almost fanatical. To his father he related the story of that youthful journey:[12]

From Idealism, which, incidentally, I had compared to and enriched with Kantianism and Fichteism, I moved to investigate the Idea in the reality itself. If the gods had formerly dwelt above the earth, they now became its centre. I had read fragments of Hegel's philosophy, the grotesque, rocklike melody of which did not appeal to me. Once again I wished to dive into the sea, but with the definite intention of finding our spiritual nature as essential, concrete and solidly rounded as the physical one.

The transition this passage suggests from a neo-Kantian world view to an Hegelian one must strengthen the grounds for a comparison with Wittgenstein, whose debt to his German philosophical heritage I have already insisted on (1.23). The Kantian influence on Wittgenstein is certainly more marked than is that of Hegel, and the converse is true of Marx; but to try to understand either Marx or Wittgenstein while taking no account of that span in the history of ideas of which Kant and Hegel are the focal figures is to be certain of misunderstanding them.

Another matter germane to the Marx–Wittgenstein affinity is the fact that Marx's earliest philosophical enquiries were connected with his legal studies. He himself records the close connection he perceived between the two subjects and his consequent efforts to work out a philosophy of law, culminating in 'a work of almost 300 pages'.[13] Now to study law is to study behaviour-governing systems of rules, and to be impelled by such a study to undertake philosophical work regarding it is to be driven by some or other form of the question, 'How is rule-guided behaviour possible?' We saw how Wittgenstein's philosophical concerns centred on the question, 'How is language possible?', and how that question led to an intensive investigation into the conceptual anatomy of rule-guided behaviour. For both thinkers, therefore, philosophical investigations are to a large extent orientated around problems connected with rules and the human institutions structured in accordance with them. That this should be so does something to explain similarities in the view that each came to take of the kind of necessity governing such institutions and of a form's relation to its content. It helps to explain, for instance, why Wittgenstein thought human language inconceivable outside of a human *Lebensform*, so that in imagining a system of linguistic rules we are also obliged to imagine the legal, cultural, religious and moral institutions which the users of that language inhabit. In like fashion, Marx always conceives of the productive forces whereby human society reproduces its life as developing within and inseparable from rule-constituted socio-economic relations. One way of portraying the later Wittgensteinian account of language is to think of semantic rules as its living form and linguistic performances in accord with those rules as its content. In the Marxian case, too, it is useful to assimilate the notions of 'rule' and 'form', so as to think of the relation in which productive forces stand to rule-governed action as being the same relation in which form stands to content.

3.21 Moral concerns

Marx's filial epistle betrays an engagement with moral dilemmas, wholly reminiscent of Wittgenstein. 'Above all', he confesses, 'I was troubled by the same contradictions between Is and Ought that is characteristic of Idealism.'[14] Hegel provided an initial resting place by suggesting in the *Phenomenology* an account of the life of the self-alienated *Geist* which must have seemed to the young philosopher very much like an account of his search for answers to the ethical questions which troubled him. It is safe to say that no philosophical system which failed to grapple with the Humean 'is'/'ought' dichotomy could have held any lasting attraction for Marx at this or at any other period of his life. This selfsame sense, that it was the urgent task of philosophy to locate moral values precisely in the realm of what is, surely does much to explain Marx's early enthusiasm for the humanised Hegelianism of Feuerbach, whom he saw as the 'destined enemy' of the later work of Schelling.[15] Wittgenstein, of course, did not believe that genuine moral values could be located in the world, but he believed that they *showed* themselves in the world, and would have sympathised with the instinct which drove the Young Hegelians to realise them there.

A remarkable upshot of Marx's urge to find the valuable in the actual was an early and very Hegelian predisposition to sympathise with attempts to inject moral considerations into putative accounts of how the world is. This emerges in the partiality he displayed in his doctoral dissertation towards Epicurean, as against Democritean, cosmologies. Measured by our standards, the mechanistic determinism of Democritean atomism seems far closer to the objectivity of natural science than does the Epicurean doctrine with its impossible attribution of spontaneity to atoms and its anthropomorphised view of inanimate nature. Yet for Marx, it is just the ethical dimension of Epicurus' vision, the inclusion in his atomism of a doctrine of free self-consciousness which renders his system superior to that of Democritus. Marx felt it entirely appropriate that Epicurus should append ethical precepts to his teaching on meteors, a teaching he believed to be 'the soul' of Epicurean natural philosophy, the principle of which, Hegel's youthful disciple argued, was 'the absoluteness and freedom of self-consciousness'.[16]

Marx was, nonetheless, aware, as Wittgenstein had been, that philosophical or quasi-philosophical attempts to explain the sum totality of the world, in the same sense that science offers explanations of natural phenomena, amounted to sterile metaphysics. This much is shown by his treatment of natural theology's attempts to prove God's existence. In the appendix to his doctoral thesis, he argued that such proofs were either 'mere *hollow tautologies*' or else logical explanations of the existence of human self-consciousness.[17] The argument Marx offers for this contention is rather scant. However, the position is in itself a noteworthy anticipation of Wittgenstein's censure of metaphysical efforts to get beyond the bounds of sense. For Wittgenstein, too, natural theology is either a foredoomed attempt to talk about what can only be shown, or else, where it is a genuine expression of religious sentiment, a kind of awed gesturing towards a feature of human self-consciousness.

In fact, Marx and Wittgenstein share a measure of common ground in their attitudes towards religious belief: for although neither could take seriously efforts to translate the language of such belief into the discourse of theoretical explanation which purported to explain the world as a creator's artifact, both closely identified sacred and moral values and were capable of being impressed by humanity's capacity to give expression to them. If what is mutual in their cultural and philosophical backgrounds is taken into account, this should not seem odd. Both came of a Christianised-Jewish ancestry, and both were heirs to a metaphysical tradition in which pietism and deism were important components. No reading of Kant or Hegel that is half-way sensitive can miss the religious sensibility which permeates their work, so it is not to be supposed that Marx, despite his frequent sneers at and caricatures of popular religiosity, was impervious to the influence of the genuine article when he met it in philosophers of their stature, any more than Wittgenstein would have been.

3.22 Political economy

If his immersion in German idealist and Greek speculation helps explain Marx's concern with religio-ethical matters, the mainsprings of his preoccupation with politico-economic realities are traceable to his early journalistic experience. As his famous article on Rhineland timber-theft legislation amply demonstrates, and his own testimony[18] and that of Engels[19] confirms, his work for the *Rheinische Zeitung* provided the first incentive to look beyond legal and philosophical systems to the economic relations and productive forces which he came to view as the ultimate determinants of political life.

Historical materialism, therefore, was not the theoretical product solely of a climate of ideas: it was also the result of a specific politico-economic state of affairs and of Marx's practical interaction with that situation, first in his role as a political journalist, and later as an active revolutionary. The evolution of his account of historical necessity is partly the story of a continual interaction between his speculative and his practical political life. Many philosophers both before and since Marx have been active politicians and men of affairs. In his case, however, the activism was an apt reflection of the philosophy he had read in his youth and the cultural atmosphere in which he read it. For the brand of Hegelianism to which the young Marx gave his allegiance is best characterised as an idealism of action, owing much to Fichte's conception of thought as a volitional activity of a reality-determining sort. The young intellectuals of Marx's student days — men like Bauer and Hess — were imbued with a romantic belief in the Promethean power of ideas and their ready translatability into a *praxis* which would revolutionise society. That Wittgenstein read some of the same idealists in the very different *milieu* of a world-weary, *fin de siecle* Vienna is, perhaps, part of the reason why political life held so little attraction for him.

3.3 History of a theory of history

The case already argued (3.11) for seeing Marx's work in terms of a progressive continuity and his theory of historical necessity as having a coherent history of development is crucial for achieving a rounded view of the theory itself. For while the story of its emergence is, on the one hand, the account of Marx's criticism of Hegelian idealism and his espousal of materialism, it is equally the saga of the discovery of a method for describing interactions between qualitatively distinct processes which originated as Hegel's dialectical method. Marx neither forgot the debt, nor lost his sense of Hegel's immense stature as a thinker. In the very preface to *Capital* which contains the famous sentences about the Hegelian dialectic 'standing on its head', Marx freely acknowledges that: 'The mystification which dialectic suffers at Hegel's hands by no means prevents him from being the first to present its general form of working in a comprehensive and conscious manner.'[20] Furthermore, Marx's assertion that his dialectical method 'is not only different from the Hegelian, but its direct opposite' must not only be set beside his acknowledgement of Hegel's precedence in founding the method, but also beside his decision to take up cudgels on Hegel's behalf against the then current German academic orthodoxy by avowing himself 'the pupil of this mighty thinker' to the extent of 'coquetting' with Hegelian phraseology in developing his own theory of value in *Capital*.[21]

Marx's seemingly conflicting attitudes towards Hegel do not contradict, but rather, complement one another. There need be no inconsistency in retaining certain Hegelian perspectives, while criticising Hegelian metaphysics and historiography where these obscure their author's best insights. Hegel's enterprise was founded on the premiss that processes in the brute-natural and in the human world — including, of course, historical processes — could be rationally understood. Reason and reality were ulti- mately reconcilable, because the former was immanent in the latter. These views (or versions of them) were shared by Marx. He also shared Hegel's opinion that a rational understanding of historical processes had to take into account the problem of human conflict, both with the elemental, and within the anthropological world, and seek internal connections within the polarities of such conflicts. What Marx criticised and ultimately abandoned was Hegel's tendency to treat these processes and conflicts as the merely epiphenomenal expression of an inner spiritual or conceptual motion which Hegelianism took to be the essential necessity governing the observable vicissitudes it sought to explain.

3.31 Exorcising essentialism

I have already remarked (1.23 and 3.01) on the parallel between Marx's critique of Hegel and the later Wittgenstein's critique of the logicist and essentialist account he had given of semantic necessity in the *Tractatus*. There is, I hold, a telling analogy between the post-Tractarian Wittgenstein's repudiation of the doctrine that language is governed by an inner logical essence and Marx's rejection of the notion that history is determined by an intrinsic conceptual fugue. The similarity is made more striking inasmuch as Wittgenstein's repudiation of logical essentialism coincides with his transition towards a view of language which is precisely historicist. The important difference, of course, is that what Hegel meant by 'logic' is at variance with the early Wittgenstein's use of the word — a use which is far more in keeping with the subject-matter of text books on modern formal logic than is Hegel's.

For the Tractarian Wittgenstein, the study of logic is a purely formal affair. 'There are', he says firmly, 'no "logical objects".' (TLP, 4.441) It is otherwise with Hegel: in his system, the dualism between form and content — or, more plainly, the difference between our thoughts and what we are thinking about — is overcome or suppressed. As he tells us in the Introduction to his *Science of logic*, in logic (or his version of it) 'the opposition in consciousness between a subjective entity existing for itself, and another similar objective entity, is known to be overcome, and existence is known as pure concept in itself, and the pure concept known as true existence.'[22] Hegelian logic is, thus, a kind of ontology; but although the Hegelian and early Wittgensteinian conceptions of the nature of logic are strongly divergent, their attitudes towards it are remarkably similar. Not only do both doctrines treat all necessity as identical to logical necessity, they both treat logic as being equivalent to what is ultimately valuable. In the *Tractatus*, the assimilation is accomplished by assigning logical form to the same realm of the unsayable as sacred and moral values inhabit, in a fashion not unreminiscent of Plato. Hegel performs the same feat by identifying the *Geist* of the *Phenomenology* with the Absolute Idea of the *Logic*: for the latter is treated by Hegel as but a further, more rigorous, expression of the self-knowledge which the former achieves once it reaches the standpoint of religion. As Taylor neatly puts it, 'Hegel sees in Christian theology the whole truth of speculative philosophy laid out in images.'[23]

The affinity between Wittgenstein's self-criticism and Marx's criticism of Hegel may, therefore, be said to consist in this: both come to repudiate variants of the philosophical doctrine that forms of life are a camouflage concealing a logical form which determines them, and to substitute for this beguiling image the idea that logical form and *Lebensform* are exoteric aspects of one another. What the transition abolishes is not logic or the power of logic, but the power of a picture which makes everything subordinate to a hidden logic.

The powerful sense of liberation which this dramatic shift of perspective accomplishes should not lead us to miss its subtle, duck-rabbitish quality. It is to the end of preserving something of this quality that I have tried to emphasise the bonds of continuity that unite both Wittgenstein and Marx's essentialist and post-essentialist phases. Neither ended his career as the enemy of logic, although both took up cudgels against the mystification of logic by essentialist metaphysicians. Both fully recognised the value and the validity of the distinction between appearance and reality, when that distinction was drawn in a properly scientific context. Indeed, Marx's own theory could not have been erected without it, and Meikle[24] goes so far as to argue that the achievement of *Capital* cannot be properly appreciated unless Marx's use of essentialist categories is taken into account. The object of Marx's and Wittgenstein's attack is not the scientists' assertion that there is more to things than often meets the eye, but the metaphysician's myth that there is never more to appearances than a shadowy and inadequate representation or misrepresentation of a Reality which is, nonetheless, their own well-ordered nature.

Marx first launched his attack during 1843 in a critical exegesis of paragraphs 261–313 of Hegel's *Grundlinien der Philosophie des Rechts und Staatswissenschaft im Grundisse*. Marx's commentary, the *Critique of Hegel's 'Philosophy of right'*, drew inspiration from his reading of Feurbach, but also, and as importantly, from the practical experience of Prussian censorship and political life which his journalism had afforded him. That experience engendered a lively scepticism regarding the notion that political contradictions existed only at the phenomenal, but not at the essential or ideal level of the historical process. 'Hegel's chief mistake', he argued, 'consists in the fact that he conceives of the contradiction in appearance as being a unity in essence, i.e., in the Idea; whereas it certainly has something more profound in its essence, namely, an essential contradiction.'[25] Just as in his *Logic*, Hegel had tried to reduce all philosophical enquiry to a series of moments in the self-development of the Absolute, so, Marx realised, Hegelian political philosophy sought to reduce concrete political institutions, like the Prussian legislature, to a moment in the self-expression of an inner logical category. Thus, Marx complains:[26]

Only for the sake of logic does Hegel want the luxury of the

Estates ... Hegel does not search for an adequate actualisation of the being-for-itself of public affairs, but contents himself with finding an empirical existent that can be dissolved into this logical category.

Analogously, in the *Investigations* Wittgenstein mercilessly exposes his Tractarian treatment of problems, which the *Tractatus* describes as 'perhaps the most concrete that there are' (TLP, 5.5563):

Thought is surrounded by a halo — Its essence, logic, presents an order, in fact, the a priori order of the world: that is the order of *possibilities*, which must be common to both world and thought. But this order, it seems, must be *utterly simple*. It is *prior* to all experience, must run through all experience; no empirical cloudiness or uncertainty can be allowed to effect it ... We are under the illusion that what is peculiar, profound, essential in our investigation resides in its trying to grasp the incomparable essence of language ... (PI, i, para. 97, original emphases)

3.32 The critique of religion

The fact that, for Hegel, the imagery of Christian belief is only a somewhat less rigorous expression of the conceptual truth he strove to express in his philosophy helps explain why, for Marx, 'the critique of religion is the prerequisite for every critique.'[27] Of course, if this slogan is taken less robustly than Marx intended, it can be made to seem to represent a standpoint which some Hegelians might be persuaded to accept. The Hegelian categories have religious resonances; but Hegel saw religious truths as having their ordinary mode of expression as representational images (*Vorstellung*) and he took it to be the task of philosophy to translate these into conceptual discourse. So long as this activity of critical philosophy remained essentially a work of translation, Hegelians might have agreed that any thoroughgoing critical philosophy presupposed a critique of religion. Marx, however, goes further. Religion is not, for him, an unrefined version of a higher conceptual truth: it is 'the heart of a heartless world', 'the soul of soulless conditions' and the 'opium of the people'.[28] To write like this is to treat theological discourse as the language of illusion, and given the theoretical achievement towards which he was trying to find his way, it is understandable that Marx should have so treated it. For until the conflation of conceptual with historical necessity has been exposed in all its guises, the conceptual labour which will produce an argument for the primacy of productive forces in explaining epochal social change cannot make headway.

How does this attitude towards religious belief compare with Wittgenstein's own carefulness in such matters? His remarks are too scattered and too tentative to permit us to draw a definitive conclusion. Certainly, he was never dismissive of religious talk or religious imagery. Equally, he believed such imagery to have a different, perhaps indefinable role in our language — certainly different from the role which images have in factual or in scientific discourse. This belief is well brought out by a remark, in the course of his lectures on religious belief, concerning Michelangelo's picture of the creation:

> It is quite clear that the role of pictures of Biblical subjects and the role of the picture of God creating Adam are totally different ones. You might ask this question: 'Did Michelangelo think that Noah in the ark looked like this, and that God creating Adam looked like this?' He wouldn't have said that God or Adam looked as they look in this picture. (LC, p. 63)

This grammatical remark draws attention to the harm that may be done when a religious picture is misassigned a role in the discourse of theory-construction. In fact, Wittgenstein speaks at several places in the *Investigations* (PI, i, paras 38, 89 and 94) of our mistaken tendency to treat the logic of our language as something 'sublime'. His own unintentional construction of a theory in the *Tractatus* has been inspired by a picture of this quasi-religious kind. He would, therefore, have found entirely congenial Marx's determination to purge putative historiographies of religious props. One suspects, however, that his own religious sensibility would have led him to think that this work of purification was as much in the interests of religion's own proper function as it was in the interests of science, and it is not clear that Marx was as much concerned to preserve a proper role for religion as he was to see that science prospered.

3.33 Philosophy as practice

In the spring of 1845, Marx penned a set of eleven *Theses on Feuerbach* in which he furthered his critique of idealism and, thereby, the account of historical necessity towards which he was moving. These *Theses* are laconic bits of draft material, and Marx did not publish them in his lifetime. However, Engels, recognising their importance, published them in 1888 in the appendix to the separate edition of his *Ludwig Feuerbach and the end of classical German philosophy*. His decision to do so reflects the prestige Feuerbachian philosophy enjoyed among the revolutionaries in the Young Hegelian movement, even if, as Mészáros[29] is so anxious to claim, Marx had substantial reservations about the approach as early as 1843. In a letter from Paris in 1844, Marx not only assures Feuerbach 'of the distinguished respect and — excuse the word — love that I have for you', but also credits him with having 'given socialism a philosophical foundation'.[30] This surely is ground enough for thinking that the qualified criticisms of his idol's positions we find in the *Theses* indicate an important turning-point in Marx's own search for a theory which would form the basis of socialist thought.

The new element introduced by these remarks is a special emphasis on the importance of the notion of practical activity for generating a genuinely materialist epistemology and account of the origins of religious life. The burden of Marx's complaint against Feuerbach — one which parallels the charges he was later to bring against the classical political economists — is that, while seeing that religious phenomena originate in human life, he fails to situate these phenomena in practical human conflicts which practice alone can eliminate.

Feuerbach stands accused of sharing with all previous forms of materialism an incomplete, reificatory and contemplative view of reality in which human activity has no part. Such activity is left to the mercies of an idealist treatment which, because it divorces theory from practice, is incapable of viewing practice itself in any but an abstract and theoretical light. There is thus a sense in which Marx sees Feuerbach as having inherited some of the worst features of both the idealist and the materialist world-views. The result of this is that, in his *Essence of Christianity*, Feuerbach 'regards the theoretical attitude as the only genuinely human attitude, while practice is conceived and fixed only in its dirty-judaical form of appearance'.[31]

By this reasoning, Feuerbach's celebrated inversion of the Christian God-made-man schema into a humanist man-made-God schema is but an anthropomorphised version of Hegelian essentialism. The escapologist's trick has failed because, although Houdini-like he has reversed his posture within his prison, he continues to treat the practices which stare him in the face as the mere material seemings which conceal the profundities of theory, so that the fly-turned-theoretician remains firmly trapped in his fly-bottle. Endeavouring to break the spell of these conceptual confusions, Marx offers a telling reminder:[32]

> The materialist doctrine that men are products of circumstances . . . forgets that it is men that change circumstances and that the educator himself needs educating . . . The coincidence of the changing of circumstances and of human activity can be conceived and rationally understood only as *revolutionising practice*.

On Marx's reading of him, Feuerbach's work dissolves the religious world into its secular basis, but overlooks the 'chief thing', which is that the apparent independence of the religious realm is explicable only by the self-cleavage of this secular basis.

> The latter must itself, therefore, first be understood in its contradiction and then, by the removal of the contradiction, revolutionised in practice. Thus, for instance, once the earthly family is discovered to be the secret of the holy family, the former must then itself be criticised in theory and revolutionised in practice.[33]

This suggests that three things are necessary to complete the work of emancipation:

(1) The religious aroma of the secular world must be recognised as the dependent product of that world.
(2) For that recognition to be fully accomplished, religion's apparent independence must be seen to result from a self-cleavage in the secular basis which it is the task of critical theory to expose.
(3) New practices must be introduced to combat and eliminate the old practices which typify the self-strife of the secular world.

135

Feuerbach may be said to have neglected (2) and (3), thus failing to achieve a unity of theory and practice; but what precisely is the role in all this of the philosophers, who, as Marx famously concluded, 'have only *interpreted* the world in various ways', whereas from the standpoint of the new revolutionary materialism, 'the point is to change it'?[34]

In my view, this last thesis is misunderstood if it is taken to be a call for the abolition of philosophy in favour of radical political activity. Yet Cohen,[35] in his exegesis of the Eleventh Thesis, while granting that it is superficial to read Marx as expressing an activist's impatience with the analytical response to illusion, does take him to be calling for a repeal of philosophy comparable to the repeal of social science entailed by the mature Marxian views of science and socialism. Cohen would have us read Marx as saying that the point is to change the world so that interpretation of it is no longer necessary. This would be a world in which theoretical explanations of the practices of socialist man needed no further elaboration in the theorist's head, as it were, because they would be revealed in those very practices. In such a world, in other words, theory and practice would achieve their proper internal union. Cohen's thought, then, is that, while Marx shares Feuerbach's urge to dispel illusion and to harmonise thought with reality, he holds that theory alone is impotent to achieve this and that only the active transformation of the world in accordance with correct theory will do the trick.

Finely nuanced as this reading certainly is, and 'somewhat novel' as Cohen admits it is,[36] as an account of Marx's judgement on philosophy, it is also rather too neat. Marx clearly intended to censure philosophical visions of a particular sort, but he cannot have intended to call for a repeal of philosophy *tout court*. Marx and Engels had, after all, arrived at their criticisms of Hegelian and Feuerbachian outlooks by a process in which wide philosophical reading and reflection played no minor part.

Marx, moreover, continued to philosophise well into the period of his maturity as a theorist and politician. The *Grundrisse*, for example, which stands midway between the *Communist Manifesto* of 1848 and the publication of the first volume of *Capital* in 1867, is full of philosophy. To a thinker, steeped in the conjectures of the pre-Socratics, who had translated Aristotle's *De anima* and who was as familiar with the post-Cartesian philosophical tradition as any man of his time, the idea that a world communist revolution would abolish philosophy or could be achieved without its aid would have seemed both utopian and repugnant. What Marx says is that philosophers (he does not say all of them) have tried to *interpret the world,* and it is to this phrase that we must attend if we are to grasp his intention. In our usual parlance, 'interpretation' can be used to mean the translation of expressions from one language into another, and it can be used to mean the *explanation* of words, phrases or sentences within the same language. We can also speak variously of interpreting a picture, a diagram or a piece of music; but there is a queerness about the notion of 'interpreting the world' (where this means offering an interpretation which will cover everything that 'is the case' and not just some aspect of it, as happens in the sciences) which should leave us unsurprised by the information that this is something some philosophers do. To offer an interpretation of the world is to purport to give a theoretical explanation of the meaning of all that there is. Philosophers who try to do this are the ones who claim to be able to tell us about 'the Meaning of Life', 'The Purpose of Being', the 'Absolutely Good' or the 'Absolutely Beautiful'. They are the metaphysicians, the super-scientists, and they number in their ranks such geniuses as Plato, Hegel and, despite himself, the Tractarian Wittgenstein.

If Marx is indeed to be understood as calling for a repeal of philosophy in the Eleventh Thesis, then it must be this kind of global metaphysics and not philosophy in general that he wanted to see replaced by the kind of practice which would change the world. This practice must be taken to include, besides such obvious activities as the political and even military mobilisation of the proletariat and its allies, forms of philosophical activity such as are critical of idealist metaphysics and supportive of materialist theory. Philosophy, on this view of it, is no longer something contemplative, but a practical, purposive activity, a form of revolutionary struggle.

Now, this view of philosophy does differ from that taken by Wittgenstein in some notable respects. There was no political partisanship in Wittgenstein's attitude to philosophy. His ideal philosopher was 'not a citizen of any community of ideas' (Z, 455). He was, moreover, almost obsessively strict in trying to keep intact the boundary between philosophy and theory in a way which Marx, who also makes the distinction, was not. This obsession was, however, a function of a critical posture towards the pretensions of metaphysics and its claims to interpret the world which Wittgenstein certainly shared with Marx. He also

most emphatically shared the Marxian conviction that philosophy, in order precisely to avoid lapses into metaphysics, had to
be treated as an activity, a practice among practices, an
assemblage of techniques involving skill. The philosopher's work
consisted in 'assembling reminders for a particular purpose' (PI,
i, 127), and the methods by which this work was done were like
'different therapies' (PI, i, 133) or like untying 'knots in our
thinking' (Z, 452).

> Almost in the way a man who is not used to searching in the
> forest for flowers, berries or plants will not find any because
> his eyes are not trained to see them . . . Similarly, someone
> unpractised in philosophy passes by all the spots where
> difficulties are hidden in the grass whereas someone who
> has had practice will pause . . . (CV, p. 29e)

3.34 'Settling accounts'

The *Theses*, while confirming and completing some of the
positions Marx adopted in the *Economic and philosophical manuscripts*
of 1844, ought also to be regarded as a draft of conceptions which
made a more finished appearance in *The German ideology*, a
collaborative work which Marx and Engels completed in 1846,
and which marks an intermediate stage in the evolution of the
theory that concerns us. It continues the subversive analysis of
Hegelianism, although its targets are the Young Hegelian
offshoots of that doctrine — Feuerbach, Strauss, Bauer and
Stirner. As Marx was later to indicate, the main purpose of the
book was self-clarificatory, the outcome of a resolve 'to settle
accounts with our erstwhile philosophical conscience'.[37] However, as Marx's phrase implies, this settlement is not simply a
severing of relations: it is rather a balancing of debts and credits
in respect of an intellectual movement towards which he and
Engels had felt a critical yet deep, and even passionate, sympathy. The Hegelian Left offered far more to the revolutionary
temperament than a critique of established religion. It represented a romantic, life-affirming humanism, which sought to
connect the abstract conceptions of Hegelian philosophy with live
issues, and to make of philosophy itself something one could live.
It is therefore no accident that the notion of a *Lebensform*, which
was to achieve such prominence in Wittgenstein's later philo-

sophy, should emerge strongly in Marx and Engels's effort to take stock of where this current of thought had led them, and of where they wished to place themselves with respect to it. For, as Sève[38] remarks, the philosophical humanism of the Young Hegelians is not simply cast aside in *The German ideology*; but real men have replaced idealised, abstract notions of man at the centre of the theoretical arena.

The chief positive upshot of this review was that Marx and Engels produced the first concise (although not their most finished) statement of their theory of historical necessity. Extracting from the notion of 'practical activity' — whose importance Marx had stressed in the *Theses* — the rather more specific concept of 'productive activity', they now argued that:[39]

(1) Men . . . begin to distinguish themselves from animals as soon as they begin to *produce* their means of subsistence, a step which is conditioned by their physical organisation. By producing their means of subsistence men are indirectly producing their material life.

(2) The way in which men produce their means of subsistence depends first of all on the nature of the means of subsistence they actually find in existence and have to reproduce.

(3) This mode of production must not be considered simply as being the reproduction of the physical existence of the individuals. Rather it is a definite form of activity of these individuals, a definite form of expressing their life, a definite *mode of life* on their part . . .

These propositions clearly signal a shift from an idealist to a realist anthropology which, moreover, is founded on explanations in terms of the production of material goods, the physical make-up of the producers and, in the last resort, on the kind of material available for transformation by this productive activity. Transmutations in the world of ideas can no longer be understood independently of these live activities and the material constraints within which they are carried out. It was not, Marx and Engels held, consciousness which determined life, but life which determined consciousness.[40]

At this juncture, once again, the grounds for treating the unfolding of the Marxian view of history and the development of the Wittgensteinian account of language as comparable processes appear particularly compelling. As they abandon Hegelian idealist categories, we find Marx and Engels substituting for the spiritualised and logicist mode of explanation, to which that doctrine ultimately reduces, unmistakably materialist conceptions of their own. Their brand of materialism, to be sure, is not to be confused with its eighteenth-century mechanist predecessors. Nonetheless, in insisting that forms of consciousness are determined by the real life of socialised humanity and that this life consists primarily in the reproduction of subsistence under determinate material conditions, they must be taken to be proclaiming that social processes and their accompanying states of consciousness are inconceivable in the absence of certain natural regularities. Such processes cannot arise in default of our world having the kind of material structure it has and exhibiting the degree of predictability which it in fact exhibits. Material regularities are therefore necessary, although not sufficient, conditions for the rise of tribal, feudal, bourgeois and socialist states of social consciousness. In putting the matter like this, moreover, the new materialism preserved such central features of the Hegelian outlook as the notion of development through active struggle and the importance of humankind's spiritual and cultural strivings after rational goals. It did not abolish the logic of Hegel's dialectical method, but used it to plot the dynamic interaction of forms of consciousness with the specific regularities in nature which made them possible. It is for this reason that Marxists have used the adjective 'dialectical' in attempting to distinguish their brand of materialism from others.

Analogously, Wittgenstein, in the settlement of accounts with his Tractarian philosophical conscience which he undertook in the *Investigations*, gains an overview of language which makes room for the constraints imposed by nature without abolishing logic. This perspective, as we saw (1.59), is such that a possible world in which objects randomly disappear and reappear, or in which gravitational laws are absent or radically different from those obtaining in our actual world, is not a world in which a language, recognisable as a human language, could accommodate itself. In a world, for instance, with a physics such that only unstable processes and no solid states could exist in it, we could not play the language-games associated with the naming of objects, and the playability of such games is one of the features which makes our language recognisable as ours. What some philosophers nowadays call 'propositional attitudes' are, by post-

Tractarian lights, unavoidably bound up with uniformities in nature which allow us to expect, believe and desire the things we do. The proverbial burned child's dread of fire is internally connected to the expectation that fire will burn which it is in the nature of fire to teach.

> The character of the belief in the uniformity of nature can perhaps be seen most clearly in the case in which we fear what we expect . . . The belief that fire will burn me is of the same kind as the fear that it will burn me. (PI, i, paras 472–3)

The new Wittgensteinian materialism has, of course, no more in common with mechanism or vulgar reductionism than did its Marxian forerunner. As Marx and Engels chose to preserve what they saw as best in their Hegelian inheritance, so, as I have been at pains to point out (1.1–1.11), did Wittgenstein preserve important elements of the *Tractatus* philosophy. Language and the material world still form an indissoluble unity; but the logic of the former has now to be understood in relation to determinations imposed by the latter.

This convergence of a materialist semantics and a materialist philosophy of history helps explain the decidedly Wittgensteinian ring of the pronouncements about language in *The German ideology*. As the later Wittgenstein emphasised the linkage of language, ideas and real-life activity, so Marx and Engels argue that: 'The production of ideas, of conceptions of consciousness, is at first directly interwoven with the material intercourse of men — the language of real life.'[41] They come very close as well to anticipating at least the spirit of Wittgenstein's arguments against semantic privacy and the Lockean model of language-use when they insist that language 'is as old as consciousness, language *is* practical real consciousness that exists for other men as well, and only therefore does it also exist for me'.[42] His own struggles to escape the metaphysical traps into which he had fallen in the *Tractatus* had convinced Wittgenstein that the new philosophers' task was 'to bring words back from their metaphysical to their everyday use' (PI, i, para. 116). Similarly, the founders of historical materialism held that philosophers had

> only to dissolve their language into the ordinary language from which it is abstracted, in order to recognise it as the

distorted language of the actual world, and to realise that neither thoughts nor language form a realm of their own, that they are only *manifestations* of actual life.[43]

More than a decade of practical experience and of reflection upon it intervenes between the intermediate version of historical materialism and the first mature expression of its fundamental principles, contained in Marx's 1859 *Preface* to his *Contribution to the critique of political economy*. This *Preface*, although rooted in the philosophical debates of the 1840s, goes well beyond Wittgenstein's conception of the proper scope of philosophy. In setting forth as it does the structural model which became the chief Marxist paradigm in the explanation and analysis of social change, it is unashamedly a general theory of the forces governing history and the mode of their interaction.

The years 1847–59 witnessed an extraordinary intensification of Marx's active political life. They were the years of the production of the *Communist Manifesto* and involvement in the Communist League, of Marx's editorship of the *Neue Rheinische Zeitung* and the publication of a mass of political commentaries in that journal and in the *New York Herald Tribune*. By the time he wrote the *Preface*, Marx had acquired first-hand experience of political life in Germany, France, Belgium and Britain. Philosophical questions still deeply engaged him, as the pages of the *Grundrisse* amply demonstrate. However, the chief issues which now confronted him were political and theoretical. His great need was to elaborate an abstract account which would explain the ultimate how and why of the concrete politico-economic circumstances which he was working to revolutionise, and which would uncover the nature of revolution itself. This need could not be satisfied by pure philosophical speculation — even the critical philosophy directed against metaphysical speculation. To meet it Marx had to become an economic researcher and historian, labouring with real data in the British Museum and railing against the utopian 'simpletons', who 'have no need for such exertions'.[44] It is at this point that the Marxian project diverges most sharply from the Wittgensteinian enterprise. Marx's life experiences challenged him to do for human history what had been done for natural history by Darwin, whose *The origin of species* appeared in the same year that the *Preface* was written.

3.4 The mature theory

In expounding his theory, Darwin made deliberate use of the metaphor of a 'struggle for existence', convinced that unless this conceit was 'thoroughly engrained in the mind, the whole economy of nature . . . will be dimly seen or quite misunderstood'.[45] Although specifying that the meaning he intends for the term 'struggle' is 'large and metaphorical',[46] Darwin nonetheless employs it centrally in the origination of his scientific account of biological processes, and this circumstance, given the notion's significance for a tradition stretching from the pre-Socratics to Hegel, was bound to win the admiration of Marx, who read *The origin of species* a year after its publication. Despite the 'crude English manner' in which — as Marx complained, first to Engels[47] and later to Lassalle[48] — Darwin developed his ideas, the founder of historical materialism saw in them a foundation in natural history for his own theory and had even wished to dedicate the second volume of *Capital* to Darwin. There is indeed a kinship of sorts between the Marxian and Darwinian doctrines. As Darwin's hypothesis required that his readers be reminded of a strife-filled reality beneath the tranquil appearance of a natural world seemingly 'bright with gladness',[49] so Marx had to emphasise the violent struggle of developing productive forces to break free of existing productive relations and to strip off the legitimising veil of ideological appearances which denied this hidden strife.

The comparison between the two theories should not, however, be overstated. Marx was critical, not only of what he took to be the crudity of Darwin's intellectual style, and of the 'pompous ignorance and intellectual laziness' of those who, like the unfortunate social economist, Friedrich Lange, made free play with the phrase 'the struggle for life' without carrying out detailed analysis of its working;[50] he was also critical of what he saw as lacunae in Darwin's own exposition. By 1866, a year before the publication of the first volume of *Capital*, we find him praising as 'a very important advance over Darwin' Pierre Trémaux's *Origine et transformations de l'homme et des autres êtres*, on the grounds that progress, which is merely accidental in Darwin, is a necessity for Trémaux and that the latter treats as necessary the palaeontological gaps which trouble Darwin.[51]

This tension between Marx's admiration for Darwin as the discoverer of a great scientific truth and as sharer of a true vision

143

of the nature of material processes, and his sense that the truth had been inadequately stated and the necessities contained in the vision insufficiently expressed, is indicative of the caste of thought which led him to choose the kind of model for his own theory of history that he did. In order to satisfy both his respect for the constraints imposed by the economic and historical data which his researches uncovered and his very Hegelian urge to trace with detailed thoroughness and subtlety the full range of internal connections which unified this data, he needed a model which, while respecting the integrity of each of its elements, would perspicuously display the necessity which ordered them.

This paradigm would have to cope with the complex task of exhibiting the *relationships* between the various aspects of the social process, showing how classes stood to the means of production, and how modes of production related to religion, law and politics. In order to achieve all this, Marx settled on a structural model, and the fact that he did so is an outcome of the standards he set himself and of his theoretical project itself which, although it perhaps lay closer to the biological sciences than it did to physics, was conceived as a distinct enterprise in its own right, with its own field of enquiry and methodology.

The 1859 *Preface* sets out the rudiments of Marx's mature theory of history in a passage which is surely a milestone in the history of social theory, and which has become a minefield of conceptual traps for scholars:[52]

> In the social production of their life, men enter into definite relations of production which correspond to a definite stage of development of their material productive forces. The sum total of these relations of production constitutes the economic structure of society, the real foundation on which rises a legal and political superstructure and to which correspond definite forms of social consciousness. The mode of production of material life conditions the social, political and intellectual life processes in general. It is not the consciousness of men that determines their being, but, on the contrary, their social being that determines their consciousness.

That this *Preface* really does contain the mature version of Marx's theory of historical necessity is shown by the fact that the notions and pattern of explanation set out there recur, without significant modification, in *Capital*, as do references to Darwin[53] and his 'epoch-making work on the origin of species'.[54] Proclaiming that Darwin had 'interested us in the history of Nature's Technology', Marx speaks of the need for a critical history of human technology and continues:[55]

> Technology discloses man's mode of dealing with Nature, the process of production by which he sustains his life, and thereby also lays bare the mode of formation of his social relations, and of the mental conceptions that flow from them. Every history of religion, even, that fails to take account of this material basis is uncritical. It is in reality much easier to discover by analysis the earthly core of the misty creations of religion, than, conversely, it is, to develop from the actual relations of life the corresponding celestialised forms of those relations. The latter method is the only materialistic, and therefore the only scientific one.

The same basic conception of historical necessity is reiterated in the third volume of *Capital*, in which the social process of production is said to be

> as much a process of material conditions of human life as a process taking place under specific historical and economic production relations ... Like all its predecessors the capitalist process of production proceeds under definite material conditions, which are, however, simultaneously the bearers of definite social relations entered into by individuals in the process of reproducing their life.[56]

3.41 The nexus of necessity

Now in none of these passages is Marx claiming that the effects of production on all levels of conscious activity are immediate, so that the emergence, say, of baroque art forms could be exhaustively explained in terms of some current mode of production. This said, it is evident that the explanatory power of his model is diminished unless we take him to be saying that, in the main, the lines of necessitation proceed upwards through the levels of the structure he mentions and not in the reverse direction. This claim does not force him to deny that superstructural activity can affect infrastructural processes; but such effects are not his major interest, and his argument does not concern them. The model which the 1859 *Preface* introduces could not have done what Marx required of it if all it were taken to be illustrating were the mutual interdependence of all elements in the base and in the superstructure.

The *Preface* mentions three levels of the structure — productive forces, relations of production and the politico-legal super-structure. The last-named two levels consist essentially of *relations* (since their form is determined by contractural rules which are, in the strict sense, artifices, designed to juxtapose human relata in certain configurations), while the most basic level is comprised of *forces*, consisting of material resources and human capacities and *powers*.

This way of putting the matter, and the whole notion of developing forces at the fundaments of a structure, further bolsters the thesis that the productive forces are the chief source of historical necessity. It also seems right to insist, as Cohen does,[57] that production *relations* alone constitute the economic structure and that the productive *forces* are not part of it. This view can be defended without trying to decide whether Cohen is right in thinking that the productive forces are basic to the structure in the special sense of being like an external plinth on which the the edifice rests, rather than like being an intrinsic part of it. (The difficulty with this construal of the metaphor is that the productive forces have also to be thought of as the *content* of the productive relations, and the connection between a plinth and the structure it sustains is not precisely that of content to form.) The best reason, it seems to me, for refusing to treat the forces of production as part of the economic structure is precisely that the latter is said to consist of 'relations', and the concept of a 'relation' is very different from the concept of a 'force' or a 'power'. To say that A exerts a force on, or has power over, B is always to say that A stands in a relation 'r' to B; but to say *simpliciter* that 'ArB' is not to say anything about forces or powers.

The postulate that the productive forces are the primary sources of historical necessity and that their level of development explains the nature of any given set of productive relations finds further support in Marx's talk of production relations *corresponding* to the productive forces. Here, once again, I think Cohen is right in taking Marx to mean that the former are appropriate to the latter, and are as they are *because* they are appropriate to

146

productive development.[58] Cohen neatly turns an objection to the effect that the correspondence of relations to forces implies no priority either way, because it belongs to the meaning of *'entsprechen'* that if x corresponds to y, then y corresponds to x, by pointing out that correspondence is not always symmetrical.[59] Falls in wrestling correspond symmetrically to points scored in fencing, but the correspondence (if there is one) between sexual promiscuity and the spread of venereal disease is not symmetrical.

The precise nature of the productive forces is a question which will be of more intensive concern to us later. Presently, we may content ourselves with observing that they obviously include such means of production as tools and raw materials and the physical and intellectual labour power which uses and shapes them. Marx explains that they determine the relations of production because of their developmental tendency which turns existing relations into fetters. The productive forces are, therefore, compelled to sunder these fetters in order to realise their developmental potential. Marx continues:[60]

> Then begins an epoch of social revolution. With the changes of the economic foundation the entire immense superstructure is more or less rapidly transformed. In considering such transformations a distinction should always be made between the material transformation of the economic conditions of production, which can be determined with the precision of a natural science, and the legal, political, aesthetic — in short, ideological — forms in which men become aware of this conflict and fight it out.

3.42 *The place of ethics*

The epochal transformations of society, then, are said to be caused by contradictions between forces comprising the content of a given tribal, feudal or capitalist mode of production and the property relations which constitute its form. The term 'contradiction', as Marxism employs it, no longer has to do with conceptual anomalies or negative stages in the World Spirit's quest for self-realisation as it did in Hegel. Here it means simply that the struggle against material scarcity, the drive to meet subsistence needs, can no longer continue under a given set of economic relations and requires the formation of new ones. This should not be taken to imply that the productive forces are merely irrational drives or that the rational ideal and profound ethical concerns of the Hegelian system have been scrapped in favour of a scientistic world-picture inspired by Darwinism. For the productive forces are postulated within a conceptual framework which presupposes human rationality in supposing that the social beings, to whom alone the theory applies, are also rational beings inasmuch as they will employ the available means to satisfy their needs and can learn what those means are. Moreover, the interpretation of historical materialism which accords primacy to the productive forces without locating them in the economic structure avoids the charge of having reduced ethics to economic relations.

It is true that the theory treats systems of ethics, as it does legal, religious and political systems, as superstructural, and hence as the ideological resultants, in the last resort, of processes originating in the infrastructure; but this is not to demean the role of ethics. On the contrary, it is to number codes of moral behaviour among the ways in which social beings recognise the necessities governing a vast area of their existence and respond to them (which is not, of course, to say that they all respond in the same way).

There is no reason either to saddle historical materialism with the dogma that nothing of immediate interest to moral philosophy can be happening at the infrastructural level. The type of necessity arising out of the character of the productive forces is only weakly analogous in its law-like operation to such natural forces as the gravitational field, and it does not set the same sorts of limits to human possibility as such forces do. Productive forces, while they certainly depend on the basic regularities in nature being as they are, must not simply be conflated with the forces of 'brute' nature. They are, in large part, human capacities which can be used to offset and overcome the obstacles that brute-nature sets to them. To see in them the source of historical necessity is not to see them as enslaving human creatures in a way which makes their moral choices irrelevant. As Cohen points out, 'men cannot be slaves of their own capacities.'[61] In the course of the next chapter, I shall try to show that the true nature of the productive forces is of profound significance for ethics.

3.5 Legitimacy

In the immediately preceding sections, I have tried to provide an outline of Marx's theory of historical necessity which throws into relief its cogency and explanatory power. To do this is not of course, to secure for the theory independent credibility, and obviously nothing like the sort of defence which might achieve this can be attempted here. Something must be said, however, on the question concerning the legitimacy of Marx's theoretical project itself — on the very idea, that is, of trying to elaborate a theory of history such as he has given us. The issue arises out of my attempt to connect Wittgenstein's thought with that of Marx, chiefly via their respective critiques of logical essentialism. We noted two things most particularly in our survey of Wittgenstein's philosophical journey. We saw, firstly, a continuing and intensifying battle to purge his reflections of that craving for generality which leads the philosopher to construct theoretical explanations of the sort that it is the scientist's business to supply; and secondly, a shift towards an anthropocentric and historicist view of language. The second feature is in many ways a natural development out of the equivalence Wittgenstein sets up between imagining a language and imagining a form of life. In imagining a language, we are imagining speakers of that language, and the more fine-grained our imaginings become, the more they will take account of the changing cultural, religious, economic and political institutions which belong to the speakers. In short, to have an overview of language is precisely to have an overview of history. In regarding this history, however, we are forbidden, even more strictly than was the case before we attained our vision of it, to venture beyond description into any sort of theory construction, and this (so the objection runs) is the trap into which Marx has fallen.

Some support for the Wittgensteinian credentials of the objection, although not for the objection in itself, can be found in one of his 1947 remarks: 'Who knows the laws according to which society develops? I am sure they are a closed book even to the cleverest of men . . . You can fight, hope and even believe without believing *scientifically*.' (CV, p. 60) The last sentence expresses a ' sentiment with which no Marxist need disagree. However, this does not detract from the possibility that the whole thought represents nothing capricious, but a real conviction, and that Wittgenstein would have genuinely found it impossible to believe in the theory of historical necessity we have just been considering. It is also possible that he might have said of it what he once wrote of Darwin and Copernicus — that what they had achieved was not a true theory but a fertile new point of view (CV, p. 18).

These speculations do not, however, serve the purpose of showing that Marx breaches the Wittgensteinian canon by moving from a philosophical critique of Hegelian essentialism to a theoretical account which, no less then Hegel's, delves beneath historical appearances to give an explanation of social development in terms of hidden forces. The charge that to attempt this is to do something illegitimate relies on an over-strict interpretation of Wittgenstein's precept which calcifies it into a dogma. This dogmatism is itself based on a misunderstanding. The intensification of Wittgenstein's anti-theoretical discipline in the post-Tractarian period is attended by the introduction of the idea of philosophy as a collection of different therapies (PI, i, 133) and a treatment of an illness (PI, i, 255). There can be little doubt that what is uppermost in Wittgenstein's mind when he employs this simile is Freudian psychoanalysis.[62]

Now psychoanalytic therapy can, notoriously, be prolonged or even interminable, because the notion of a psychoanalytic 'cure' has blurred edges. That this should be so has to do with the persistent and recurrent nature of the disease and with the supposition that the only appropriate antidote to it is self-knowledge, which can never be complete. Thus, analyst and analysand engage in an indefinitely extendable dialogue, during the course of which the analysand's account of his symptoms and dreams, his recollections of his life-history, reveal new and sometimes astounding manifestations of his sickness. It is no accident, then, that when Wittgenstein began to liken his mode of philosophising to a therapy, he introduced the interlocutor-device, thereby inserting into his text the atmosphere of just such a dialogue. Nor is it accidental that, when reading the *Investigations* in particular, we should be struck by the way in which misleading pictures are erased, only to be revived again at some fresh turn in the argument. The point of this procedure is to intimate that such pictures are the product of an urge to theorise as powerful as the libidinous drives which manifest themselves in the discourse of analysands in the consulting room. Like those drives, however, the theoretical impulse has appropriate as well as inappropriate modes of expression. Just as sexual activity can be creative and fulfilling, so not all theorisings are perverse and misleading, but are often liberating and constructive. As psycho-analytic therapy can redirect basic psychic energies into fertile channels, so philosophical therapy can guide the impulse to create explanatory conceptual structures into areas in which they can be restrained by facts. This is precisely what Marx claimed to have done with his demystification of the Hegelian dialectic.

It would really be absurd to attribute to Wittgenstein, whose heroes had been the physicists Hertz and Boltzman, a general mistrust of scientific theory. What he mistrusted was a disposition — to which idealist metaphysics is especially prone — to produce theories which were not answerable to the facts. The specific reason underpinning this suspicion is that theories, whether they are legitimate or not, often involve proposals for revisions of ordinary language. Thus, Freud, to cite an example of Wittgenstein's, proposes to call even anxiety dreams 'wish-fulfilment dreams' (CV, p. 44). Such proposals may be entirely legitimate; but if they are, this can only be because they explain the familiar world in which our ordinary usage of language is at home better than comparable theories do and not because they merely transport us from familiar vantage points to interestingly strange ones. If a theory only does the latter, then the linguistic reforms it proposes are idle and will produce pictures that mislead. This will always be the case when, as in philosophical speculations, there is no factual court of appeal. 'Philosophical problems arise when language *goes on holiday*.' (PI, i, 38)

If this interpretation of the Wittgensteinian doctrine on the place of theory is a faithful one, then he could have had no grounds for objecting to a theory of history which originated out of just the sort of attempt to curb the pretensions of metaphysics that he himself had made. For Marx, whose labours in the British Museum correspond to Darwin's years of careful observation on the *Beagle*, can scarcely be accused of ignoring facts or neglecting to explain them in a fashion which tried to preserve the all-too-familiar realities of exploitation and oppression which were the lot of subordinate classes in general and the proletariat in particular. Whether the explanation he offers really does bridge the gap between appearance and reality is, of course, the subject of debate between Marxists and anti-Marxists. However, this dispute ought, properly speaking, to be carried on between competing schools of social science and not between social scientists and philosophical therapists.

3.51 Evaluations

A word must be said at this point concerning what comparative evaluation is to be made of the Marxian and Wittgensteinian contributions. Our discussion so far has skirted this question, concentrating instead on Marx and Wittgenstein's common struggle against the Hegelian and Tractarian versions of the logical essentialist world-picture. These two versions are likenesses of the same fundamental archetype. Both offer a sublimely perfect vision of a pure logical order beneath the phenomenal veil. In both cases the supra-phenomenal revelation turns out to be the mirror image of the instrument — Fregean logical notation in the Tractarian case, dialectical logic in the Hegelian instance — which reveals its hidden structure. To have devised, independently, techniques of escape from this perennial illusion is, taken in itself, an achievement which sets Marx and Wittgenstein on a level in so far as the merit of their originality as philosophers is concerned. However, the intellectual products of their respective criticisms of essentialism differ strikingly, and this has not a little to do with the fact the Hegelian dialectic pretends to be a 'logic' of *processes*, while the logic of the Tractatus makes no such strange claim. In the light of this difference, it is understandable that Wittgenstein's later philosophy, despite its historicist character and although it makes full allowance for alterations in the linguistic landscape, gives nothing like a full account of linguistic change. Marx, on the other hand, made it his business not only to describe, but to explain, how historical change was possible, and on this count alone his contribution (on the assumption that his theory is the correct one) must be reckoned among the greatest ever made to human self-knowledge.

3.6 The ethical dilemma

We have already noted that explanation of the workings of the historical dynamic in terms of the base–superstructure model does not obliterate ethical considerations (3.42), and some emphasis has already been laid on the dangers of segregating Marx's interests as a mature social scientist from his ethical preoccupations (3.01–3.1). The vision of communism in which his science of social change culminates is, in its portrayal of human life, lived in conditions of free creativity and harmonised emancipation, as much a moralist's as it is a theoretician's vision. Even such a writer as Kamenka, who is prepared to liken modern communist party governments to oriental despotisms[63] is at pains to argue that Marxism has ethical foundations and that

> Marx perceived in himself and in others the characteristic ways in which goods work. He saw that evils were divisive and goods co-operative, that apparent harmony between evils always involved an element of resistance . . . He saw the incoherence and dependence enshrined in any morality that elevated ends and subordinated activities: he realised the different roles played by 'rules' in the morality of freedom and the morality of security and protection.[64]

Nonetheless, the base–superstructure model continues to pose enigmas to friends and foes of historical materialism. There seems to be a feeling abroad that if the model explains what Marx thought it explained, then it must be explaining morality away in an illicitly reductionist fashion; and, on the other hand, that its explanatory power is diminished if it is understood as according moral values the kind of importance in economic and political life that some philosophers think proper.

Thus, Lukes, in an exchange with Cohen, argues that 'one cannot identify the powers and constraints embodied in norm-governed economic relationships independently of the norms which . . . govern them.'[65] The basis of his case is the indispensability of normativity to the descriptions of the power relations which constitute the infrastructural level of Marx's model for any given mode of production, and the apparent intractability of the dilemma he finds here moves him to conclude that the model ought to be scrapped.[66] Cohen, who, as he points out, is defending not a concept of non-normatively based power, but of non-normative power *simpliciter*, can retort that the indispensability of A to B and the fact that A is not explained by B do not in combination show that B cannot be described in A-free terms.[67]

We may wonder whether this response really touches the deeper issues involved here: for the picture of a full-scale liberation of value-neutral productive forces by a series of revolutions which will culminate in the unfettered productivity of communist society is a bewildering as well as a heady image, and it can awaken a lively fear of losing one's ethical moorings — a sense that one's moral identity would be at risk in such a world.

Cohen himself seems to have felt something like this sort of disquietude. Five years after publishing his vigorous defence of his version of historical materialism, *Karl Marx's theory of history*, Cohen announced that Marx's philosophical anthropology seemed false to him in that it appeared one-sidedly to stress humanity's relation to the objective material world and to neglect men's relation to the self which Hegel had made his chief concern.

This confession was not, from the perspective of Cohen's reading of Marx, to be seen as a complete volte-face: for it was the anthropology, not the theory of history, which Cohen took to be false, and the former treats human creativity as something natural to humankind, while the latter shows men producing out of the necessity which scarce resources create. For all that, Cohen's difficulty seems serious enough. There was, he claimed,[68]

> a human need to which Marxist observation is commonly blind, one different from and as deep as the need to cultivate one's talents. It is the need to be able to say not what I can do but who I am, satisfaction of which has commonly been found in identification with others in a shared culture based on nationality, or race, or religion, or some slice or amalgam thereof.

Two things must be said concerning this candid declaration. Firstly, it is just not plausible completely to divorce Marxist anthropology from the Marxist theory of history, even if, for some purposes of exposition, it may be desirable to treat them separately. Even Cohen, who hesitates to connect the two doctrines, concedes that both have production at their centre.[69] The rational capacities which enable men to perceive, predict and pre-empt the onset of conditions of scarcity are the very same capacities which belong to what may be thought of as the intellectual and imaginative side of human labour power. They are part of the forces of production and help explain their tendency to develop as they do. The productive forces are to the conditions of unfettered productivity, envisaged in Marx's philosophical anthropology, what means are to ends in ethically interesting courses of action, at least in the sense that defective means are liable to infect the ends they are meant to serve.

Secondly, the human need Cohen identifies to discover an identity within a shared culture is certainly also a moral need and a very real one (although how Cohen can accuse Marxists of being 'blind' to it, in the light of the participation of communist parties in national liberation struggles in Vietnam, Latin America and South Africa is something I do not understand). To be part of a cultural, national or religious community is to be bound by bonds of obligation, trust and respect to other members of that community. It is precisely obligatory bonds of this sort which the Hegelian term of art, *Sittlichkeit* or 'concrete ethics' (which Lovibond explains in terms of obligations to sustain the institutions which embody a shared way of life) tries to capture. It was surely one of Hegel's great insights, and one which owed not a little of its inspiration to his reading of the Greeks, that *Geist* can find no self-realisation outside of human communities whose members are linked to one another by ethical ties of this sort, and that the famous unity of the real with the rational is possible only when Reason finds its resting place within a moral reality.

On this view, Cohen is quite right to draw back before a vision of unrestrained productivity, albeit of the most creative and 'artistic' sort, made possible by the action of value-neutral productive forces. For the alarming sense of moral weightlessness that this utopian image evokes is the parent of an intuition that the communist society towards which we are travelling is a radically unstable one, more threatened with dissolution and decay than any previous social formation we have known. For if *sittlich* obligation is taken to be something ideological, then it will disappear when the ideological contests and concealments which are a function of class struggle disappear, and there will be nothing to preserve the cohesion of the communist community, save the new communards's rational perception that to do so is in their own best interests. However, 'rational' here has a far narrower meaning than it did in Hegel's mouth or, indeed, in the mouths of many philosophers who preceded him. It carries no heavier moral baggage than the enlightened self-interest of creative individuals, emancipated from the last bonds imposed by scarcity. Of course, it may be said that it is clearly not in their self-interest to exchange, by counter-revolution, their communist lot for any pre-communist one; but this rather begs the question, since it is precisely their sense of selfhood under communism that is in question. This is the true ethical dilemma, posed by the Marxist theory of history on any interpretation of it which treats the forces of production as value-free: for as we have insisted all along, it is these forces which the base–superstructure model portrays as being *primarily* responsible for the social changes which lead to communism, and it is their free play which chiefly characterises communist society. In the next and final chapter, I shall try to resolve this dilemma by showing that these forces are not void of moral power.

Notes

1. K. Marx and F. Engels, *Collected works*, vol. 2 (Lawrence and Wishart, London, 1979), pp. 103–4.

2. K. Marx, *The eighteenth Brumaire of Louis Bonaparte* in K. Marx and F. Engels, *Collected works*, vol. 2 (Lawrence and Wishart, London, 1979), p. 104.

3. A.T. Van Leeuwen, *Critique of earth* (Lutterworth Press, Guildford and London, 1974), p. 225 f.

4. R.P. Wolff, 'Reflections on literary style and social theory. The case of Karl Marx's *Capital*', University of Massachusetts, Amherst, unpublished, original emphasis.

5. L. Althusser, *For Marx*, Ben Brewster (trans.) (Allen Lane, The Penguin Press, London, 1969), p. 59, original emphasis.

6. D. McLellan, *Marx before Marxism* (Macmillan, London and Basingstoke, 1970), p. 37.

7. Althusser, *For Marx*, p. 116.

8. D. McLellan, *Karl Marx* (Macmillan, London, 1973), p. 303.

9. J. Hoffman, *The Gramscian challenge. Coercion and consent in Marxist political theory* (Basil Blackwell, Oxford, 1984), pp. 23–4.

10. K. Marx, *Capital*, vol. 1, I.S. Moore and E. Aveling (trans.) (Lawrence and Wishart, London, 1954), p. 340.

11. S. Lukes, 'Marxism, morality and justice' in G.H.R. Parkinson (ed.), *Marx and Marxism* (Cambridge University Press, Cambridge, 1982), p. 177 f. For an attempt to deal with the paradox in terms of a distinction between morality as *Recht* and morality as emancipation, see S. Lukes, *Marxism and morality* (Clarendon Press, Oxford, 1985), pp. 27–47.

12. K. Marx, 'Letter to Heinrich Marx' in *The letters of Karl Marx*, S.D. Padover (trans.) (Prentice Hall, Englewood Cliffs, New Jersey, 1979), p. 9.

13. Marx, 'Letter to Heinrich Marx', p. 5.

14. Ibid., p. 5.

15. K. Marx, 'Letter to Ludwig Feurbach' in Padover (ed.), *The Letters*, p. 5.

16. K. Marx, *The difference between the Democritean and Epicurean philosophy of nature* in *Collected works*, vol. 1 (Lawrence and Wishart, London, 1975), pp. 68–72.

17. Ibid., p. 104, original emphasis.

18. K. Marx, *Preface* to *A contribution to a critique of political economy* in *Selected works* (Lawrence and Wishart, London, 1968), p. 180.

19. F. Engels, 'Letter to R. Fischer', quoted by McLellan in *Karl Marx*, p. 57.

20. K. Marx, *Capital*, vol. 1, p. 29.
21. Ibid.
22. G.F. Hegel, *Science of logic*, vol. 1, W.H. Jonston and L.G. Struthers (trans.) (George Allen and Unwin, London, 1929), p. 71.
23. C. Taylor, *Hegel* (Cambridge University Press, Cambridge, 1975), p. 211.
24. S. Meikle, *Essentialism in the thought of Karl Marx* (Duckworth, London, 1985), esp. pp. 61–70.
25. K. Marx, *Critique of Hegel's 'Philosophy of right'*, Joseph O'Malley (ed.), Annette Jolin (trans.) (Cambridge University Press, Cambridge, 1976), p. 91.
26. Ibid., p. 64.
27. K. Marx, *Introduction* to *A contribution to the critique of Hegel's 'Philosophy of right'* in O'Malley (ed.), *Critique*, p. 131.
28. Ibid.
29. I. Mészáros, *Marx's theory of alienation* (Merlin Press, London, 1970), pp. 234–5.
30. K. Marx, 'Letter to Ludwig Feuerbach (in Bruckberg)' in Padover (ed.), *The letters*, pp. 34–5.
31. K. Marx, *Theses on Feuerbach* in *Selected works* (Lawrence and Wishart, London, 1970), p. 28.
32. Ibid., pp. 28–9, original emphasis.
33. Ibid., p. 29.
34. Ibid., p. 30, original emphasis.
35. G.A. Cohen, *Karl Marx's theory of history. A defence* (Clarendon Press, Oxford, 1978), pp. 338–41.
36. Ibid., p. 338.
37. K. Marx, *Preface to the critique of political economy* in *Selected works* (Lawrence and Wishart, London, 1970), pp. 182–3.
38. L. Sève, *Man in Marxist theory*, J. McGreal (trans.) (Harvester Press, Sussex; Humanities Press, New Jersey, 1978), p. 76.
39. K. Marx and F. Engels, *The German ideology* in *Collected works*, vol. 5, p. 31, original emphasis.
40. Ibid., p. 37.
41. Ibid., p. 36.
42. Ibid., p. 44, original emphasis.
43. Ibid., p. 447, original emphasis.
44. K. Marx, 'Letter to Joseph Weydemeyer' in Padover (ed.), *The letters*, p. 71.
45. C. Darwin, *The origin of species* (Everyman Library, London and New York, 1967), p. 67.
46. Ibid., p. 68.
47. K. Marx, 'Letter to Engels' in Padover (ed.), *The letters*, p. 139.
48. K. Marx, 'Letter to Ferdinand Lassalle' in Padover (ed.), *The letters*, p. 452.
49. Darwin, *The origin of the species*, p. 67.
50. K. Marx, 'Letter to Ludwig Kugelmann' in Padover, (ed.), *The letters*, pp. 273–4.
51. K. Marx, 'Letter to Frederick Engels' in ibid., p. 215.
52. K. Marx, '*Preface to A contribution to the critique of political economy*, in

K. Marx and F. Engels, *Selected works* (Lawrence and Wishart, London, 1968), p. 181.

53. Marx's reservations about Darwin's method of presentation must have pertained, mainly, to its undialectical character. Gruber suggests that Darwin was well aware of the philosophical issues involved and had given them considerable thought, but covered his philosophical tracks in his published work. In that case, we cannot exclude the possibility that Darwin, on his side, had philosophical as well as prudential considerations in mind when, as Gruber reports, he declined Marx's offer to dedicate the second volume of *Capital* to him. See H.E. Gruber, *Darwin on man. A psychological study of scientific creativity* (Wildwood House, London, 1974), pp. 71–2.

54. K. Marx, *Capital*, vol. 1, p. 323, n.

55. Ibid., p. 352 n.

56. K. Marx, *Capital*, vol. 3 (Lawrence and Wishart, London, 1959), pp. 818–19.

57. G.A. Cohen, *Karl Marx's theory of history*, p. 28.

58. Cohen, *Karl Marx's theory of history*, p. 136.

59. Ibid. pp. 136–7.

60. K. Marx, *Preface*, pp. 181–2.

61. Cohen, *Karl Marx's theory of history*, pp. 147–8.

62. For a recent and careful treatment, see B. McGuinness, 'Freud and Wittgenstein' in B. McGuinness (ed.), *Wittgenstein and his times* (Basil Blackwell, Oxford, 1982), pp. 27–43.

63. E. Kamenka, *The ethical foundations of Marxism* (Routledge and Kegan Paul, London, 1962), p. 199.

64. Ibid., p. 195.

65. S. Lukes, 'Can the base be distinguished from the superstructure?', *Analyse und Kritik*, vol. 4 (1982), p. 220.

66. Ibid., p. 222.

67. G.A. Cohen, 'A reply to four critics of *Karl Marx's theory of history*', *Analyse und Kritik*, vol. 5, no. 2 (1983).

68. G.A. Cohen, 'Reconsidering historical materialism', *Nomos*, XXVI, J.R. Pennock and J.W. Chapman (eds) (New York and London, 1983), p. 235.

69. Ibid., p. 241.

70. S. Lovibond, *Realism and imagination in ethics* (Basil Blackwell, Oxford, 1983), pp. 63–5.

4

Values in History

4.0 Introduction

I present in this chapter an argument to justify the integration of
the semantico-ethical theory, developed in Chapter 2, and the
Marxian account of historical necessity just rehearsed. The route
to be followed runs from an analysis of what the term 'productive
forces' ought properly to include, through the reasons for
counting language among such forces, to the conclusion that
value-preservation is among the necessary conditions for the
occurrence of epochal historical change. Two sorts of gain attend
the possibility of this argument being thought sound: most
importantly, it would show that Marxists are bound by the value-
laden character of their own explanatory model to take account in
some or other fashion of the need to preserve moral values — an
example would be the South African Communist Party's refusal
to countenance indiscriminate violence against innocent civilians
— and it would militate against the thought that communist
society is a prospect which threatens our sense of identity as
members of a moral community. Additionally, it would further
strengthen the case for treating Marxian and Wittgensteinian
thought as affined by showing that the same account of moral
necessity was complementary to both.

Before any of this can be done, however, a debt which is
perhaps overdue ought now to be paid. The question as to what
kind of internal necessity makes language possible is a transcendental question, and the theory whereby I have tried to
answer it is specially reliant on that form of argumentation
known as a Transcendental Argument. It seems sensible, then, to
begin this chapter with a general discussion of such arguments,
and to say something more specifically about the sort of
Transcendental Argument on which my theory depends.

4.1 Transcendental arguments

The least controversial thing to be said about transcendental reasoning is that its modern origins are in Kantian critical philosophy. Thus, Transcendental Arguments (henceforth TAs), both in their typical and in their deviant varieties, are best understood in the general light of Kant's own projects and in the context of the dialectical tradition which he inaugurated. In his introduction to the first *Critique*, Kant explains: 'I entitle *transcendental* all knowledge which is occupied not so much with objects as with the mode of our knowledge of objects insofar as this mode of knowledge is to be possible *a priori*.'[1]

Properly Kantian TAs, then, are justifications for synthetic *a priori* knowledge-claims — i.e. propositions which are true of the world we experience, but which are necessarily true and independent of such experience. Significantly, Kant modelled his TAs on certain juridical instances in civil law in which rights or entitlements are in dispute. That he took inspiration from a legal rather than a logico-mathematical model, favours the view that, although he took this mode of argumentation to be an entirely reasonable and compelling form of response to sceptical challenges, he probably did not think of it as a readily formalisable deductive mode with relations of strict entailment holding between premisses and conclusion. More likely, he saw his TA form as an argumentative strategy which an advocate might employ in order to get a reasonable judge into a position from which the reasonableness of the claim before him would seem indubitable and any challenge to its reasonableness would be revealed as illegitimate.

The challenges Kant sought to expose as illegitimate were those seeking to undermine our convictions about such matters as the existence of external objects, the reality of causal connections and the existence of a self whereby the perceptual manifold could be unified and made coherent. His motive in taking up cudgels against the straw man of Cartesian scepticism was intrinsic to his goal of devising a philosophical system which would match Newtonian physics in the apodicticity of its principles, while reconciling the claims of rationalism and empiricism. Even this vast enterprise was integral to a still wider area of concern, encompassing his quest for justifications of moral and religious faith. If Wood[2] is right in arguing that this latter aspect represents the foundation of Kantian epistemology and that the critical philosophy itself is a religious outlook, then it will not seem odd if the TA form turns out to possess features which refer us back to a Socratic conception of philosophy as a self-questioning activity, and so to attitudes and enigmas associated with certain essentially religious points of view.

The standard TA form is deceptive in its apparent simplicity. It takes as first premiss some indubitable experiential fact or set of facts, goes on to adduce some necessary condition of our having the experiences we indubitably do have, and concludes that we have no option other than to believe that the condition actually obtains. The effect of a successful TA is, therefore, to show that it is inconsistent to give less credence to a condition which has been shown to be necessary for the having of a given type of experience than the level of belief which accompanies the experience itself. Thus, for instance, the sceptic who doubts the existence of external objects will find himself convicted of inconsistency before the 'tribunal of reason', if he continues to express his doubts, once it is established, firstly, that he does have experiences of the relevant type and cannot, so to speak, help having them; and secondly, that the existence of external objects is a necessary condition of his having just the experiences he concedes he has.

4.11 Typical features

Two identifying features can be extracted from the above account. The first is that a genuinely Kantian TA is always grounded in some form of *experience*. Kant, after all, specifically designed the TA form in order to establish necessary conditions for conceptualised experience. Thus, in trying to determine whether a putatively transcendental chain of reasoning is of authentic Kantian ancestry, it must always be useful to ask if whatever it takes as its starting-point can plausibly be said to fall under the description of something experienced. Arguments founded on perceptual occurrences easily pass this test. It is less obvious that arguments — like that rehearsed in Chapter 2 — which aim to establish the necessary conditions for the possibility of language do so. I shall deal with this difficulty shortly. The matter is of some weight, because if no restriction of this sort governs the admissibility of candidate TAs, it will be open to unscrupulous or careless philosophers simply to claim that they are relying on a TA whenever ordinary deductions fail to suit their purposes. On the other hand, the restriction should not be over-zealously applied, since not all arguments concerning experience need be concerned with it in the context of the classical epistemological problems inherited by Kant.

The second feature, which also bears importantly on matters soon to be dealt with, is that *bona fide* TAs are, in the last resort, arguments *ad hominem*. They are so in that they seek to convict the sceptic of inconsistency on the grounds that his sceptical utterances do not square with the fact that he, being what he is, is uttering them. They try to show him that, because of what he is, he has *no title* to doubt what he claims to doubt, no right to call what he does 'doubting'.

It is easy to see how the *ad hominem* element enters into the structure of *a priori* knowledge-claims. The conceptualisation of experience is readily representable as something persons *do* to the 'raw' data of experience, not, of course, volitionally, but in virtue of the way people are constituted. Such knowledge as we can have of the conditions of our experience can then plausibly be described as being what Hintikka calls 'maker's knowledge'.[3] Kant is, as Hintikka notices, explicit on the point. He speaks, in the first *Critique*, of reason having 'insight only into that which it produces after a plan of its own'.[4] He says also that 'we can know *a priori* of things only what we ourselves put into them.'[5] Likewise, in the *Critique of judgement*, he says reflective judgement is able only to 'give as a law from and to itself' the transcendental principle that particular empirical laws are to be treated as if an understanding had furnished them to cognition.[6]

The indispensability of the *ad hominem* element to the TA should act as a brake on its being too freely employed. Equally, there are many argumentative contexts (moral argument is a good example) in which it is legitimate and even prudent to draw an interlocutor's attention to pertinent facts about himself, especially when these conflict with things he feels inclined to say.

4.12 Dialectical and transcendental reasoning

These two features — groundedness in experience and dependence on *ad hominem* argument — can be made to serve as explanatory guidelines in tracing the spread of the TA form into those reaches of the dialectical tradition in modern philosophy which most concern us. For that tradition can fruitfully be described as an attempt to resolve, by recourse to the Socratic conception of philosophy as a mode of self-knowledge, the problems posed to experience, firstly by Cartesian, and then by empiricist theories of knowledge. Its self-reflective dimension, in particular, allowed the TA structure to be more or less naturally absorbed into Hegel's more complex dialectical pattern of argumentation: for as Alexander points out, Hegel appraised Kant as having failed to develop the implications of his reflection, but never as having begun with a false step.[7]

For Hegel, Kant's critical philosophy represented the most rigorous formulation to date of the thesis that being determines itself and that its reflections are self-justifying. Thus, the argument in the *Phenomenology*, whereby Hegel arrives at his conception of Spirit as Notion, begins with an examination of 'sense-certainty' and its inadequacies, in much the same way as Kant sets out in the Aesthetic and Analytic of the first *Critique* to criticise vulgar empiricism. The Hegelian 'deduction' of Spirit as Notion is reminiscent of the Kantian 'deduction' of the transcendental unity of apperception. Indeed, Hegel says of the latter doctrine: 'It is one of the profoundest and truest insights to be found in the *Critique of pure reason* that the *unity* which constitutes the nature of the Notion is recognised as the original synthetic unity of apperception.'[8]

A shared conception of philosophy as a mode of reflection which puts itself in question is a basic source of such empathy as Hegel felt for Kantian thought and explains why the TA form, or variants of it, were so naturally absorbed into the intricate movement of Hegel's dialectical reasoning. Yet there must be costs as well as benefits attached to investment in TAs, for although the great advantage of a well-directed TA is that it silences sceptical doubts by getting the sceptic to recognise things about himself that made his doubts seem empty, the *ad hominem* argument which settles the issue also ensures that it will not be settled finally. For in employing this strategy, one opens up ancient and dangerous questions as to who and what we take ourselves to be, and so introduces an element of open-endedness into conceptual investigations which, once introduced, will be difficult to seal off again.

Two related factors have contributed to contemporary Anglophone philosophers's difficulties in arriving at an adequate concensus concerning the nature and capacities of TAs. The first is a prevalent antipathy to the kind of grand-scale philosophising that Kant and Hegel typified, and the image of philosophy as a self-critical mode of access to ultimate self-knowledge that went with it. The second is the fact that, as a result of the combined impact of the Fregean revolution in logic and the birth of positivism, modern Anglo-American philosophy is and has been largely analaytical and undialectical in its methods, and more inclined to be impressed by the possibilities and achievements of formal logic than either Kant or Hegel (or Marx, for that matter) were or could have been.

The confluence of these factors gave rise to the idea that, if TAs were to be of any use, they had either to be treated as if they were, or be modified until they became, a species of *reductio ad absurdum* proof, the premisses of which formed an unbroken chain of formal deduction. Only as such could they function within the prudent limits of the 'research programmes' which so many analytical philosophers aspired to carry out.[9] This attitude left its mark on the debate which followed Strawson's[10] use of TAs in his descriptive metaphysics and Shoemaker's[11] use of them against scepticism about the existence of other minds. Thus, Korner[12] argued that TAs, as exemplified in the first *Critique*, could never succeed because it was logically impossible to demonstrate the uniqueness of a categorical schema; while Stroud[13] held that TAs, as instanced in Strawson and Shoemaker's anti-scepticism, rested on a version of the verification principle and were, therefore, redundant if verificationism was sound doctrine and impossible if it were not. Gram[14] proposed a like dilemma by claiming that an epistemic premiss necessarily grounded conclusions for perceptions under a description, and that such premisses could only be used in a TA, either to infer what they were supposed to establish by assuming it, or by inference from what is in fact perceived, thereby rendering the premiss superfluous.

These assaults had an interesting result in that, while they by no means forced the champions or reformers of the TA to embrace dialectics and eschew analysis, they did induce them to shift to perspectives which allowed them to view the argument forms in question in a less formalistic and a less positivistic light. Broadly summarised, the approaches offered in this, more recent, literature took two compatible forms. It was argued

(1) that TAs were not a version of verificationism, and
(2) that they did serve to establish conceptual connections
of some kind, even if these were not of the sort to be looked
for in a formally valid deductive proof.

We may interpret (1) as an anti-positivist stance and (2) as signalling a movement away from logical formalism. Some philosophers, notably Hacker,[15] and in a more recent and extensive treatment, Genova,[16] have concentrated on rebutting the charge of verificationism. Others have focused on defending the claim that TAs do establish genuine, if weaker, relations between premises and conclusions. The latter group includes Strawson himself, who, in supporting the claims of naturalism against scepticism, accepts that even if TAs do not 'succeed in establishing such tight or rigid connections as they initially promise, they do at least indicate or bring out conceptual connections, even if only of a looser kind'.[17]

A good reason for limiting our expectations along the lines Strawson suggests is that no relation of entailment seems establishable between our possession of a given concept — albeit a concept necessary to our experience — and the actual existence of some object. That reason has been adduced by Grayling[18] in favour of the adoption of what he calls 'B-option TAs' — i.e. arguments designed to show only the indispensability of certain concepts to our conceptual scheme or to our having experiences of a certain kind. This alternative would not settle sceptical doubt at a single stroke, but it might do so at a double stroke, if it could be shown that ours was the only conceptual scheme possible for us.

This defensive posture will seem less defeatist if we attend to the direction that the *ad hominem* component can impose on conversations in which TAs play a prominent role. As we saw, this feature makes refutation of the sceptic turn on the circumstance that his putative doubts fail to square with some ineliminable and shared facet of his make-up. He will be told that his scepticism cannot be reconciled with the fact that he is a sentinent creature, or a language-user, or a member of a moral community, and so on. However, this way of putting matters leaves it open to the sceptic to reply — even if he concedes that, being what he is he could not doubt what he claims to doubt, and that he presently has all the relevant self-knowledge he could have — that there is a sense in which the case against him is not finally closed and is, indeed, indefinitely reopenable. His response relies on the thought that, while self-knowledge can be adequate in given circumstances and for a given purpose, it cannot be adequate *simpliciter*. Further justification for a plea that the question be left open may be sought in the idea that who and what we are depends on unfathomable and changing circumstances in nature or in history; but once the claim that the growth of our self-knowledge cannot be limited in advance is allowed to stand, we are forced to allow for the possibility that the sceptic's disease may break out again in a new form. That concession is avoidable only on pain of denying the very possibility that deepened self-insights will raise fresh questions as to what it *means* to be sentinent, equipped with a language, or a moral agent, thus recreating the very climate of perplexity in which scepticism can flourish.

The inability of the TA form to foreclose the possibility of further debates with sceptics, far from showing that this mode of reasoning is obsolete, points to the sort of importance it really has, the uses to which it can be put and the kind of seriousness due to it. We should not say of a line of argument successfully employed in a legal action to show that Brown's behaving thus-and-so constituted negligence, say, within the meaning of the statutes, that it proved nothing just because similar arguments about negligence were sure to ensue again. We recognise that the argument may have to be restated to meet changed circumstances or changes in the law. However, that does not make its general form redundant, nor does it mean that the judge who was persuaded by it was wrong to find against Brown in the first place. For this judge is not in the same case as the geometrician who writes 'QED' in a proof with a faulty or missing premiss. The latter's 'proof' was not really a proof, inasmuch as it failed to demonstrate what he thought it did. Furthermore, we know that very serious issues are decided in cases like Brown's — i.e. cases in which what is at issue is not some matter of fact, but the construal of a statute — and that grave consequences may attend such decisions. It is just because of the gravamen that can attend legal decisions of this kind that a tradition of precedents is allowed to play a role in judicial decision-making and questions of meaning are made subject to a process of interpretation and re-interpretation, rather than being decided once for all by a stipulative definition.

Analogously, a TA which has been effective against one or another form of sceptical doubt achieves more than a pyrrhic victory. Its accomplishment is not nullified by the consideration that it may need to be restated in new terminology in order to meet renewed sceptical challenges, themselves clothed in new terminological disguises. Like their legal cousins, ancestor-TAs have a role to play in determining the outcome of later disputes, and it is a mark of our regard for the issues at stake that this should be so.

The true source of our resistance to this form of argument-ation's employment does not, then, lie in its inability to produce proofs of a rigorously deductive sort. It is to be sought, rather, in the reservations some philosophers have felt about the vision of philosophy and its directions, which is, as I have argued, unavoidably associated with thinking that relies on TAs. In so far as these philosophers wish to distance themselves from the dialectical tradition, they are right to suspect transcendental reasoning, for the association is more than circumstantial. Because it relies so heavily on arguments *ad hominem*, the TA form creates an almost irresistable image of philosophy as a spiralling pattern of discourse, comprised at every turn in the sequence of knowledge-claims or theses and sceptical antitheses, mediated in each case by the perennially open question: 'Who am I?' This, of course, was the picture that Hegel made a life's work of elaborating in explaining how Reason overcomes the different, yet recurrent conceptual crises encountered on the successive stages of its journey to self-realisation. Marx, it should be noted, showed the fullest grasp of how the dialectic achieved this shape, and of what he was accepting in accepting its general form, when he observed:[19]

> Theory is capable of seizing the masses once it demon-strates *ad hominem*, and it demonstrates *ad hominem* once it becomes radical. To be radical is to grasp matters at the root. But for man the root is man himself. The manifest proof of the radicalism of German theory is the fact of its issuing from a resolute positive *transcendence* . . .

If, as I have been arguing, Wittgenstein has a place within the dialectical tradition, should we not expect him to employ some form of TA in his later wrestlings with scepticism? The answer is not straightforward. Wittgenstein was not an imitator of the classically Kantian TA, any more than Hegel and Marx had been. To be that, he would have had to believe that it made sense to talk of 'knowing' one's own experiences, and he was firmly convinced that it did not. We may *have* experiences of one kind or another, remember having had them, predict, on the basis of those memories, that we will have the same experiences again and we may certainly *know*, on the basis of what they tell us and the behaviour we observe in them, what experiences others have. However, I cannot be said to know, say, that *I* am in pain, because none of the variety of criteria which allow me to identify other sufferers and ascribe pain to them applies in my own case. In fact, no criteria determine my saying 'I am in pain' (PI, i, 404).

If, then, we regard Kantian TAs as introspective techniques whereby knowledge-claims about external reality are founded on putative knowledge of 'internal' subjective experiences, then this is not the path traced in the Wittgensteinian refutation of scepticism. If we take a broader view, however, both of the possibilities inherent in transcendental reasoning and of Wittgenstein's long and complex arguments against scepticism and the very possibility of a private language, we can discern the same general strategy that distinguished Kant and Hegel's anti-Cartesian project from rationalism and empiricism. For Wittgenstein's anti-sceptical arguments depend at crucial places on getting the sceptic to acknowledge the ordinary experiences of the world he shares with the rest of us, as well as the techniques we and he commonly employ in describing such experiences. The next step is to get him to compare these with the distortions which warp both experience and linguistic techniques when he is doing philosophy as he, the sceptic, does it. The cure is effected when the sceptic perceives that his philosophical contortions are futile, are part of no playable language-game, just as 'a wheel that can be turned though nothing else moves with it, is not part of the mechanism' (PI, i, 271). Thus, the sceptic is invited to remember the unphilosophical moments when he exclaims at the blue of the sky — moments in which 'the idea never crosses your mind that this impression of colour belongs only to *you*' (PI, i, 275, original emphasis). When the interlocutor protests that he at least *means* something definite when he looks at a colour and names his (private) impression of colour, Wittgenstein responds that this is to treat the colour-impression like a detachable membrane and adds that such a treatment 'ought to arouse our suspicions' (PI, i, 276). In such ways of directing the sceptic's attention to what he is and to what he normally experiences, we can detect the experiential appeals and *ad hominem* arguments which are the hallmarks of the TA form.

4.2 The core-game argument

Central to the theory of core-language-games, outlined in Chapter 2, was an argument, directed at moral sceptics and, most importantly, at moral cynics, which resembles some of the TAs we have been discussing. In essence, this argument moves from the assertion (1) that language — understood as a network of gradeable language-games — is something which all humans, not in some way crippled or otherwise disadvantaged, use or are capable of using, through the premiss (2) that value-preservation is a necessary condition for any imaginable language, to the conclusion (3) that no language-user can self-consistently use language to express cynical attitudes or sceptical doubts about such values as truthfulness, trust, just-dealing and reverence.

This argument's title to be regarded as a *genuine* piece of transcendental reasoning (and not just an unsound attempt at deduction disguised as a TA) is chiefly bolstered by the fact of its containing an *ad hominem* component which, as we have just been noticing, plays an important role in all TAs, even when they deviate from the Kantian norm in other ways. If someone objects that, on the other hand, the argument is concerned with language and not with the possibility of experience, I shall respond that this is something of a quibble. For it is as clear that we speak as it is that we have experiences, so a TA can get started where my argument starts just as well as anywhere else. What is true is that the range of experiences of which we are capable is tied to the depth and breadth of our mastery of language. The sensibility that distinguishes Bach's compositions from Vivaldi's, a Cezanne from a Manet, is an active and educated sensibility whose perceptions must be so bound up with the activities associated with command of language as to be virtually (although not actually) indistinguishable from them.

However, although my argument concerns language and not experience, what was said of experience in the Wittgensteinian refutation of epistemological scepticism is equally true of language in my attempted refutation of moral cynicism. For although I may know *that* I said such-and-such to so-and-so and in which language I said it, and may also know *how* to speak a given language, knowing that I know this (in the sense of having confidence in my ability to repeat past performances), I cannot be said to have said anything if I say in any language that I *know* I can speak or that I am speaking. In this last case, *Doubt* can get no grip, and the missing holdfast must be fatal also to his partner *Certainty*. Linkage of these three concepts is inevitable in a TA: for as Wittgenstein aptly puts it, 'The game of doubting itself presupposes certainty' (OC, 115), and 'In a law-court, for example, "I am certain" could replace "I know" in every piece of testimony.' (OC, 8)

It appears, then, that the core-game TA is unlike the general run of properly Kantian TAs in just the way that makes Wittgenstein's TA deviant. However, this is not a disqualifying weakness: on the contrary, it simply renders the grounds on which it is initiated incorrigibly resistant to sceptical assaults in a way which would otherwise have been impossible. It does, however, give the appearance of obliging someone who uses it to take sides in the dispute between realists and anti-realists, which has been a prevalent theme of some recent Oxford philosophy.

As I understand it, anti-realists are committed by their doctrine to a denial of the objectivity of the truth of various kinds of statement. In particular, anti-realism repudiates the doctrine that the meaning of a sentence is given by its truth-conditions independent of our recognitional capacities — i.e. independent of our ability to recognise whether things in the world are or are not thus-and-so. By these lights, the realist conception of truth as objectively determined and transcending verification- or assertion-conditions ought to be abandoned.

Now the conclusion of the TA that concerns us limits itself to asserting only that language-users cannot *self-consistently* doubt the objectivity or disregard the importance of certain moral values. It does not claim to demonstrate directly, in accordance with the principle of bivalence, the objective existence of these values. It is therefore arguable that this way of putting the matter, in appealing, not to truth itself, but only to the unquestioning acceptance of what we cannot help but think true, implies commitment to a version of anti-realism.[20] If this were correct, it might render suspect this essay's pretences to be a defence of moral realism and make the project of grafting the core-game theory onto an account of historical necessity, which is taken by its exponents to be a realist theory, seem artificial.

The best way with this difficulty is to start by conceding that the moral realist's position, at least in the form in which I am defending it, is, so to speak, tinged with subjectivity, and it is on this account that it appears to converge with anti-realism. However, this subjective taint (if it matches that description) is not the sort of which the anti-realist can make use, nor is it such as to disentitle moral realists who admit to it to call themselves by that name. The TA on which my brand of moral realism relies makes no mention of 'recognitional capacities' and is entirely silent on the question as to whether truth can be verification-transcendent, as realists think it can and anti-realists proclaim it cannot. This is no mere evasion. The topics with which we are concerned are ethical, moral and historical, not epistemological, so talk of recognitional capacities and of verification procedures is conspicuously inapposite, given the issues before us. There is indeed a sort of subjectivity in which the anti-realist who wishes to talk the language of moral realism may feel he can afford to traffic. He may feel inclined to say that his moral evaluations are a subjective matter only in the sense that colour identification is a subjective matter. Both, he admits, depend on our recognitional abilities: but, he may add, appeal to these abilities in the case of moral values no more illegitimises someone's claim to call himself a moral realist, than it debars someone, who claims really to see the colours he correctly identifies, from calling misidentifications perceptual failures. There is no need for me to comment on the merits of this ingenious argument, for it is not the argument I employ. The TA on which my moral realism hinges has no more of a subjective shape than its *ad hominem* dimension confers, and this deals, not with 'knowing subjects', but with language-users and historical agents. There is no dealing here in epistemological certainties or in uncertainties either: for as I have just explained, there is no dealing in knowledge or certainty at all.

It has, indeed, been something of a mistake for moral realists to have allowed themselves to be drawn into the debate between realists and anti-realists through the adoption of such labels for their position as 'naturalist', 'descriptivist' and even 'cognitivist'. By so doing, they have implicitly accepted the premiss from which their 'anti-naturalist', 'prescriptivist' and 'non-cognitivist' opponents often proceed — i.e. that the issue is an epistemo-logical one, to be decided within the confines of Cartesian or Lockian theories of knowledge and with special reference to the so-called 'truth-theories' which have been parasitic on them. We do not need a 'theory' of truth to help us decide whether moral values play the sustaining role that I have argued they do play in the unquestioned (because unquestionable) reality of our lives and our language. What we do need to do is to examine that reality and our lives, considered as inseparable from it, and this is what the TA form helps us to do.

4.3 Labour power and moral powers

Let us return now to the Marxist theory of history and the role which is to be assigned to language and the values which sustain it within the base–superstructure model which Marx used to depict the workings of historical necessity. The question is not a new one, nor have orthodox Marxist theoreticians failed to address it. Stalin, whose abilities as a theorist it has become fashionable to underrate, discusses the matter in a polemic directed at the disciples of the Soviet linguist N.Y. Marr. His answers are illuminating, although, in my view, they take insufficient account of the possibilities allowed for by Marx's model and of the variety of distinctions which must be drawn between and within its various regions. Stalin says unambiguously that language is not part of the superstructure. His reason for this denial is that:[21]

> The superstructure is not directly connected with production, with man's productive activity. It is connected with production only indirectly through the economy, through the base, through the prism of changes wrought in the base by the changes in production ... Language, on the contrary, is connected with man's productive activity directly, and not only with man's productive activity, but with all his other activities in all spheres of work, from production to the base and from the base to the superstructure.

The intuition underlying this argument seems sound enough. One does feel disinclined to say that changes in the basic productive relations generate *language* in the same way as they are said to give rise to new legal forms and political institutions. The latter are, as we saw (3.41), relations in which social beings stand to one another, relations which may indeed require or be accompanied by appropriate linguistic innovations. However, such adaptations will themselves be activities — using old expressions in a new way, devising new descriptions to fit changed circumstances — not relationships which have resulted from activity of just this practical sort.

Yet Stalin's emphasis on the directness of the link between language and productive activity invites the supposition that language ought to be numbered among the productive forces which determine the superstructure in the last instance. However, this conclusion too is resisted. Although conceding that 'there does exist a certain analogy between language and the implements of production',[22] Stalin rejects the alternative of classifying it as such. He is equally suspicious of the idea that language is, so to speak, intermediate between the base and the superstructure. This is not straightforwardly incorrect, inasmuch as the sense in which we speak of language as a 'tool' is not the sense in which a tool, *qua objective* productive force, is a means of production. It may be impossible to envisage tool-making and tool-use in the absence of language; but it is implausible that language in and of itself, and in the absence of such objective forces as tools and raw materials, could produce material wealth. Nor is support to be found in the relevant texts for the postulation of some middle zone between infra- and superstructure which could accommodate language, and no explanatory purpose would be served by such a strategy, so long as language must be thought of, as we have tried all along to think of it, as inseparably tied to the human form of life. Nonetheless, Stalin completely fails, despite his own insistence on the direct connection between language and productive activity, to canvass the possibility that language might be sited among the *subjective* forces of production, along with such inherently human capacities as intellect and skill, although such a prospect can find textual justification and does nothing to diminish the base–superstructure model's explanatory power.

4.31 Objective and subjective forces

The distinction between objective and subjective productive forces is explicitly drawn by Marx. He speaks in *Capital* of the separation 'of subjective labour power from the objective conditions of labour' as being the 'real foundation in fact, and the starting point of capitalist production'.[23] In the *Grundrisse* he explains:[24]

The community itself appears as the first great force of production; particular kinds of production conditions (e.g.

stock-breeding, agriculture) develop particular modes of production and particular forces of production, subjective, appearing as qualities of individuals, as well as objective [ones].

Another passage in the chapter on capital makes it clear that he equates the subjective forces with what he there calls 'the intellectual' forces of production.[25] Marx also speaks of what he calls 'general social knowledge' as being a *direct force of production*.[26] Although he provides no list of productive forces, it is fairly obvious that the forces that Marx calls 'objective' will include such raw materials as are transformable into use-values, tools for effecting the transformation, and places in which the process of production is carried out, such as farms, factories and storage facilities.

Subjective productive forces are such as inhere in human subjects. They are the powers that agents bring to bear on objective productive forces in order to transform them into values. As Marx conceives of it, the production of value is such that the objective and subjective forces mutually require one another before it can occur. The question at once presents itself as to whether and in what terms we ought to assign priorities to these two forces.

Cohen tackles this issue by saying that the 'source of the development of the productive forces is subjective', but that it 'needs an objective medium which the stated conditions supply'.[27] These 'stated conditions' are the materials, tools and spaces just mentioned, and Cohen's way of putting the relation between the objective and subjective forces, while preserving their dialectical interdependence, nonetheless shows that the latter, in being a *source of development* have a kind of primacy, since it is the *development* of the productive forces which primarily determines social change. These subjective forces, then, constitute everything Marx means by labour power in the definition he offers of it in *Capital*: 'By labour power or capacity for labour is to be understood the aggregate of those mental and physical capabilities existing in a human being, which he exercises whenever he produces a use-value of any description.'[28]

That Marx regards physical as well as mental capabilities as constitutive of labour power shows that by 'subjective productive forces' he does not mean, as an absolute idealist might, something purely spiritual or mental, but only something which is intrinsic to human subjects. This emerges later in his discussion of capitalist production, when he says: 'Man himself, viewed as the impersonation of labour-power, is a natural object, a thing, although a living conscious thing, and labour is the manifestation of this power residing in him.'[29]

Interpretation of such passages demands care in balancing the Hegelian and materialist conceptions which co-exist in them. Man personifies certain of the productive forces, and that is the point of calling them 'subjective'. These forces must not, however, be conflated with Hegel's *Geist*, for they are not purely spiritual forces, nor is that which personifies them a purely spiritual being. The physiology of social beings is as relevant to the study of their productivity as is their psychology. Labour power, therefore, is a sum of physical and mental forces which belong to the material world in belonging to the human residents of that world. However, to say this is not to gainsay the obvious, but nonetheless important, truth that in the production of use-values, the intellectual faculties — especially the powers of reasoning, imagining and abstracting — must be regarded as pre-eminent elements in the make-up of the subjective productive forces. Because even quite rudimentary forms of production are inconceivable without such powers, as much would be clear even without the textual evidence supplied by Marx. As it is, we have the famous passage from his discussion in *Capital* of the labour process:[30]

We presuppose labour in a form that stamps it as exclusively human. A spider conducts operations that resemble those of a weaver, and a bee puts to shame many an architect in the construction of her cells. But what distinguishes the worst architect from the best of bees is this, that the architect raises his structure in imagination before he erects it in reality. At the end of every labour process, we get a result that already existed in the imagination of the labourer at its commencement.

The recognition that imagination and intellection were central to the subjective productive forces prompted Marx not only to make the radical division between human labour and animal activity that he makes in this passage, but also to distinguish what he called 'co-operative' from 'universal' labour. The latter represents the historical store of the collective achievements made possible by the subjective forces of production. It is the reservoir of humankind's theoretical and technological progress, which constitutes both the level of development of the productive forces at any given stage and the possibility of their further development. Once again, Marx's way of drawing the distinction is reminiscent of Hegel:

> Both kinds play their role in the process of production, both flow one into the other, but both are also differentiated. Universal labour is all scientific labour, all discovery and all invention. This labour depends partly on the co-operation of the living, and partly on the utilisation of the labour of those who have gone before. Co-operative labour, on the other hand, is the direct co-operation of individuals.[31]

4.32 Labour and language

It is true that Marx does not say specifically that language is a productive force or a constituent of labour power: but assuming as I do that he took it to be so, there is no special reason why he should have made a point of saying so. He was not engaged in elaborating a philosophy of language or constructing a 'theory of meaning': his concern was with theories of history and of political economy. The 'linguistic turn' was one that philosophy had yet to take, so he would not have had the preoccupations we tend to take for granted and would have felt no compelling need to spell out the role of language in his scheme of things. The proposition that human labour in its fullness includes human language is one that someone trained in the Hegelian tradition might very well take for granted.

It is very difficult, moreover, to see how Marx could have failed to include language within the scope of labour power, as Stalin was content to do, when the prominence that the above-cited passages accord to rationality, imagination and scientific ingenuity is taken into account. Marx, the materialist, could scarcely have envisaged these faculties as existing in men independent of their material realisation in the audial and visual mediums which language provides. Indeed, his earlier rejection of Hegel's logical essentialism would have driven him to say that our reasonings and imaginative discoveries just were their material realisation in our public expressive behaviour. Nor can it be accidental that Marx's way of distinguishing human architecture from insect constructions is reminiscent of Wittgenstein's distinction between animal signals and human speech (**PI**, i, 25). When Marx thought about human productive activity and its development, he was inevitably driven to thoughts about language and its development, and he makes the comparison explicitly in the *Grundrisse*.[32]

Furthermore, it really does not seem feasible that Marx could have described 'universal' labour in the terms he did without believing that it involved discourse and developments in discourse. We have no right to assume that he was unmindful of the fact that advances in science usually depend on and often amount to no more than innovations in symbolism and the discovery of new techniques for talking about the way things are.. Even the most cautiously orthodox exegesis of Marx on this point ought to be able to accommodate the thought that the conception of language as a form of labour power is implicit in the distinction between objective and subjective productive forces.

This conclusion can be supported by an independent argument, showing that the ability to use language is essential to productive activity. What blocks ready acceptance of this proposition is the thought that some productive operations are so rudimentary that animals or machines can perform them, and indeed the very possibility of mechanised production depends on this being so. Moreover, it will not do to rest the case for including language among the productive forces on examples of sophisticated operations which clearly require it, because the base–superstructure model's power to explain *all* epochal change depends partly on its being able to cope with societies in which production is precisely rudimentary.

Let us try to meet this difficulty by supposing two cases, (a) and (b), in which precisely the same basic operation — pounding with a pestle, say — is being performed. The pestle need only be of a very primitive sort, and the pounding need require the bare minimum of dexterity. The sole difference between the cases is that in (a) the operation is performed by a machine, of a sort so elementary that nobody will want to attribute to it the capacities that some philosophers have wished to attribute to computers and the like; while in case (b) the operator is a human person. What chiefly distinguishes the two operations? The difference is surely that they are differently initiated: in case (a) we speak of the operation being 'set in motion', an efficient cause being provided by a genuine agent, who performs a genuinely volitional action by throwing a switch or pulling a lever. In case (b), a verbal or gestural command sets the operator to work, as happens in the language-game played by Wittgenstein's builders. Thus, understanding and meaning enter into this example as they do not in case (a), and when we speak of the actions done in case (b) as being 'mechanical' actions, this is only an elliptical way of saying that they are very simple actions.

The requirements of meaning and understanding cannot be eliminated from (b) by imagining that the operation is initiated, not by another's command or even by a command the agent 'gives to himself', but by the flashing of a light or the sound of a whistle, mechanically produced. That innovation merely pushes the problem of explaining how the operator begins to expend his *physical* labour-power one step further back: for the response will be that the light or whistle act in case (b) as they do not in case (a), as signs or signals which the operator must *interpret correctly* if the work is to commence or continue. In other words, there must be rule-guided activity here, activity which is precisely *internally* related to understanding in being an instantiation or exemplification of it.

Neither is anything gained by imagining that the case-(b)-operator is involuntarily compelled to operate the pestle by a mechanically produced stimulus. This scenario simply reduces (b) to (a) by robbing the human operator of those faculties which distinguish him from a machine. The fact is that we are not, in case (a), witnessing the expenditure of labour-power properly so-called, but rather the *result* of the labour expended in the human activities of devising and constructing the machine and setting it in motion, and all these activities presuppose understanding and its evincements. We may conclude, therefore, that:

(1) language is a necessary condition for production in that labour-power is not expendable except by language-users, and
(2) that the case for classifying language among the subjective forces of production is made.

Of course, if it were only the case that language stimulated or enabled production, (1) would not be sufficient for (2). Such ideological phenomena as the Protestant work ethic may be considered necessary for production without being part of the forces of production in Marx's sense. However, the above argument does establish (2) by insisting on the internal connection between understanding an instruction and the productive activity by which such understanding is manifested.

4.4 Forces and powers

There is no need to repeat here the arguments elaborated in Chapter 2 which showed the indispensability of value-preservation to the internal coherence of language. The conclusion that language is among the productive forces which necessitate historical development leads inevitably to the proposition that the self-same moral necessity which was seen to be at the core of language plays a role in conditioning the historical process itself, in the sense that it sustains that process by sustaining language. It should no longer seem merely contingent that animals, who have neither language nor morals, have no history or historical development either.

It may be objected, however, that a force is not a power and that, *a fortiori*, a productive force is not a moral power. It is useful, in this regard, to start by reminding ourselves that the Marxian phrase for the ultimate determinants of the historical process is *Produktivkrafte*, which translates more literally as 'productive powers' than as 'productive forces'.[33] Nonetheless, it is not, strictly speaking, true that everything we designate as a productive force ought also to be classified as a power. Implements of production and raw materials *have* productive power, but they are not themselves powers. Still, labour power, as we have explained it (4.31), is a genuine power. It is the power to initiate, control, devise and sustain processes which produce use-values and create wealth.

Of course, powers are not all of a kind. Some powers are physical, others psychological or intellectual, and some sorts of power lend themselves to coercive employments, while yet others exercise only a restraining influence on some sorts of action. Moral powers strike me as being of this last sort. They set limits or constraints on what we may do or say and define the boundaries between ourselves and things or persons we must respect if we wish to preserve such values as truthfulness, justice and reverence. It is in setting these ethical limits that, as has been argued, they also establish, from 'within', as it were, the limits between coherent and incoherent discourse. It is of some importance — and a fact to which Holland has drawn attention in his penetrating discussions of Plato's ethics[34] — that geometry is a better guide to the understanding in this matter than is the mathematics of utilitarian ethics, arithmetic. For moral powers, in curbing rather than stimulating activity, resemble the boundaries of a geometric figure, beyond which are the limitless possibilities of formlessness. Such forms of power as are quantifiable arithmetically — steam-power, electric-power, atomic-power and so forth — are just the sorts which lend themselves to the calculations of the utilitarian (who need not, of course, be a moral cynic) and the moral cynic himself. These kinds of power can be multiplied to *seemingly* limitless extents, and it is this fascinating property which tempts the cynic to forget that the theories and pseudo-theories he devises or concocts about power and how to achieve more of it, as well as his calculations and miscalculations of the possibilities of dominance over others, are themselves made possible only by the enabling constraints which moral powers impose.

4.5 An 'Hegelianised' base?

A different sort of objection may arise from the suspicion that, by importing the notion of a moral power into the Marxist theory of history at the level of the productive forces, I have in effect Hegelianised the base of the base–superstructure model, thereby transforming it from a conceptual tool in a materialist explanation into a mere trope of idealist metaphysics. The whole novelty and advantage of Marx's account, so this objection runs, is that it explains our moral and spiritual lives in terms of material forces and powers, and to make our moral powers part of that explanation is to re-invert the dialectic that Marx was so anxious to set on its feet.

To this I would respond that I have Hegelianised the base, only to the extent that Marx himself permitted it to remain Hegelianised. I have been at pains to emphasise that the influence of Hegel on Marx's thought is far deeper and more enduring than commentators like Cohen and Althusser have been prepared to allow. It follows that the Marxist explanation of how epochal change is generated is misunderstood, unless account is

taken of the very real sense in which Marx believed Hegel to have
arrived at a vision, albeit a distorted one, of the truth. As Meikle
puts it:[35]

> Marx rejects the idealist starting point, but he does not
> reject Hegel's thought root and branch. He rejects it as
> a fantastic inversion of the truth, not as a falsehood. He
> retains the potent categorical structure developed by
> Hegel . . .

While I therefore allow that the viability of my account of the
role played by moral powers in determining historical change
depends on allowing the Hegelian features of Marx's thought to
emerge, I do not agree that the base has thereby been idealised or
the material character of the productive forces lost to sight. The
fear that this has happened stems from a misunderstanding of the
meaning of 'materialism' as Marx employs the term. Marxists are
emphatically not obliged to deny the existence of spiritual
realities, nor are they committed to any radically physicalist
doctrine concerning the forces sustaining social processes. All
dialectical materialism requires is a belief in the knowability of
material objects and processes and in the independence of these
from the consciousness of epistemic subjects, coupled with the
stipulation that such spiritual things as there are cannot exist
independently of the material conditions which determine their
possibilities in the last instance. These are all propositions which
a thoroughgoing Hegelian would have to deny; for although they
allow for enriched, organicist and holistic explanations of
change and are, thus, prophylactic against atomistic and
reductionist brands of materialism, they disallow spiritualistic,
logicist or idealist metaphysics, and debar explanations in which
spiritual forces are the sole primary determinants of material
events.

These rules for a dialectical materialist account have been met
at each stage in the elaboration of my account of semantic and
historical necessity. The core-language-games, whose function is
value-preservation, are not said to be the sole, but only among
the necessary conditions for semantic coherence. They are, like
all of language, dependent for their existence on the existence of
the material world and the basic natural regularities operative in
it. The so-called autonomy of grammar does not contradict, but
rather requires, that this be so. Nowhere have I claimed that

either natural or normative regularities are in any sense unknowable or dependent on the consciousness of language-users.

Furthermore, as regards historical materialism, it is freely acknowledged that objective and subjective productive forces are interdependent, and that the former are nothing other than material things and processes of a relatively unmysterious kind. Even at the ultimate level of subjective productivity or labour power, there is no pretence that language and the moral powers enabling it are sole occupants of the region. Obviously physical strength and physiological make-up are among the factors which constitute labour-power. Equally obviously there must be material conditions which allow for the identification and re-identification of human individuals, be they considered in their .aspect as labourers or as users of language. Thee individuals must be supposed to have bodies and the ability to use them in set ways, before any preservation of their moral values or the generation of use-values can take place.

4.6 Conclusion

Our examination of Wittgensteinian semantics and further enquiry into Marxian historiography have yielded a picture according to which the preservation of moral values must be counted among the necessary conditions for the existence of language (conceived of as Wittgenstein came to conceive of it), and for historical change (understood as Marx understood it). These values, it transpires, are genuine powers, capable of conferring coherence on the vast field of human linguistic activity and of contributing, by so doing, to the dynamic whereby social formations are created and decease. Like most philosophers' pictures, this one is, doubtless, capable of misleading us. Yet philosophers can, in the last resort, avoid such pictures only at the cost of marginalising the interest of what they have to say. In particular, they cannot avoid them if they wish to combat the influence of other world-pictures which they think dangerous or stultifying.

I submit that the picture of a world unified and vitalised by moral powers is less dangerous than the empiricist picture of a world that is morally dead. The latter image has been with us since the eighteenth century and it has fed the cynicism of politicians, who have sought the assistance of a variety of theories — systems analysis, structuralism and even positivistic versions of Marxism — in their pursuit of power and in their struggle to retain it. It has inhibited interest in moral philosophy among students of political science — a field once held to be virtually indistinguishable from ethics. More seriously, the image of a morally lifeless world has encouraged a form of international brinkmanship by leading statesmen to think that coercive power is the only power that counts, so that our present world has become the most dangerous place our kind has ever inhabited.

However, beyond asserting that my account has more truth and less danger in it than the doctrines which ethical non-cognitivists and moral cynics favour, I do not want to make further claims for its powers of explanation. I do not, for instance, claim that each revolutionary liberation of productive forces leads to an increased dominion of the moral powers over the lives of men. That is a millinearian vision which some have found enticing, but philosophy done in a sober spirit ought not to embrace it. There can be no warrant, either in observation or in logic, for the supposition that peoples at a lower level of economic development, having a less complex mode of social interaction or more rudimentary languages than ours, are morally worse off than we are or can expect to be. I have argued only that our moral values *sustain* the possibility of our language and our lives together, and am content to observe Wittgenstein's silence as to what more they may do.

Notes

1. I. Kant, *Critique of pure reason*, N. Kemp Smith (trans.) (Macmillan, London, 1974), A11/B25, original emphasis.
2. A.W. Wood, *Kant's moral religion* (Cornell University Press, Ithaca and London), 1970.
3. J. Hintikka, 'Transcendental arguments genuine and spurious', *Nous*, vol. vi, no. 3 (1972), p. 274. For a criticism of Hintakka's reading of Kant's idea of a mode of knowledge, see A. Grayling, *The refutation of scepticism* (Duckworth, London, 1985), pp. 79–83.
4. I. Kant, *Critique of pure reason*, B xiii.
5. Ibid., B xviii.
6. I. Kant, *Critique of judgement*, J.H. Bernard (trans.) (Macmillan, London, 1914), pp. 18–19.
7. J.D. Alexander, 'Kant, Hegel and the problem of grounds', *Kant-Studien*, no. 70 (1979), p. 467.

8. G.F. Hegel, *Science of logic*, A.V. Miller (trans.) (Allen and Unwin, London, 1969), p. 584, original emphasis.

9. For notable exceptions to this tendency, see C. Taylor, 'The validity of transcendental arguments', *Proceedings of the Aristotelian Society*, vol. 53 (1979), pp. 151–65; and R. Rorty, 'Transcendental arguments, self-reference and pragmatism' in P. Bieri, R.P. Horstman and L. Krüger (eds), *Transcendental arguments and science* (Reidel, Dordrecht, Boston and London, 1979), pp. 77–103. Rorty's article is an attempt to connect TAs with the historicist tradition.

10. P.F. Strawson, *Individuals* (Methuen, London, 1959).

11. S. Shoemaker, *Self-knowledge and self-identity* (Ithaca, New York, 1963).

12. S. Körner, 'The impossibility of transcendental deductions', *The Monist*, vol. 51, no. 3 (July 1967), pp. 317–31.

13. B. Stroud, 'Transcendental arguments', *The Journal of Philosophy*, vol. 15, no. 9 (May 1968), pp. 241–56.

14. M.S. Gram, 'Transcendental arguments', *Nous*, vol. v, no. 1 (February 1971), pp. 15–26.

15. P.M.S. Hacker, 'Are transcendental arguments a version of verificationism?', *American Philosophical Quarterly*, vol. 9, no. 1 (1972), pp. 78–84. Interestingly, although Hacker concluded in this paper that the 'Kantian turn' in recent philosophy may have brought us closer to Koningsberg in the 1780s than to Vienna in the 1920s (p. 85) — by which I take him to mean that Wittgenstein was closer to Kant than to positivism — in the revised edition of his *Insight and illusion*, pp. 211–14, he is firm in holding that it is a mistake to take Wittgenstein to be constructing TAs in the private language argument of the *Philosophical investigations*.

16. A.C. Genova, 'Good transcendental arguments', *Kant-Studien*, no. 4 (1984), pp. 469–95.

17. P.F. Strawson, *Scepticism and naturalism: some varieties* (Methuen, London, 1985), p. 23.

18. A. Grayling, *The refutation of scepticism* (Duckworth, London, 1985), pp. 17–113.

19. K. Marx, *Introduction* to *A contribution to the critique of Hegel's 'Philosophy of right'* in Joseph O'Malley (ed.), *Critique of Hegel's 'Philosophy of right'*, by K. Marx, Annette Jolin (trans.) (Cambridge University Press, Cambridge, 1976), p. 137 original emphasis.

20. For an argument linking weak or 'B-option' TAs to anti-realism in respect of perceptual discourse, see Grayling, *The refutation of scepticism*, pp. 110–13.

21. J. Stalin, 'Marxism and linguistics' in B. Franklin (ed.), *The essential Stalin* (Croom Helm, London, 1973), p. 411.

22. Ibid., p. 431.

23. Marx, *Capital*, vol. 1, p. 535.

24. K. Marx, *Grundrisse*, M. Nicolaus (trans.) (Penguin, Harmondsworth, 1973), p. 495.

25. Ibid., p. 502.

26. Ibid., p. 706, original emphasis.

27. G.A. Cohen, *Karl Marx's theory of history. A defence* (Oxford University Press, 1978), p. 42.

28. Marx, *Capital*, vol. 1, p. 164.

29. Ibid., p. 196.

30. Ibid., p. 174.

31. Marx, *Capital*, vol. 3, p. 104.

32. Marx, *Grundrisse*, p. 85.

33. For an elaboration of this point, see Cohen, *Karl Marx's theory of history*, pp. 37–8.

34. R.F. Holland, 'Absolute ethics' in *Against empiricism* (Basil Blackwell, Oxford, 1980), pp. 134–5.

35. S. Meikle, *Essentialism in the thought of Karl Marx* (Duckworth, London, 1985), p. 41.

Bibliography

Works by Marx and Engels

Engels F., (1970) *Socialism: Utopian and Scientific,* in *Marx–Engels, Selected Works,* Lawrence and Wishart, London, pp.394–428

—— (1976) *Principles of Communism,* in *Marx–Engels, Collected Works,* vol. 6, Progress Publishers, Moscow and Lawrence and Wishart, London, pp.341–357

Marx K., (1954) *Capital,* vol. 1, S. Moore and E. Aveling (trans.), F. Engels (ed.), Lawrence and Wishart, London

—— (1956) *Capital,* vol. 2, F. Engels (ed.), Lawrence and Wishart, London

—— (1959) *Capital, A Critique of Political Economy,* vol. 3, F. Engels (ed.), Lawrence and Wishart, London

—— (1970) *Preface to a Contribution to the Critique of Political Economy,* in *Marx–Engels Selected Works,* Lawrence and Wishart, London

—— (1973) *Grundrisse,* M. Nicolaus (trans.), Penguin, Harmondsworth

—— (1975) *Difference Between the Democritean and Epicurean Philosophy of Nature,* in *Marx–Engels, Collected Works,* vol. 1, Progress Publishers, Moscow and Lawrence and Wishart, London, pp.25–106

—— (1975) *On the Jewish Question,* in *Marx–Engels, Collected Works,* vol. 3, Progress Publishers, Moscow and Lawrence and Wishart, London, pp.146–174

—— (1975) *Economic and Philosophical Manuscripts of 1844,* in *Marx–Engels, Collected Works,* vol. 3, Progress Publishers, Moscow and Lawrence and Wishart, London, pp.229–326

—— (1976) *Theses on Feuerbach* [original version], in *Marx–Engels, Collected Works,* vol. 5, Progress Publishers, Moscow, pp.3–5

—— (1976) *Theses on Feuerbach* [edited by Engels], in *Marx–Engels, Collected Works,* vol. 5, Progress Publishers, Moscow, pp.6–9

—— (1976), Critique of Hegel's *'Philosophy of Right',* Joseph O'Malley (ed.), Annette Jolin (trans.), Cambridge University Press, Cambridge

—— (1979) *The Eighteenth Brumaire of Louis Bonaparte,* in *Marx–Engels, Collected Works* vol. 11, Lawrence and Wishart, London, pp.99–197

—— (1979) The Letters of Karl Marx, Saul K. Padover (trans.), Prentice Hall, Englewood Cliffs, New Jersey

Marx K. and Engels F., (1967) *The Communist Manifesto,* S. Aveling (trans.), with *Introduction and Notes* by A.J.P. Taylor, Penguin, Harmondsworth

—— (1975) *The Holy Family, or Critique of Critical Criticism,* in *Marx–Engels, Collected Works,* vol. 4, Progress Publishers, Moscow and Lawrence and Wishart, London, pp.5–211

—— (1976) *The German Ideology. Critique of Modern German Philosophy According to its Representatives Feuerbach, B. Baver and Stirner, and of German Socialism According to its Various Prophets,* in *Marx–Engels, Collected Works,* vol. 5, Progress Publishers, Moscow, pp.19–539

—— (1976) *Manifesto of the Communist Party*, in *Marx–Engels, Collected Works*, vol. 6, Progress Publishers, Moscow and Lawrence and Wishart, London, pp.477–519

Works by Wittgenstein

Wittgenstein L., (1961) *Notebooks 1914–1916*, G.H. von Wright and G.E.M. Anscombe (eds), G.E.M. Anscombe (trans.), Basil Blackwell, Oxford
—— (1961) *Tractatus Logico-Philosophicus*, D.F. Pears and B.F. McGuinness (trans.), Routledge and Kegan Paul, London
—— (1967) *Letters from Ludwig Wittgenstein with a Memoir*, B.F. McGuiness (ed.), L. Furtmuller (trans.), Basil Blackwell, Oxford
—— (1929) 'Some Remarks on Logical Form', *Proceedings of the Aristotelian Society*, supp.vol. 9, pp.162–171
—— (1965) 'Wittgenstein's Lecture on Ethics', in *Philosophical Review*, vol. 84, pp.3–26
—— (1958) *The Blue and Brown Books*, Basil Blackwell, Oxford
—— (1978) *Remarks on the Foundations of Mathematics*, G.H. von Wright, R. Rhees and G.E.M. Anscombe (eds), G.E.M. Anscombe (trans.), Basil Blackwell, Oxford
—— (1958) *Philosophical Investigations*, G.E.M. Anscombe and R. Rhees (eds), G.E.M. Anscombe (trans.), Basil Blackwell, Oxford, 2nd ed
—— (1967) *Zettel*, G.E.M. Anscombe and G.H von Wright (eds), G.E.M. Anscombe (trans.), Basil Blackwell, Oxford
—— (1969) *On Certainty*, G.E.M. Anscombe and G.H. von Wright (eds), D. Paul and G.E.M. Anscombe (trans.), Basil Blackwell, Oxford
—— (1977) *Remarks on Colour*, G.E.M. Anscombe (ed.), L.L. McAlister and M. Schättle (trans.), Basil Blackwell, Oxford
—— (1966) *Lectures and Conversations on Aesthetics, Psychology and Religious Belief*, C. Barrett (ed.), Basil Blackwell, Oxford
—— (1979) 'Remarks on Frazer's Golden Bough', J. Beversluis (trans.), in C.G. Luckhardt (ed.), *Wittgenstein Sources and Perspectives*, Harvester Press, Hassocks, pp.61–81
—— (1980) *Culture and Value*, G.H. von Wright and H. Nyman (eds), P. Winch (trans.), Basil Blackwell, Oxford

General Literature

Alexander J.D., (1979) 'Kant, Hegel and the Problem of Grounds', in *Kant–Studien*, vol. 70, pp.451–470
Althusser L., (1969) *For Marx*, Ben Brewster (trans.), Allen Lane, The Penguin Press, London
—— (1971) *Lenin and Philosophy and Other Essays*, Ben Brewster (trans.), New Left Books, London
Anscombe G.E.M., (1958) 'Modern Moral Philosophy', in *Philosophy*, vol. 33, pp.1–19

Bibliography

—— (1959) An Introduction to Wittgenstein's *Tractatus,* Hutchinson, London

—— (1968) 'On Brute Facts', in J.J. Thomson and G. Dworkin (eds), *Ethics,* Harper and Row, New York, pp.71–75

Ayer A.J., (1968) 'Can there be a Private Language?' in G. Pitcher (ed.), *Wittgenstein, A Collection of Critical Essays,* Macmillan, London, pp.251–266

—— (1985) *Wittgenstein,* Weidenfeld and Nicolson, London

Baker G.P., (1979) *'Verehrung und Verkehrung',* Waismann and Wittgenstein, in C.G. Luckhardt (ed.), *Wittgenstein Sources and Perspectives,* Harvester Press, Hassocks, Sussex, pp.243–285

Baker G.P. and Hacker P.M.S., (1980) *Wittgenstein Understanding and Meaning,* Basil Blackwell, Oxford

—— (1984) *Scepticism Rules and Language,* Basil Blackwell, Oxford

—— (1985) *Wittgenstein Rules, Grammar and Necessity,* Basil Blackwell, Oxford

Barker P., (1980) 'Hertz and Wittgenstein', in *Studies in History and Philosophy of Science,* vol. 11, no. 3, pp.243–256

Blackwell K., (1981) 'The Early Wittgenstein and the Middle Russell', in I. Block (ed.), *Perspectives on the Philosophy of Wittgenstein,* Basil Blackwell, Oxford, pp.1–30

Bolton D., (1982) 'Life-Form and Idealism', in G. Vesey (ed.), *Idealism Past and Present,* Royal Institute of Philosophy Lectures, Series 13, Press Syndicate, University of Cambridge, pp.269–284

Boltzman L., (1960) 'Theories as Representations', in *Philosophy of Science,* A. David and S. Morgenbesser (eds) Meridian Books, New York, pp.245–252

—— (1974) *Theoretical Physics and Philosophical Problems,* B. McGuinness (ed.), D. Reidel Publishing Co., Dordrecht and Boston.

Broda E., (1983) *Ludwig Boltzman,* Ox Bow Press, Connecticut

Canfield J., (1981) *Wittgenstein Language and World,* University of Massachussets Press, Amherst

Cavell S., (1979) *The Claim of Reason,* Clarendon Press, Oxford

Churchill J., (1983) 'The Coherence of the Concept "Language-Game"', in *Philosophical Investigations,* vol. 6, no. 4, pp.239–258

Cioffi F., (1981) 'Wittgenstein and the Fire Festivals', in Irving Block (ed.), *Perspectives on the Philosophy of Wittgenstein,* Basil Blackwell, Oxford, pp.212–237

Cohen G.A., (1978) *Karl Marx's Theory of History. A Defence,* Oxford University Press, Oxford

—— (1983) 'A Reply to Four Critics of *Karl Marx's Theory of History',* in *Analyse und Kritik,* vol. 5, no. 2, pp.195–223

Cohen G.A., (1983) 'Reconsidering Historical Materialism', in J.R. Pennock and J.W. Chapman (eds), *Nomos,* vol. 26, *Marxism,* New York and London, pp.227–251

—— (1985) 'Nozick on Appropriation', in *New Left Review,* no. 150, pp.89–105

Dampier-Whetham W.C.D., (1930) *A History of Science,* Cambridge University Press, Cambridge.

Bibliography

Darwin C., (1967) *The Origin of Species*, Everyman, London and New York

Davidson D., (1984) *Inquiries into Truth and Interpretation*, Oxford University Press, New York

Donagan A., (1968) 'Wittgenstein on Sensation', in G. Pitcher (ed.), *Wittgenstein. The Philosophical Investigations*, Doubleday, Garden City, New Jersey, pp.324–351

Douglas M., (1966) *Purity and Danger*, Routledge and Kegan Paul, London

Drury M.O'C., (1981) 'Conversations with Wittgenstein', in Rush Rhees (ed.), *Ludwig Wittgenstein: Personal Recollections*, Basil Blackwell, Oxford, pp.112–189

—— (1983) 'Letters to a Student of Philosophy—I', D. Lee (ed.), in *Philosophical Investigations*, vol. 6, no. 2, pp.76–102

—— (1983) 'Letters to a Student of Philosophy—II', D. Lee (ed.), in *Philosophical Investigations*, vol. 6, no. 3, pp.159–174

Dummett M., (1968) 'Wittgenstein's Philosophy of Mathematics' in G. Pitcher (ed.), *Wittgenstein the Philosophical Investigations*, Macmillan, London, pp.420–447

—— (1978) *Truth and Other Enigmas*, Duckworth, London

—— (1981) 'Frege and Wittgenstein', in I. Block (ed.), *Perspectives on the Philosophy of Wittgenstein*, Basil Blackwell, Oxford, pp.31–42

Durkheim E., (1915) *The Elementary Forms of the Religious Life*, George Allen and Unwin, London

Eagleton T., (1982) 'Wittgenstein's Friends', in *New Left Review*, no. 135, pp.64–90

Easton S.M., (1983) *Humanist Marxism and Wittgensteinian Social Philosophy*, Manchester University Press, Manchester

Falck C., (1985) 'The Process of Meaning-Creation: A Transcendental Argument', in *Review of Metaphysics*, vol. 38, pp.503–528

Foot P., (1978) *Virtues and Vices and Other Essays in Moral Philosophy*, Basil Blackwell, Oxford

Frege G., (1950) *The Foundations of Arithmetic*, J.L. Austin (trans.), Basil Blackwell, Oxford

—— (1952) *Translations from the Philosophical Writings of Gottlob Frege*, P. Geach and M. Black (eds.), Basil Blackwell, Oxford

Geach P.T. (1967) 'Good and Evil', in P. Foot (ed.), *Theories of Ethics*, Oxford University Press, Oxford, pp.64–73

Genova A.C., (1984) 'Good Transcendental Arguments', in *Kant-Studien*, vol. 4, pp.469–495

Geras N., (1985) 'The Controversy About Marx and Justice', in *New Left Review*, no. 150, pp.47–85

Gram M.S., (1971) 'Transcendental Arguments', in *Nous*, vol. 5, no. 1, pp.15–26

—— (1971) 'Privacy and Language', in E.D. Klemke (ed.), *Essays on Wittgenstein*, University of Illinois Press, Urbana, Chicago and London, pp.298–327

Gramsci A., (1978) *Selections from Political Writings, 1921–1926*, Quintin Hoare (trans. and ed.), Lawrence and Wishart, London

Grayling A., (1985) *The Refutation of Scepticism*, Duckworth, London

Gruber H.E., (1974) *Darwin on Man. A Psychological Study of Scientific Creativity*, Wildwood House, London

Hacker P.M.S. (1972), *Insight and Illusion*, 1st edition, Oxford University Press, Oxford

—— (1972) 'Are Transcendental Arguments a Version of Verificationism?', in *American Philosophical Quarterly*, vol. 9, no. 1, pp.78–85

—— (1979) 'Semantic Holism: Frege and Wittgenstein', in C.G. Luckhardt (ed.), *Wittgenstein Sources and Perspectives*, Harvester Press, Hassocks, Sussex, pp.213–242

—— (1981) 'The Rise and Fall of the Picture Theory', in Irving Block (ed.), *Perspectives on the Philosophy of Wittgenstein*, Basil Blackwell, Oxford, pp.85–109

—— (1986) *Insight and Illusion*, 2nd edition, Oxford University Press, Oxford

Hare R.M., (1952) *The Language of Morals*, Oxford University Press, Oxford

—— (1963) *Freedom and Reason*, Oxford University Press, Oxford

—— (1967) 'Geach: Good and Evil', in P. Foot (ed.), *Theories of Ethics*, Oxford University Press, Oxford, pp.74–82

Hegel G.W.F., (1929) *Science of Logic*, vol. i, W.H. Jonston and L.G. Struthers (trans.), George Allen and Unwin, London

—— (1949) *The Phenomenology of Mind*, J. Baillie (trans.), George Allen and Unwin, London, Humanities Press, New York

—— (1969) *Science of Logic*, A.V. Miller (trans.), Allen and Unwin, London

—— (1970) *Hegel's Philosophy of Nature*, A.V. Miller (trans.), Oxford University Press, Oxford

Hertz H., (1956) *The Principles of Mechanics*, W.E. Jones and J.T. Walley (trans.), Dover Publications, New York

Hintikka J., (1972) 'Transcendental Arguments: Genuine and Spurious', in *Nous*, vol. 6, no. 3, pp.274–281

Hintikka M.B. and Hintikka J., (1986) *Investigating Wittgenstein*, Basil Blackwell, Oxford

Hoffman J., (1983) *Marxism, Revolution and Democracy*, B.R. Grüner, Amsterdam

—— (1984) *The Gramscian Challenge. Coercion and Consent in Marxist Political Theory*, Basil Blackwell, Oxford

Holiday A., (1985) 'Wittgenstein's Silence: Philosophy, Ritual and the Limits of Language', in *Language & Communication*, vol. 5, no. 2, pp. 133–142

Holland R.F., (1980) *Against Empiricism*, Basil Blackwell, Oxford

Ilyenkov E.V., (1977) *Dialectical Logic, Essays on its History and Theory*, H. Campbell Creighton (trans.), Progress Publishers, Moscow

—— (1982) *The Dialectics of the Abstract and the Concrete in Marx's Capital*, S. Syrouatkin (trans.), Progress Publishers, Moscow

—— (1982) *Leninist Dialectics and the Metaphysics of Positivism*, New Park Publications, London

Isenberg A., (1968) 'Deontology and the Ethics of Lying', in J.J.

Thomson and G. Dworkin (eds), *Ethics*, Harper and Row, New York, pp.163–185

Janik A. and Toulmin S. (1973) *Wittgenstein's Vienna*, Weidenfeld and Nicholson, London

Janik A., (1979) 'Wittgenstein, Ficker and *Der Brenner*' in C.G. Luckhardt (ed.), *Wittgenstein Sources and Perspectives*, Harvester Press, Hassocks, Sussex, pp.161–189

Kamenka E., (1962) *The Ethical Foundations of Marxism*, Routledge and Kegan Paul, London

Kant I., (1914) *Critique of Judgement*, J.H. Bernard (trans.), Macmillan, London

—— (1943) *Critique of Pure Reason*, J.M.D. Meiklejohn (trans.), Dent, London

—— (1953) *Prolegomena to Any Future Metaphysics*, P.G. Lucas (trans.), Manchester University Press, Manchester

—— (1974) *Critique of Pure Reason*, N. Kemp-Smith (trans.), Macmillan, London

Kenny A., (1966) 'Cartesian Privacy', in G. Pitcher (ed.), *Wittgenstein. The Philosophical Investigations*, Macmillan, London, pp.352–370

—— (1973) *Wittgenstein*, Penguin, Harmondsworth

—— (1981) 'Wittgenstein's Early Philosophy of Mind', in Block op.cit., pp.140–147

—— (1984) *The Legacy of Wittgenstein*, Basil Blackwell, Oxford

King J., (1981) 'Recollections of Wittgenstein', in R. Rhees (ed.), *Wittgenstein: Personal Recollections*, Basil Blackwell, Oxford, pp.83–90

Klemke E.D., (1971) 'The Ontology of Wittgenstein's *Tractatus*', in E.D. Klemke (ed.) *Essays on Wittgenstein*, University of Illinois Press, Urbana, Chicago, London, pp.104–119

Kolakowski L., (1978) *Main Currents of Marxism*, vol. 1, *The Founders*, P.S. Falla (trans.), Oxford University Press, Oxford

Körner S., (1967) 'The Impossibility of Transcendental Deductions', in *The Monist*, vol. 51, no. 3, pp.317–331

Kripke S.A., (1982) *Wittgenstein on Rules and Private Language: An Elementary Exposition*, Basil Blackwell, Oxford

Leavis F.R., (1981) 'Memories of Wittgenstein', in R. Rhees (ed.), *Wittgenstein: Personal Recollections*, Basil Blackwell, Oxford, pp.62–82

Lee D. (ed.), (1980) *Wittgenstein's Lectures, Cambridge 1930–1932*, Basil Blackwell, Oxford

Locke J., (1959) *An Essay Concerning Human Understanding*, A. Campbell-Fraser (ed.), Dover, New York

Lovibond S., (1983) *Realism and Imagination in Ethics*, Basil Blackwell, Oxford

Lukes S., (1973) *Individualism*, Basil Blackwell, Oxford

—— (1982) 'Can the Base be Distinguished from the Superstructure?', in *Analyse und Kritik*, vol. 4, no. 2, pp.211–222

—— (1982) 'Marxism, Morality and Justice', in G.H.R. Parkinson (ed.), *Marx and Marxisms*, Cambridge University Press, Cambridge, pp. 177–206

—— (1985) *Marxism and Morality*, Oxford University Press, Oxford

Bibliography

McDowell J., (1978) 'Are Moral Requirements Hypothetical Imperatives?', in *Proceedings of the Aristotelian Society*, supp.vol. 52, pp.13–30
—— (1979) 'Virtue and Reason', in *The Monist*, vol. 62, no. 3, pp.331–350
McLellan D., (1970) *Marx Before Marxism*, Macmillan, London and
Basingstoke
—— (1973) *Karl Marx*, Macmillan, London
McGinn C., (1984) *Wittgenstein on Meaning*, Basil Blackwell, Oxford
McGuinness B., (1979) 'Wittgenstein's "Intellectual Nursery Training"',
in *Wittgenstein, The Vienna Circle and Critical Rationalism*, Proceedings of
the 3rd International Wittgenstein Symposium, Kirchberg am
Wechsel, pp.33–40
McGuinness B., (1981) 'The So-Called Realism of Wittgenstein's
Tractatus' in Block, op. cit., pp.60–73
—— (1982) 'Freud and Wittgenstein', in B. McGuinness (ed.),
Wittgenstein and his Times, Basil Blackwell, Oxford, pp.27–43
Malcolm N., (1958) *Ludwig Wittgenstein: A Memoir*, Oxford University
Press, London, New York and Toronto
—— (1982) 'Wittgenstein and Idealism', in G. Vesey (ed.), *Idealism Past
and Present*, Royal Institute of Philosophy Lectures, Series 13, Press
Syndicate University of Cambridge, pp.249–368
Mays W., (1979) 'Wittgenstein in Manchester', in *Language, Logic and
Philosophy*, Proceedings of the 4th International Wittgenstein Sym-
posium, Kirchberg/Wechsel, Austria, pp.171–178
Meikle S., (1985) *Essentialism in the Thought of Karl Marx*, Duckworth,
London
Mèszàros I., (1970) *Marx's Theory of Alienation*, Merlin Press, London
Moran J., (1972) 'Wittgenstein and Russia', in *New Left Review*, no. 73,
pp.85–96
Nielsen K., (1985) 'On Finding One's Feet in. Philosophy: From
Wittgenstein to Marx', in *Metaphilosophy*, vol. 16, no. 1, pp.1–11
Nyíri J.C., (1982) 'Wittgenstein's Later Work in Relation to Conservatism',
in B. McGuinness (ed.), *Wittgenstein and his Times*, Basil Blackwell,
Oxford, pp.108–120
Pascal F., (1981) 'A Personal Memoir', in Rush Rhees (ed.), *Ludwig
Wittgenstein: Personal Recollections*, Basil Blackwell, Oxford, pp.26–62
Pears D., (1971) *Wittgenstein*, Fontana/Collins, London
—— (1979) 'The Relation Between Wittgenstein's Picture Theory of
Propositions and Russell's Theories of Judgement', in C.G. Luckhardt
(ed.), *Wittgenstein Sources and Perspectives*, Harvester Press, Hassocks,
Sussex, pp.190–212
—— (1981) 'The Logical Independence of Elementary Propositions', in
Irving Block (ed.), *Perspectives on the Philosophy of Wittgenstein*, Basil
Blackwell, Oxford, pp.74–84
Phillips Griffiths A. and MacIntosh J.J., (1969) 'Transcendental
Arguments', *Proceedings of the Aristotelian Society*, supp.vol. 43, pp.165–
193
Pitcher G., (1964) *The Philosophy of Wittgenstein*, Englewood Cliffs, New
Jersey
Pitkin H.F., (1972) *Wittgenstein and Justice*, University of California Press,
Berkeley, Los Angeles, London

Plato (1974) *The Republic,* D. Lee (trans.), Penguin, Harmondsworth

Rhees R., (1966) 'Can There Be a Private Language?' in Pitcher (ed.), op. cit., pp.267–285

—— (1981) 'Postscript', in *Ludwig Wittgenstein: Personal Recollections,* Basil Blackwell, Oxford, pp.190–232

—— (1982) 'Wittgenstein on Language and Ritual', in B. McGuinness (ed.), *Wittgenstein and his Times,* Basil Blackwell, Oxford

—— (1984) (ed.) *Recollections of Wittgenstein,* Oxford University Press, Oxford

Ring M., (1983) 'Baker and Hacker on Section One of the *Philosophical Investigations',* in *Philosophical Investigations,* vol. 6, no. 4, pp.259–275

—— (1986) 'Reply to Siemens', in *Philosophical Investigations,* vol. 9, no. 3, pp.225–228

Rorty R., (1971) 'Verificationism and Transcendental Arguments', in *Nous,* vol. 5, no. 1, pp.3–14

Rorty R., (1979) 'Transcendental Arguments, Self-Reference and Pragmatism', in P. Bieri, R.P. Horstman and L. Krüger (eds), *Transcendental Arguments and Science,* Reidel, Dordrecht, Boston and London, pp.77–103

Rubenstein D., (1981) *Marx and Wittgenstein,* Routledge and Kegan Paul, London, Boston and Henley

Russell B., (1903) *The Principles of Mathematics,* Allen and Unwin, London

—— (1905) 'On Denoting', in R.C. Marsh (ed.), *Logic and Knowledge,* Allen and Unwin, London, 1956, pp.41–56

—— (1908) 'Mathematical Logic as Based on The Theory of Types', in Marsh, op. cit., pp.59–102

—— (1918) 'The Philosophy of Logical Atomism', in Marsh, op. cit., pp.177–281

Searle J., (1969) *Speech Acts,* Cambridge University Press, Cambridge

—— (1983) *Intentionality,* Cambridge University Press, Cambridge

Sève L., (1978) *Man in Marxist Theory,* J. McGreal (trans.), Harvester Press, Sussex, Humanities Press, New Jersey

Shoemaker S., (1963) *Self-Knowledge and Self-Identity,* Ithaca, New York

Siemens R.L., (1986) 'Merrill Ring on Baker and Hacker', in *Philosophical Investigations,* vol. 9, no. 3, pp.216–244

Sraffa P., (1960) *Production of Commodities by Means of Commodities,* Cambridge University Press, Cambridge

Steedman I., (1977) *Marx after Sraffa,* New Left Books, London

Stalin J., (1972) *Marxism and Problems of Linguistics,* Foreign Languages Press, Peking

—— (1973) 'Marxism and Linguistics', in B. Franklin (ed.), *The Essential Stalin,* Croom Helm, London, pp.411–431

Stenius E., (1960) *Wittgenstein's Tractatus,* Basil Blackwell, Oxford

—— (1981) 'The Picture Theory and Wittgenstein's Later Attitude to It', in Irving Block (ed.), *Perspectives on the Philosophy of Wittgenstein,* Basil Blackwell, Oxford

Strawson P.F., (1969) *Individuals,* Methuen, London

—— (1966) *The Bounds of Sense,* Methuen, London

—— (1971) *Logico-Linguistic Papers,* Methuen, London

—— (1985) *Skepticism and Naturalism: Some Varieties,* Methuen, London

Bibliography

Stroud B., (1968) 'Transcendental Arguments', in *The Journal of Philosophy*, vol. 65, no. 9, pp.241–256

—— (1968) 'Wittgenstein and Logical Necessity', in G. Pitcher (ed.), *Wittgenstein. The Philosophical Investigations,* Macmillan, London, pp.477–496

Taylor C., (1972) 'The Opening Arguments of the *Phenomenology'*, in Alasdair MacIntyre (ed.), *Hegel A Collection of Critical Essays,* University of Notre Dame Press, Notre Dame and London, pp.151–187

—— (1975) *Hegel,* Cambridge University Press, London, New York and Melbourne

—— (1979) 'The Validity of Transcendental Arguments', in *Proceedings of the Aristotelian Society,* vol. 53, pp.151–165

Van Leeuwen A.T., (1974) *Critique of Earth,* Luttleworth Press, Guildford and London

Von Wright G.H., (1966) 'A Biographical Sketch', in Malcolm N., *Ludwig Wittgenstein: A Memoir,* Oxford University Press, London.

—— (1979) 'The *Origin and Composition of Wittgenstein's Investigations'* in C.G. Luckhardt (ed.), *Wittgenstein Sources and Perspectives,* Harvester Press, Hassocks, Sussex, pp.138–160

—— (1982) 'Wittgenstein in Relation to his Times', in B. McGuinness (ed.), *Wittgenstein and his Times,* Basil Blackwell, Oxford, pp.108–120

Waismann F., (1951) *The Principles of Linguistic Philosophy,* R. Harré (ed.), Macmillan, London

—— (1979) *Wittgenstein and The Vienna Circle,* J. Schulte and B. McGuinness (trans.), Basil Blackwell, Oxford

Wilkerson T.E., (1970) 'Transcendental Arguments', in *Philosophical Quarterly,* vol. 20, pp.200–212

—— (1976) *Kant's Critique of Pure Reason,* Oxford University Press, London

Williams B., (1974) 'Wittgenstein and Idealism', in G. Vesey (ed.), *Understanding Wittgenstein,* Royal Institute of Philosophy Lectures, vol. 7, Macmillan, London, pp.76–95

Winch P., (1958) *The Idea of a Social Science,* Routledge and Kegan Paul, London

—— (1972) *Ethics and Action,* Routledge and Kegan Paul, London

—— (1981) 'Im Anfang war die Tat', in Block, op. cit., pp.159–178

Wolff R.P., (N.D.) 'Reflections on Literary Style and Social Theory. The Case of Karl Marx's *Capital'.* Unpublished

Wood A.W., (1970) *Kant's Moral Religion,* Cornell University Press, Ithaca and London

—— (1981) *Karl Marx,* Routledge and Kegan Paul, London, Boston, Melbourne and Henley

Wright C., (1980) *Wittgenstein on the Foundations of Mathematics,* Duckworth, London

Zabeeh F., (1971) 'On Language Games and Forms of Life, in Klemke, op. cit., pp.328–373

Index